THE ANTHROPOLOGY GRADUATE'S GUIDE

This book is dedicated to our families,
present and past,
who believed in and supported us
as we follow our paths, passions, and dreams
no matter how different from their own.

THE ANTHROPOLOGY GRADUATE'S GUIDE

FROM STUDENT TO A CAREER

Carol J. Ellick

Joe E. Watkins

Left Coast
Press Inc.

Walnut Creek, California

Left Coast Press is committed to preserving ancient forests and natural resources. We elected to print this title on 30% post consumer recycled paper, processed chlorine free. As a result, for this printing, we have saved:

3 Trees (40' tall and 6-8" diameter)
1 Million BTUs of Total Energy
325 Pounds of Greenhouse Gases
1,567 Gallons of Wastewater
95 Pounds of Solid Waste

Left Coast Press made this paper choice because our printer, Thomson-Shore, Inc., is a member of Green Press Initiative, a nonprofit program dedicated to supporting authors, publishers, and suppliers in their efforts to reduce their use of fiber obtained from endangered forests.

For more information, visit www.greenpressinitiative.org

Environmental impact estimates were made using the Environmental Defense Paper Calculator. For more information visit: www.papercalculator.org.

LEFT COAST PRESS, INC.
1630 North Main Street, #400
Walnut Creek, CA 94596
Left Coast Press Inc. *http://www.LCoastPress.com*

Library of Congress Cataloging-in-Publication Data:

Ellick, Carol J.
  The anthropology graduate's guide : from student to a career / Carol J. Ellick, Joe E. Watkins.
    p. cm.
  Includes bibliographical references and index.
  ISBN 978-1-59874-568-9 (hardcover : alk. paper) —
  ISBN 978-1-59874-569-6 (pbk. : alk. paper)
  1. Anthropology—Vocational guidance. 2. Anthropology—Study and teaching (Higher)
  I. Watkins, Joe E. II. Title.
  GN41.8.E55 2011
  301.023—dc22
                                        20100536
Printed in the United States of America

∞ The paper used in this publication meets the minimum requirements of American National Standard for Information Sciences—Permanence of Paper for Printed Library Materials, ANSI/NISO Z39.48–1992.

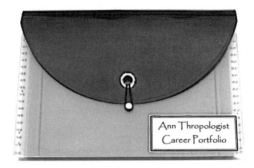

Ann Thropologist
Career Portfolio

CONTENTS

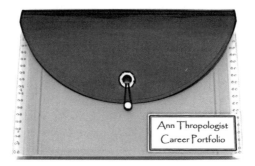

Ann Thropologist
Career Portfolio

ACKNOWLEDGMENTS

Special thanks to the University of New Mexico Anthropology Department, Avenues to Professionalism students. They were the test group for much of the content of this book, and they continued to provide quotes and comments throughout the writing process. The proof that the process works lies in the successes of these students. Granted the "study population" is small, but they are successful. We hope that their portfolios and experiences continue to build within the field of anthropology and that the cumulative effects are enjoyable and successful careers.

Thanks also to the friends and colleagues in our network and to the friends and colleagues in their networks. Without their advice, comments, and recommendations, this book would be much thinner and just plain boring. The network (and our thanks) extend to those individuals in the offices of our professional organizations. We particularly thank the Society for Applied Anthropology for putting us on the trail of Dr. Riall Nolan, Purdue University. Dr. Nolan wrote the book *Anthropology in Practice: Building a Career Outside of the Academic* (Directions in Applied Anthropology). We thank him for sharing his time and his wisdom, and for the list of applied anthropologists to contact for their stories.

When our publisher said "Broaden," we appealed to those outside our network and were rewarded with immediate responses from anthropologists in applied and academic careers who volunteered to help. They each took time from their incredibly busy schedules to write a career story for inclusion in this book. Their contributions broadened this book, and it is much the better for it. To each, we extend our thanks; and we can only hope that the book measures up to their perceived standards.

We thank our archaeological and anthropological friends who took time to review, edit, and comment on the initial drafts. Amanda M., Brian F., Kelley H.-G., and Larry Z., we owe you beyond your worth!

And, last but not least, we thank the founder and family of Left Coast Press, Inc. Mitch, we appreciate your vision, wisdom, experience, and patience, but most of all, your friendship. Thanks for listening to the spark of an idea and showing up for dinner with a contract.

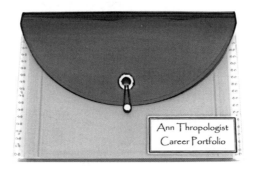

CHAPTER 1

FROM STUDENT TO A CAREER

"Why should it be the student's primary responsibility to bridge the gap between training and the working world? It should be . . . the working world, the students, and those doing the training working together in a continuous discourse—each has their own unique perspectives and contributions."
    —Gwen Mohr, journal comment, Avenues to Professionalism class

INTRODUCTION
(WHY YOU NEED THIS BOOK)

Do you want a career in anthropology? If you do—and we mean, if you *really* do—then you need this book. Why? Because it presents strategies that will assist you in transitioning from your career as a student to your career in your chosen discipline. It provides information on using the anthropological skill set when applying for jobs, analyzing your career path, and fitting into the workplace. The stories, scenarios, and activities presented in this book will help you learn how to best present your knowledge, skills, and abilities to prospective employers.

Now, since you've made it to paragraph two and haven't put the book down, we can assume that you've reached and hold fast to the conclusion that you would like to pursue a career in anthropology. Who are your role models? What topic, covered in class, got your mind spinning? What does a career in anthropology mean to you and how do you get it? The question then becomes, how do you bridge the gaps between classroom knowledge, field experience, a job, and a career?

GOING FOR IT

Not all job application processes are the same; if they were, we wouldn't have enough to fill a book. The federal government, for example, has learned to harness technology and has created a clearinghouse for all its advertised positions. Choose this path and your future is but a button click away. Want a job in academia? Jump to Chapters 13 and 14. (But don't skip the other chapters. Even though the academic process is different, there is value in the information provided in the other chapters. They provide background and balance.) Want to challenge what you've learned about anthropology so far? Open yourself up to the vast opportunities in nonprofit organizations and the public sector. That's really where we can help.

THE MYTH PERPETUATED

You have just completed twelve years of pre-collegiate education, plus presumably an additional three or more years. During this time, your educational role models, for the most part, have been teachers, instructors, and professors. Professors have probably played the greatest role in influencing your choice of major. They are experts within their field, but they probably are experts within only one track of their field, the academic track.

Myth #1

You may have heard outright during mentoring sessions or whispered in the hallowed halls that to do anything less than complete a Ph.D. and follow in academic track is not "real" anthropology. Not true, not true, not true. A recent publication by the National Association for the Practice of Anthropology notes, "it is estimated that from 42 to 60 percent of Ph.D. anthropologists and virtually all M.A. anthropologists work outside the academy" (Guerrón-Montero 2008: 1). So many anthropologists can't be doing something that is not "real anthropology." Pay special attention to the personal stories and quotes presented throughout this book. These people provide a taste of reality, not gossip from those who've never ventured beyond the ivory tower. Do the research; don't accept secondhand, unverified data.

Myth #2

One of the greatest fears of parents is that their child will select a college major in a field that has too much competition for too few jobs. (And that their kid will come back home jobless and hungry, with dirty laundry, long hair, and . . . oh wait, that was Carol's parents' fear!)

Myth Busters
Yes, there are a lot of graduates competing for "that job." According to the statistics listed in the *American Anthropological Association 2009–2010 Guide* (AAA 2009–2010), during the 2008–2009 school year, 8,561 students graduated with a bachelor's degree, 1,236 graduated with a master's, and 503 graduated with a doctorate in anthropology. Don't be discouraged! The market is open for those who look. In 2009, a broad-reaching survey was conducted by the American Anthropological Association (AAA) and the AAA Committee on Practicing, Applied and Public Interest Anthropology (CoPAPIA). The full report is due out later this year (Fiske at al. 2010), but a blog post on August 10, 2010 (AAA 2010b) reports that 66 percent of the students graduating with a master's degree in anthropology found jobs within six months of graduation, 82 percent within a year. Since we don't have the full report, we can't tell you what these students went into or if they are working within their chosen field, but they got a job! Compare this with the findings of the National Association of Colleges and Employers. According to the 2009 Student Survey, "19.7 percent of 2009 graduates who applied for a job actually have one" (Berman 2009).

This is good news! Maybe going into anthropology was a smart move on your part. And, just think, these are real statistics that you can quote to your mother when she asks, "What can you do with a degree in anthropology?"

Stories

Telling you our stories is fun but provides a rather narrow focus within the field of anthropology, so we've used our network to reach out to anthropologists across the discipline. Their stories are presented here and interspersed throughout the chapters; they are also included in Appendix 2. These are the stories of individuals with seasoned careers, people who helped form the theories and practices within the profession that you learned about during your educational career.

Organization of this Book

Originally we thought the book would follow the syllabus that was developed for a semester-long class. It has, but teaching a group of people who are sitting in front of you is different than putting the words on paper in a way that imparts that same level of knowledge. At first, we made a straightforward attempt to follow our course outline. Then, when it became apparent that that wasn't going to work, it took months to get over the shock and to wrap our minds around another approach. Then, it took a while to overcome procrastination and writer's block. Any of this sound familiar? We all go through it. Even the most proficient writers have to gain enough confidence in the knowledge of their subject in order to write. So, we started writing.

The resulting book has been tweaked somewhat to fit the textbook-based instructional format. This said, the overall goal remains the same. It is designed to prepare you for your career by teaching strategies that can assist you in obtaining a job in your desired discipline. We are writing primarily about employment in the non-academic track of anthropology—our path—but many of the techniques offered here are applicable to almost any of the other social sciences. Sure, each social science has certain quirks specific to its discipline, but the broad outlines and approaches we suggest are similar.

Sections and Chapters

There are three sections to this book. The first section, Preparation, provides background information about anthropology and about obtaining a career in anthropology. The chapters within this section offer tips for developing the base you will need to continue with this process.

The second section, Product Development, is dedicated to the development of the job application components. These components and products will be kept in your portfolio, updated as needed, and provided to potential employers during the application process.

The chapters in the last section of the book, Set Yourself Apart, are intended to help you stand out among the several thousands of other anthropology graduates. They provide ideas and exercises to help build your knowledge, skills, and abilities beyond those of your competition. These last few chapters are intended to stimulate ideas and options to get you out there to grasp your dream job.

WHY US?

We are Carol Ellick and Joe Watkins. Together we have worked within the field of anthropology—primarily archaeology—for nearly 70 years. (The reality of this is nearly as scary as typing it. We can't be this old!) Through our careers, we have worked for government agencies, universities, and within the private sector. In this day and age, a successful career in anthropology involves creativity and flexibility. While we both trained as anthropologists, Joe is currently employed in the Native American Studies Program at the University of Oklahoma, and Carol just started a firm called Archaeological and Cultural Education Consultants (ACEcs). Both fall under the category of "applied" or "practicing" anthropology.

Carol's Story

Carol's interest in anthropology began during a family drive across country when she was fourteen years old. There was no way to know at that time that the questions she asked herself in Mesa Verde National Park would form the basis of her career. She single-mindedly pursued her interest by taking classes related to anthropology, archaeology, geology, history, and the environment, to the exclusion of much else, while completing her bachelor's degree. Her first paid position as an archaeologist was on the Chief Joseph Dam Cultural Resources Project along the Columbia River in Washington. Carol participated in subsequent cultural resource management (CRM) projects along that stretch of river and on projects in Oregon, California, and Arizona. Like many other archaeologists of the 1970s and 1980s, Carol made her living by working for various universities and private CRM companies. The way she managed to stay out of the unemployment lines was by working in the field during the summers and by illustrating artifacts and maps for publication during the off-season. Since 1990, she has focused on developing the field of public outreach and education. Within this subfield of archaeology, "public archaeology," she became the first person to create and manage a full-time public outreach and education department within a for-profit anthropological consulting firm. The completion of a master's of arts in education, specializing in curriculum and instruction, helped her bridge the professions of education and archaeology. Her specialty for more than twenty years has been the development of educational materials for K–12 grades based on traditional cultural and scientific information. Recently, this specialization has given her the opportunity to work internationally, in Australia and Japan.

Joe's Story

Until discovering an archaic period projectile point on the family homestead in southeastern Oklahoma, Joe thought he was going to be a paleontologist. (Of course, he was only ten years old, so dinosaurs are as good as it gets.) But it was the words of his Choctaw grandmother that made the difference. She said that the projectile point was made by people who lived in the area before the Choctaw, but that it was important not to let that unwritten history get lost. Joe obtained his bachelor's of arts degree from the University of Oklahoma, and then went to graduate school at Southern Methodist University, where he earned his M.A. in 1977. He worked in all aspects of cultural resource management—crew member, crew chief, contractor, and consultant—for public and private organizations as well as for state and federal agencies. He went back to complete his doctorate at Southern Methodist University in 1994, his dissertation focusing on the ethical practice of anthropology and anthropologists' relationships with indigenous groups worldwide.

Sometimes a career is a single job at a single university held for the term of one's working life. More often, though, a career is made up of what you've accomplished within the profession. The key is that you aim to do what you enjoy and, hopefully, one day you'll look back and realize that somehow you've done it; your jobs have become a career.

HOW WE CAME TO WRITE THIS BOOK

In 2005, we attended a graduate student symposium sponsored by the graduate student association at the University of New Mexico. It was painful. We sat and listened, watched and cringed. It was obvious that while these students might know their research topic, they had never been taught how to prepare an oral presentation with PowerPoint slides for a "professional" conference. Instead of simply complaining about the inadequacies of their college education, we decided to do something about it.

Our first undertaking was the development of a somewhat comical, personally animated and illustrated talk entitled "How to Give a Professional Presentation." This project led to the development of an outline for a book (this book) and a semester-long class entitled "Avenues to Professionalism: How to Obtain Your Career in Anthropology." The class worked, and we think the book will make our approach accessible to an even wider range of students.

CONTRIBUTORS

In addition to our words and ideas, this book contains contributions from the students who took our class, Avenues to Professionalism, at the University of New Mexico, Department of Anthropology, in Fall 2006. The class was geared to upper division undergraduate and graduate students. Students evaluated the course every three weeks. By the end of the term, they unanimously voted this course the most important class they'd taken during their college careers to date. They said, "Every student should take this course. It should be part of the core curriculum."

The book also benefits from the incredibly helpful comments and personal stories of our reviewers (and friends). We have included many of these suggestions, acknowledging credit to the reviewers by citing their names.

We also sent a plea out to anthropologists in our networks and in the networks of the people who contacted us. The outcome was an incredible response from the applied and academic anthropological communities. Within several short weeks, we received more than 25 career stories from people who gave permission to use their stories in whole or part. The book would not provide nearly as complete a picture of the options in the field of anthropology without the stories of these individuals. Many stated that they wished that such a book had existed when they graduated.

We hope the readers of this book will find it as useful.

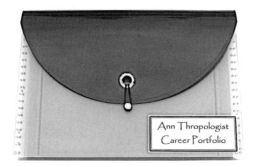

Ann Thropologist
Career Portfolio

SECTION I
PREPARATION

This first section, Preparation, provides background information about anthropology and obtaining a career in anthropology. The chapters within this section offer tips to help you develop the base you will need to get started in your career development.

Chapter 2 describes what you need to do before you begin delving further into the book. Chapter 3 describes some of the fields and specialties within anthropology, as well as job qualifications based on educational level. Chapter 4 covers professionalism and standards; and Chapter 5, a transitional chapter, looks at the jobs you have held and helps you recognize and record the knowledge, skills, and abilities that you've accumulated to this point.

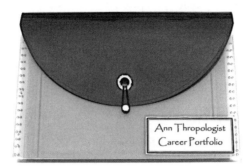

CHAPTER 2

GETTING ORGANIZED

"This class laid out the information and structure that I needed to transition from student to professional. If the book contains the same information that was in this class, everyone will find it helpful."
—Anonymous evaluation comment, Avenues to Professionalism class

INTRODUCTION

We know that you're ready to read the book and are ready to apply for and land the first job of your career, *but* there are a few things that need to be done first to make it easier for you to succeed.

BEFORE YOU BEGIN

The successful completion of this book and the procurement of a job involves more than just reading the text. There are three products that we recommend you create before continuing with the rest of text. If you create these, as directed, as you read this chapter, you will have a place to store completed documents. Completing these will allow you to keep resources handy and organized throughout your job search.

The first product that you will create is a journal. Undoubtedly, at some point in your life, you've been required to keep a journal for personal or class use. And, as you pursue your career in anthropology, you will also keep field journals. However, the journal created here is most likely a bit different from those others.

The second item you will create is a portfolio. This is where you will keep all the documents you produce as you proceed through the chapters of the book. It will hold your applications, your professional information, and your career goals. This portfolio will be one of the things you grab the minute you even start thinking about looking for a new job.

The third product is a written contract. The contract will identify past knowledge, skills, and abilities, as well as put into words what you would like to achieve in the transition between your career as a student and initiating your professional career.

The production of these three components will help you organize your thoughts, keep track of materials, and provide a base for the measurement of your progress. The skills practiced during the completion of these tasks will be beneficial in any future job.

THE JOURNAL

"Now, I am not one who has ever kept a journal for any reason, so at first I thought that was the biggest pain in the ass ever. But, I soon found myself focusing my thoughts on the particular points or issues of professional conduct, etc. as they were presented. Journaling required you to be 'present' for each thought, addressing them singularly and then as parts of a whole, because no matter how many things may be crossing your mind, it is very hard to **write** about more than one at a time—you have to focus and concentrate. Although it was sort of a 'forced march' in the beginning if I wanted a good grade, it became habitual to address and re-address thoughts, insights, and those 'ah-ha' moments in the journal. In fact, I can even go back to it to see if I still agree with things I wrote or, moreover, to see that some actually make more sense now."

—Matt Dawson, Director
Passport in Time Clearinghouse, SRI Foundation

We've heard the argument that, in this age of technology, we should "go paperless" and provide instructions for creating and maintaining the journal on the computer. There are programs set up for journaling and, yes, you will be required to maintain journals in certain jobs and contexts, but jotting something down that comes to mind when you are riding the bus, sitting on the beach, or having a snack at McDonalds is difficult if your computer is sitting on your desktop at home. What if you have one of those "aha" moments like Matt did, or find that elusive reference, and you don't have the computer and document to type it into? It is much easier to carry a pencil and notebook than it is a computer. In addition, there is something more personal about writing by hand and turning a page than typing keys and scrolling down the page.

The journal to be used in this context can be as simple as a 10¢ spiral notebook or as exotic as a handmade, leather-bound journal. The choice is yours. Select something that you will feel comfortable using and that will last you through the job search process (bearing in mind that the job search is not a one-time thing). The paper and binder are not important. What *is* important is that you use it throughout the process. Your journal will become your personal reference library. It will be a catalog of your search, containing all your data, notes, and comments, not only while preparing yourself for your first job, but also through the initial stages of your career.

Journal Layout and Structure

Your journal is your place for notes, information, data, ideas, and daily reflections. Journals are structured and formatted to fit the specific needs of this process. It is important that you format your journal to use the front and back sides of each page, so make sure that you select a writing implement that does not bleed through the paper.

Your journal should be structured with odd and even pages. The odd-numbered pages are for your notes, information, and data. The even-numbered pages are for thoughts and ideas.

Structure for the journal:

■ Number the front side and back side of each sheet in the notebook.

■ The first three sheets of paper (both sides, meaning pages 1–6) will be the title page and Table of Contents for your journal.

■ Label the top of page 1 "Title Page" (see Figure 1). Label the back of this page, "page 2."

■ Pages 3–6 are for your Table of Contents (see Figure 2). As you enter information into your journal, flip back to your Table of Contents and list the titles and page numbers. This will help you find information in the future.

■ Data, general notes, and information go on the odd pages. The even pages are to be used for thoughts and ideas.

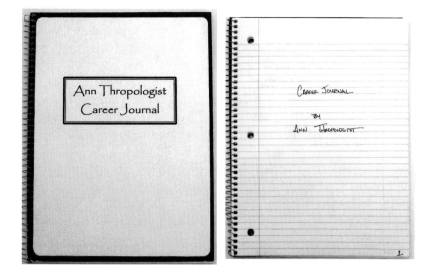

Figure 1. Cover and title page of Ann Thropologist's journal.

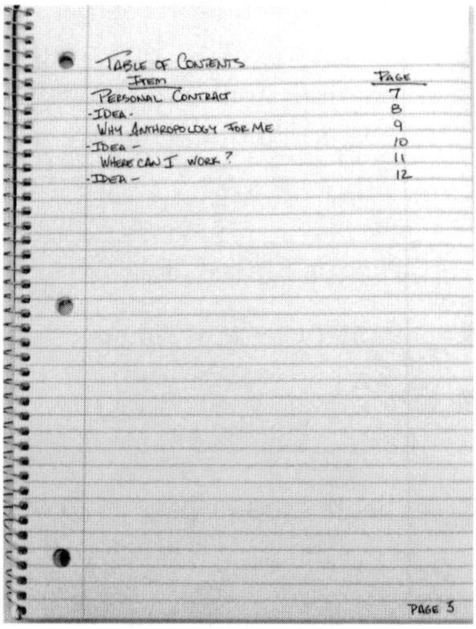

Figure 2. The Table of Contents begins on page 3.

■ Actual journal entries begin on page 7.

■ If necessary, maps, illustrations, or other outside information can be pasted onto pages in the journal. These additions always go on the odd-numbered pages.

Journal writing requires the discipline to record information. Journal-keeping skills—reading, researching, analyzing, creating, inventing, discussing, and thinking—are essential to any career in anthropology and will help you learn how to think beyond the normal processes. In addition, keeping a journal will help remind you of the things that you want to do, try, or just think about occasionally. You should use your journal as a method to track your progress. It is important that you learn to write easily, and that you don't self-censor your thoughts too often or too much.

THE PORTFOLIO

"I can't believe how useful the portfolio has been. I know exactly where my résumé is and can put my hands on it when I need it."
—Erin Hudson, Cultural Resource Technician, USDA Forest Service

The same rule applies to the portfolio as to the journal: it can be as basic or as creative as you'd like to make it. The difference, however, is that while the journal is for you and only you, the portfolio should be used as a container for all job application and career-related materials. In addition, you may take it to job interviews so that you have your curriculum vita, résumé, and letters of reference at your fingertips.

The portfolio is the "binder" that holds this process together (see Figure 3). To keep you organized, we've provided a section called "For the

Figure 3. Sample portfolio.

Portfolio" at the end of each chapter, which describes the document(s) that was (were) just created, polished, or procured during the exercises.

Portfolio Layout and Structure

Your portfolio should contain final (clean) copies of your contract, curriculum vita, résumé, personal biography, letters of reference, five-year plan, and other products created during the career preparation process. When purchasing your portfolio, consider getting one that is wide and tall enough to accommodate dividers or has the sections built into the container. There should be a minimum of eight to ten sections to your portfolio (Figure 4).

Figure 4. Your portfolio should accommodate dividers or sections.

Set up the sections of the portfolio as follows:

- Journal
- Personal contract
- Curriculum vita
- Résumé
- Biography
- Cover letters/letters of introduction
- Letters of reference
- Five-year plan and ethics statement

■ Job application forms

■ Other (including maybe this book…)

So, what are you waiting for? *Stop reading* and run to the store to make your first investment toward your post-student life and your career.

PERSONAL CONTRACT

What have you done? What classes have you taken that will prepare for your job in anthropology? What knowledge do you have? What skills and abilities? How do you connect seemingly unrelated pieces of your life with your career goals?

The purpose of the personal contract is to state where you've been and what you know as well as where you would like to be. There is nothing wrong with pipe dreams—nor are they necessarily unobtainable. The key to reaching your dreams is to set up small, measurable steps that can be achieved along the way.

Periodically, we encounter people who reminisce about their early interest in anthropology or archaeology, and we listen to their stories about how they couldn't find a job or needed a career that would support them. They didn't believe they could reach their dream. In fact, if you aren't sure, or you try to grasp the brass ring without getting used to riding the horse, it's just not going to happen. (Well, maybe it happens for the lucky, but for most of us, it requires lots of work.)

So, the personal contract is a good place to start. It provides a base, a point to reflect on so that you can evaluate your progress.

Drafting Your Personal Contract

Drafting a personal contract allows you to state your specific goals, as well as to lay out the steps needed to realize them. You have the opportunity to review what you have accomplished and what you want to achieve, and to detail the process to get you there. It also provides you with a statement that can be referenced in case you get side-tracked, or to review when assessing progress.

To begin, write a one- or two-page statement that identifies what you've done in relation to what you'd like to accomplish. This statement will serve as the basis for your "contract" for your transition from student to professional and ultimately stands as the outline for your plan to pursue a career in the field of anthropology.

You may wish to outline your contract in your journal or type it into your computer. The finished contract should be typed, spell- and grammar-checked, produced on a clean sheet of paper, and filed in the second section of your portfolio. You may wonder, because this contract is for your personal use and not distributed to others, why you should go to the trouble of producing a final clean copy. Here's why: It is a good idea to get in the habit of producing only the highest quality. When employers have to choose between two equally qualified individuals, they will look at the details.

Your contract should have a title at the top of the page and be laid out in paragraph format. The following questions and discussions are provided for you to use as a base. Reflect on the following topics and write a couple of sentences that relate to each in your journal or draft. Use what you have written to help refine your thoughts and draft your contract.

1. What is your specific area or discipline of interest? For the purpose of this exercise, think about what drew you to the field of anthropology, what you like, and what you think you would like to do. If you have no idea, don't panic. There is plenty of time to narrow your field and focus on a specialty. Besides, you may not have had the opportunity yet to learn about, to volunteer, or to work in every subfield or area. You don't have to lock yourself in; experience and experiment. For more information (which will potentially increase confusion with the variety of choices) on the fields of anthropology, please read Chapter 3.

2. Where would you like to be, geographically? You might wonder if this is important. It may not be for you, but for many it is. If you choose (or chose) a graduate school based on a particular area of study, you may have unknowingly predetermined where you will live or work. For example, if you are interested in cultures of the Pacific Northwest, then you would seek a program with strengths in that topic. The program or professors and the contacts you make while in that program will provide you with the background to work within that area. More than likely, the program will be located in the Pacific Northwest, not in the Southwest, Northeast, Plains, or Southeast.

3. What classes, projects, and educational experiences have you had that relate to your proposed career? List the most relevant. Think of classes outside of anthropology that may also have relevance. Are you planning to work in Mexico or Spain? What in your Spanish classes or study abroad would be particularly helpful to future employment, and how would you make it attractive to an employer? Are you artistically inclined? Would you be able to illustrate artifacts if given the chance? What classes have you taken that would help?

4. What would you like to accomplish within the transition from student to professional? Reading this book and completing the exercises will put you on the right path, but what else will benefit you? Are you planning to volunteer with an agency or organization that would help you build your résumé? How are your computer skills? Where and how could you get the training that would fill in the gaps? Are you in the last semesters of school? What would help you complete your current course of study in the least stressful, most productive manner?

5. How many hours per week will you spend reading this text, working on your journal and portfolio, completing the exercises, and researching career related topics? Make a plan and stick to it. As with exercising or studying, it's easy to procrastinate or find excuses to do something else. You will get back what you put in, so if you really want a career in anthropology (or anything else), you need to apply yourself. The people who have jobs that just land in their lap are few and far between. Even if you're good, you will need to put forth an effort to get and keep that job.

6. How will you evaluate your progress and accomplishments? The book will provide guidelines, but how will you know if you are on track? Consider using your journal for weekly reflection. What have you done this week that will put you that much closer to your career? Also consider how you will reward yourself for the positive achievement of your goals. A reward doesn't have to be food, and it doesn't have to be expensive. How long has it been since you took a couple of hours for a walk? Read a book that wasn't a required text? Watched a favorite movie or just sat with your eyes closed and listened to music?

The main point of this exercise is to provide a place to start, to get you thinking about where you've been and where you would like to go, and to provide the mechanism for evaluating your progress, the final exercise in Chapter 15. The job search or establishment of a career can seem overwhelming. Hopefully, by building a firm base, it will become less daunting.

SUMMARY

This chapter offered suggestions for the development of three products—the journal, the portfolio, and the personal contract—that will aid you in your job and career quest. We realize it's human nature to think "I'll come back and do this later," but experience has taught us it's better to do this right now, before going on to the next chapter.

FOR THE PORTFOLIO

This chapter provided the guidance for the production of the portfolio, the framework for the journal, and the creation of the personal contract. You now have the container for holding the products that will assist you in obtaining the jobs that will ultimately lead to your career. At this time, place your journal in the front section of your portfolio and your personal contract into the second section.

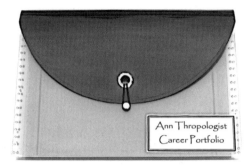

CHAPTER 3

I WANT TO BE AN ANTHROPOLOGIST...

"I chose to pursue archaeology as a subject of study and as a career so that I may help Native American communities, specifically my Pueblo, with the many issues these communities have with archaeology. . . . I intend to pursue a career in cultural resource management while working directly with or for my Pueblo."

—Joseph (Woody) Aguilar
University of Pennsylvania Anthropology Ph.D. student
San Ildefonso Pueblo member

INTRODUCTION

In this chapter, we ask you to look at why you decided to become an anthropologist. Once we establish that this is your dream, we take you through the process of clarifying for yourself what field of anthropology

31

you'd like to work in. The information we provide is intended to give you some ideas of what can be done with a degree in anthropology, how it can be applied to jobs in general, and, more specifically, what you can do with a bachelor's, master's, or doctoral degree in anthropology. Working professionals have sent us stories of their paths to careers. These are presented here; additional stories appear in Appendix 2. The career choices presented in this chapter fall mainly within the applied or practicing field of anthropology; additional information on academic careers is covered Chapters 13 and 14.

WHY ANTHROPOLOGY?

How did I decide that I wanted to become an anthropologist? What drew me to this profession over other possibilities? Take a moment to reflect and address these questions in your journal.

Several years ago, Carol began to listen to stories that people would tell about when they got interested in anthropology, how they got interested, and when they actually got to take a formal class. In response, she developed an activity that uses a set of four questions that assess when and how people got interested in anthropology. The questions are:

■ How old were you when you got interested in anthropology?

■ Who introduced you (parent, park ranger, teacher)?

■ What got you interested (museum display, *National Geographic,* Indiana Jones movies)?

■ What grade were you in when you took your first anthropology class or had it presented in a class (fourth-grade social studies, high school history, sophomore college class)?

Carol has presented these questions to a number of college anthropology classes, workshops, and conferences, and although no systematic statistical analysis has been conducted to date, the responses have been fairly uniform. The majority of people responded that they got interested between the ages of five and twelve. Most people learned about anthropology from a parent, although teacher comes in as a close second. The answers to what got them interested had the most variation, but museums, *National Geographic* magazine, and national parks all rated quite highly. (And, yes, Indiana Jones occasionally gets mentioned.) But it is the answer to the final of the four questions that provides real insights. Most people indicated that while they may have started their interest in anthropology in grade school, they didn't get to take their first anthropology class until they were in college. School didn't create, foster, or feed the interest. Everyone had to do it for themselves.

How would you answer the questions? How have you fostered your interest over time? How do you take this passion and interest and use it to get a job? Everyone can amass classes and experience, so it will be your passion and skills that will help win that job over another applicant with the same qualifications. How will you continue your interest and enthusiasm as people tell you that you need to find a real career or that you need to find a job that will pay money or that the job will go to someone else? If you don't think you've got the drive, getting that job will be difficult. If you do have the drive, we hope to provide you with tools that will make the difference.

There is no right time to enter the field of anthropology, and there is no right path to follow. There are as many paths as there are people. That said, some choices can make getting jobs easier.

ANTHROPOLOGY

You picked up this book, so there has to be an interest. Have you started your job search? Are you looking only at jobs with "Anthropologist Needed" in the ad, or have you considered jobs that can use the amazing skills that a background in anthropology has provided?

What skills has your background in anthropology given you? Citing a paper by the American Anthropological Association (*http://www.aaanet.org/profdev/careers/Careers.cfm*), Kedia (2008: 23) notes that anthropologists are "careful observers of humans and their behavior" and that anthropology students are exposed to a "range of social, behavioral, biological and other scientific research methods [that supplement] statistical findings with descriptive data gathered through participant observation, interviewing, and ethnographic study." These skills, in conjunction with "careful record-keeping, attention to details, analytical reading ... social ease in strange situations, [and] critical thinking" are marketable skills that many employers need.

Jana Fortier, Ph.D., Department of Anthropology, University of California, San Diego, responded to our request for helpful advice for students entering the field of anthropology with a wonderfully written, detailed list of anthropological skills. She presented it as a "gift" toward the book project. And it is an incredible gift to share with you.

Dr. Fortier's Statement on Developing Skills

Students of anthropology invariably take classes concerning research methods, but once you leave academia, it is time to look for work in the marketplace. If you do a search in a jobs database, such as "monster.com," you might type in the key phrase "cultural anthropologist," yet only a handful of job offerings will pop up onto your computer screen. Analogous to disciplines such as mathematics, philosophy, and history, it is more the skills you have acquired rather than the degree title that are needed by potential employers. So for those of us who love to work using our skills as applied cultural anthropologists, it is important to develop skills that are recognizable and sought after by employers.

In my case, it turned out that the employers mostly have been government agencies who need someone to write reports or other documents after having done ethnographic research. Some of these agencies have been the City of San Diego, the California Transportation Department (Caltrans), the local Marine Corps Air Station, the local Naval Facilities; and some private groups, including museums, CRMs (cultural resource management firms), and some non-profits. What these employers have in common is that they seek someone who can do cultural and historical research, conduct valid interviews and surveys, write excellent reports, and do it all with common sense, enthusiasm, and professionalism.

Each ethnographer develops a distinct method, based on his or her past experience and interests. In my case, these are some of the "skills" that I have in my kit (and ones you could type into "monster.com" and find jobs). They are not all necessary for any one contract, but I have used these in many cases.

Records searching—The government agencies with whom I have worked require research into certain databases. These have included Sacred Lands file searches, California Historic Resources Information System research, searching records in the San Diego Historical Society, artifact searches in the local anthropology museum, review of information in the National Register of Historic Places, review of laws involving CRM such as NAGPRA. One skill you will learn is to transform your library database search skills as a student into one of competence using other professional databases.

Videography and photography—I used to say that I specialize in taking pictures of people working. Studs Terkel would have been proud of me. Ethnographers need to take well-composed pictures and videotaped interviews, but we especially need to be able to stuff as much cultural information into our images as possible. Practice taking pictures of "congealed knowledge" more than of peoples' faces. In my work, I have images of people cutting usable plants, transforming them into rope, shoes, and other cultural artifacts; of people doing pottery, ironsmithing, pipe making, growing grains, threshing, teaching children, building irrigation ditches, and recreating ancient Andean terraces. When it comes time to write reports, a handful of well-composed photos illustrating your main points will bring a high quality and authenticity to your work.

Design structured interviews—This is when research design classes come in handy, but also you may want to keep a research design folder of articles and some books on hand for reference. You can effectively translate your studies of various types of research into a carefully structured research proposal for a client. I've had to use such methods as daisy-chain interviews, sampling to ensure equal numbers of diverse social classes, sets of key issues to be discussed, and key vocabulary such as native plant names. Other methods such as time allocation studies are useful, but the time frame for contract work may not allow for these more time-consuming methods. Your interviews are precious moments. Let your interviewee talk as much as they want. Don't rush and say "I have to go at 5 pm." Respect the lovely sliver of memories that you are collecting. Remember how important it is to prepare; think about how to conduct your interviews, and leave yourself enough time to carry out as many interviews as possible. My usual regret is that I only got *x* number of interviews or that I interrupted someone while they were speaking. In applied work, we often have less time and yet the reports need to be of high quality.

Transcription and data analysis—This is the place for ethnographers to slow down, spend more time reviewing the material. Transcribe all the important conversations; look for key ideas, phrases, and bits that will have the most impact in a report. Think about the goals of the report and the contracting agency.

Report writing—Don't be afraid to write that "lame first draft." Just start writing! Then polish, polish some more, and review it for sentence flow and simplicity. When busy people read your report, the paragraphs have to have "hooks" and "anchors" and other edges for your reader to remember. Use memorable quotes from interviews; devise beautiful word-images; use alliteration and other rhetorical devices from your favorite non-fiction writers.

It's never too late to stretch yourself and learn more skills. For example, I found that recording cultural geographic information using a GPS handheld device has proved useful. I have recorded information about plant gathering sites, sites of stories and myths, sites with natural resources such as vernal pools, and toponymic sites with significant cultural information about these special places. The GIS map specialists with whom I've worked have enjoyed putting together maps of these places, and they bring an additional dimension to agency reports.

There are jobs out there for those of us who choose to study cultural anthropology. But we do not always have to call ourselves "anthropologists." We can use our anthropology skills in such work as program coordinator, program manager, clinical research specialist, cultural research specialist, records analyst, grants specialist, science writer, etc.

The trick, as many practicing anthropologists will tell you, is to help convince the prospective employer that your anthropology skills will help you do the job better than a non-anthropologist would. Your degree and knowledge are composites of the classes you took, the internships you held, and the background you acquired.

The Four-Field Approach

Most of us in the "older" generation of anthropologists went through what is called the "four-field approach" to anthropology: being exposed to classes covering cultural anthropology, physical anthropology, linguistic anthropology, and archaeology. It was from this base that we decided which path to follow. Today, degrees can be individualized and multidisciplinary. What else did you study? Could your other interests be pulled in to provide additional skills that might interest an employer? If you didn't get the four-field base, do a bit of research because there is a chance that your area may relate well to another and may provide potential overlaps that could increase your hiring potential. Michelle M. Carnes, Ph.D., wanted to be an anthropology/women's studies professor. She graduated in 2009 with a degree in social/cultural anthropology (race, gender, and social justice). While working on her degree, she found work with the federal government, and that is where she stayed. (See her career story in Appendix 2.)

A more important point that we'd like to make here is that no matter which subfield you enter, it will still fall under the anthropology umbrella. So, if you are planning on a career in archaeology, bear in mind that the material culture you are excavating was once a piece of people's lives and that those people may be ancestors of living peoples today. Consider how what you do affects other researchers around you or the descendants of those around you (see Chapter 4, Professional Qualifications, Standards, and Ethics). *What you do affects others.* You should be an anthropologist first and an archaeologist second. The concept of "do no harm" is not exclusive to medical science.

To the Nth Degree

A question that hangs over most students' heads (and that we often get asked) is, what degree do I need to get a job? If you haven't asked yourself that question, you might. If your aspiration is to develop an archaeologically based seasonal round that would move you from summer projects in the Pacific Northwest to winter field projects in the Arizona sun, or if you want to do short-term ethnographic research for marketing companies so that you can stay on ski patrol at Snow Basin in the winter, then you may not need more than a bachelor's degree. If you want to direct these projects, then you will probably need at least a master's degree. If you want to become the next Jane Goodall or Dian Fossey and study nonhuman primates in the hopes of throwing additional light on human behavior, then you should count on completing a doctorate.

The above examples are *generalizations*. There are people who have made successful careers moving from technician to supervisor to director who have a bachelor's degree coupled with years of experience. But in today's culture, that is the exception rather than the rule. Even in a government setting, you can only climb so high on the General Schedule (GS) pay scale before you have to either move on to a new region and a new job or add a degree. It takes *both* education and experience to build a successful career. Look at the jobs that actually interest you before deciding that you want to take your education to its ultimate completion by getting a Ph.D. Make sure that by getting a Ph.D. you will not walk into the job market overqualified for the positions that interest you.

What You Can Do with a Bachelor's Degree

What you do with a B.A. or B.S. degree depends on your area of interest, but no matter what field you've entered, be prepared to be hired in an entry-level position. The actual work you do will depend on the employer and the project. If, for example, you plan to become an archaeologist, a bachelor's degree would qualify you to work as a laboratory technician or a field technician. Those entering cultural anthropology might find a position as a poll taker, market researcher, or assistant caseworker. Going into biological anthropology? You might look for positions in public health, at museums, zoos, or agencies conducting forensic studies. Entry-level jobs for linguistic anthropologists can be found primarily in the social services and governmental research programs.

What You Can Do with a Master's Degree

At most academic institutions, an M.A. or M.S. can be earned in as little as two years. Some master's programs require a minimum number of classes before the student must pass a set of comprehensive exams aimed at demonstrating knowledge. Other programs require internships and a research paper or thesis for graduation, in addition to the classes.

A master's degree will get you a middle-management type of job. This may not sound very appealing when phrased this way, but in practical terms it means that you would have the qualifications to work at the project management level, do your own research, or coordinate programs. This said, we would not recommend walking out of a college or university and into a management position without first gaining some field experience in that area. Field experience gives you practical knowledge that you simply cannot gain any other way (see Chapter 10, Internships and Volunteering). Believe us when we say that skipping the field experience prior to becoming a crew chief or project manager will not only be frustrating to you, it will create frustration and animosity among the crew. Those entering master's-level positions will need not only technical knowledge of a specific topic, but also the ability to analyze and synthesize information for site or project reports. Some community colleges or schools that focus on undergraduate degrees will hire professionals with a master's degree, but competition at that level is getting more intense, and more and more professors at the community college level have a Ph.D. Basically, if being a professor is your goal, then you will need a Ph.D.

What You Can Do with a Doctorate of Philosophy

A Ph.D. is the highest degree awarded by departments of anthropology. According to the ideal timeline, a Ph.D. can be completed in as few as two years following the master's. In reality, very few individuals complete their coursework and dissertation within this time frame. When planning your path, think realistically. Will you be devoting all of your time to getting a degree? If not, it might take you five to seven years to accomplish the coursework, the research, and the writing required to produce a dissertation.

The successful completion of a doctorate indicates the ability to conduct independent research, to analyze, synthesize, and evaluate information, and to write and defend a dissertation. A doctorate will get you a management-level job and put you at the top of the employment food chain. With a Ph.D., you have the credentials to be considered for a tenure-track position at the university level. Outside of the university context, you could be a research director or principal investigator and manager of your own consulting firm.

MIXING AND MATCHING

Before we venture into the discussion on applied versus academic careers, we'd like to mention the benefits of mixing and matching interests, programs, and degrees. Above, we talked about the old-fashioned four-field approach that still exists in many anthropology departments. We touched on the interdisciplinary major, but we would like to reinforce the idea that getting a double major, or a second concentration, or even degrees in related disciplines gives you more options. The strongest careers we've seen are from people who brought two distinct professions together: an R.N. and a cultural anthropology M.A.; M.D. and biological anthropology Ph.D.; anthropology B.A. and education M.A.; anthropology B.A. and Native American Studies M.A. All of these individuals created their own unique careers based on their unique qualifications.

That said, you need not go so far as obtaining a second degree. If you have a talent or specialized training, think how it can fit together with your formal education to make you stand out in the eyes of potential employers.

ACADEMIC VERSUS APPLIED

There are essentially two professional tracks that can be followed within the field of anthropology: academic and applied/practicing. Riall Nolan (2003: 16) says, "Academic anthropology is a discipline: anthropological practice is a profession." The academic track generally requires a Ph.D. and puts the applicant in the position to apply for jobs within colleges and universities. Some academic anthropologists have an applied research focus, but again, the qualification here is a Ph.D. (See Appendix 2, Career

Stories, and additional information in Appendix 3, Resources.) There are applied anthropologists who work within the academic environment, and they are constrained by the same levels of internal requirements as other academic positions. For this book, however, we choose to combine applied and practicing anthropological positions under the "applied" banner.

Because applying for academic jobs (and other types of jobs that an academic anthropologist would look for) is different from what is required in the applied track, we have dedicated two separate chapters exclusively to the academic career path. For more information on the options within the academic track and the job application process, see Chapters 13 and 14.

The "academic" exception is teaching at the pre-collegiate level. We consider this more of an applied anthropology position and so have included teaching high school in this chapter.

"There is a moment, when it all comes clear; when you realize that what you do isn't an academic exercise, but matters to people, real people. It can be meeting with tribal elders who are relying on you to identify remnants of their past; neighbors rallying around a school full of memories and a lost way of life; or an African village trying to emerge into the 21st century without losing its voice. Once I experienced this moment, I never looked back. I knew what I wanted to do; I wanted to be a contract archaeologist."
—Jeffrey H. Altschul, Ph.D., RPA, Founder, Statistical Research, Inc.

The Applied Tracks

Colleges and universities produce more graduate students than the academic track can accommodate. According to an article published in the *Chronicle of Higher Education* (Montell 2000), the American Anthropological Association "estimates that roughly half of recent doctoral recipients in the field will take jobs in government or the private sector." Since most professors have only ever worked in an academic setting, they often lack the experience to provide guidance beyond the institutional walls. Another problem we have found in discussing careers with our colleagues is that careers outside of the academy are looked down upon by many anthropology professors. Such opinions are changing. In a recent article in the *Chronicle of Higher Education* by Audrey Williams June (June 2010), the Executive Director of the AAA is quoted as saying the association has "made a concerted effort to try to reach out to [those anthropologists outside of academe] and to be relevant." In the same article, Linda A. Bennett, a professor of anthropology at the University of Memphis, is quoted as saying, "People think that anthropologists are either practitioners or academics, but it's not that linear."

Do not simply accept that a job outside of a major university is unworthy of your brilliance. There is nothing wrong with you if you desire something other than that ivory-tower position, and there is nothing wrong with *accepting* something other than that ivory-tower position.

> *"I feel like I never made a clean transition from student to career because I have never been in a for-profit company. . . . We academics are so spoiled! It's grueling, but it's rather a lot like being a grad student in some ways, and the transition isn't as harsh."*
> —Kelley Hays-Gilpin, Professor, Northern Arizona University

Unlike the academic track, the applied track can be entered at any level of education, from a B.A. to a Ph.D. Careers within the applied track can be found within governmental agencies and the private sector, or within businesses that are solely anthropological in nature or those that employ anthropologists for particular roles and perspectives.

The term "applied anthropology" is generally accepted to mean taking anthropological ideas, concepts, and information and applying them to contemporary issues. Some applied anthropologists, such as Genevieve Bell (*http://www.intel.com/pressroom/kits/bios/gbell.htm*), work in large corporations, using anthropological techniques to help the organization deal with worker training, marketing, or other aspects of the corporate world (also see Elizabeth K. Briody's career story, Appendix 2). Some anthropologists use their training to help develop programs to alleviate social issues (see Jennifer Cardew Kersey's career story, Appendix 2). Even archaeologists do applied anthropology when they "apply" archaeology to help federal, state, local, and tribal agencies comply with laws to help projects achieve compliance (see Michelle M. Carnes's career story, Appendix 2).

The Academic Exception: High School

Some high schools in the United States offer anthropology, archaeology, or forensic anthropology classes. (Forensic anthropology has become particularly popular since the introduction of the television "CSI" series.) Anthropology and archaeology classes are usually available as electives through the social studies or history department. Most states require their teachers to have a teaching certificate, in addition to a major in history or anthropology, but some states will hire individuals with a master's degree and some education training. Private and charter schools may have more flexible certification requirements. If teaching high school is of interest, you should check with the department of education for the state where you'd like to teach, before completing your studies.

If you do decide to become a high school teacher, be prepared to enter under the auspices of teaching core courses and inserting an anthropological perspective within them. When given the opportunity, you may be able to teach anthropology as a stand-alone class.

Regardless of the level you plan to teach, consider taking some education classes. If you are working, or taking a full course load, you may be able to find alternatives to the traditional university program. Many universities now offer weekend and evening classes geared to working adults. One of the most important elements of education training is practice (student) teaching. This is where you get your real classroom experience. Teaching might seem like an ideal job: I mean we've just spent how many years behind a desk? But, being on the other side of the desk can be a real shock. Carol did her student teaching with an incredible master teacher in a fourth grade classroom. It was probably one of the most amazing educational experiences of her career, but she realized that to be the teacher she wanted to be, she'd have to work 24 hours a day, 365 days a year, and there was no way she could make that sort of commitment at that point in her life.

CAREER STORIES

There are more career options in applied anthropology than you can imagine. Perhaps the easiest way to highlight the diversity is to describe our own career paths and present you with some career stories of others who have pursued an applied path. We include four career stories here that you can read and use with the "Where Can I Work?" exercise on page 47 later in this chapter. Additional stories can be found in Appendix 2.

Joe Watkins, Ph.D.
Director, Native American Studies, University of Oklahoma
My first job out of college within the field of anthropology was as an archaeologist for a federal agency. I was able to take advantage of my field experience and my education to influence the practice of archaeology in the southeastern United States. The area where I worked had three large reservoir projects going: the Tennessee-Tombigbee Waterway, the Richard B. Russell Reservoir, and the Tellico Dam projects. While I wasn't doing field work, I was able to get into the field to review the work that other ar-

chaeologists were doing. I also learned a great deal about federal contracting and the types of archaeological research that could be done with federal assistance.

After leaving the federal agency, I started my own archaeological consulting firm in Oklahoma. I was able to get some small contracts primarily in the southern and central Great Plains, but also in other parts of the United States. I was responsible for obtaining the contract, doing the fieldwork, analyzing any artifacts found during the fieldwork, and writing up the final report, all while working on the finances. I also worked as a crew member and crew chief for other contracting firms when I didn't have my own contracts.

For a time I was out of archaeology, working for a nonprofit legal services organization and a museum, but I eventually went back to doing what I enjoyed the most. I worked for large and small private consulting firms, as an archaeologist for the University of Oklahoma doing cultural resources inventories for the Oklahoma Department of Transportation, and then as an agency archaeologist in the Southern Plains Region of the Bureau of Indian Affairs. In all those jobs, I was responsible for writing large and small reports to agencies, to supervisors, or to interested groups, as well as writing clear, concise letters outlining what I had done or was proposing to do.

After I completed my Ph.D. in 1994, I felt the need to "give back" to the discipline. I wrote about my experiences as a Native American archaeologist; I revised my dissertation and got it published; I got involved in national anthropological organizations and local tribal ones; I "gave back" with a vengeance! Ultimately, as a result of all these activities, I landed a job at the University of New Mexico and now at the University of Oklahoma. I love the students and the teaching (but could do without the administrative aspects of it). I now struggle to find time to write and to conduct research, but I still find archaeology to be as rewarding as it was more than 40 years ago when I started.

Carol J. Ellick, M.A.
Archaeological and Cultural Education Consultants

I was lucky. My first paid position in anthropology was the summer prior to the completion of my B.A. I spent that summer and part of the fall working as a laboratory technician and as an assistant pedologist (soil scientist) on a large contract archaeology project. It was my first taste of fieldwork, and perhaps not my best, but overall it was exactly what I'd hoped for—outside, in the sun, using my mind, and getting paid for it. This job was my first in cultural resource management (CRM), the area in which I would end up spending the majority of my time for the first 30 years of my career. It sounds simple, but it hasn't been. Working as a field technician or crew chief took applying to every possible agency and organization that may have won contracts during the previous season.

During my career as a field archaeologist, I worked for CRM programs in anthropology departments and for private companies. If a field project was only a few weeks long, I could find myself working for two, three, and possibly four employers in one year. Some years, I worked in three different states! The only part that wasn't fun was sending letters of application and filling out federal and state forms during tax season. And, when I use the term "field archaeologist," I don't just mean digging holes in the dirt. I spent my summers on crews walking survey, excavating, drawing stratigraphy, gridding sites, and doing cartography. I stamped bags in the lab, processed artifacts, and prepared samples for analysis. I worked as a field and lab technician, crew chief, lab manager, and project supervisor. During the off-season, I used my artistic talents and illustrated artifacts and finalized maps for publication. I worked for the Forest Service, Bureau of Land Management, three major universities in Washington State, an uncountable number of archaeological consulting firms, and a school district. The way I figured it, my mark of success was staying out of the unemployment lines.

The longer I worked, the more specific my area of interest became, until I ultimately settled into archaeological education and public outreach. While working in this field, I worked for for-profit and not-for-profit companies and organizations. I also held workshops, lectured at universities, and taught university classes. Over time, this all added up to a career.

Robynne Locke
ICF International

About halfway through my M.A. in cultural anthropology at the University of Denver, I began to be concerned about what I was going to do after graduation. I wasn't sure if continuing on to a Ph.D. program was something I was ready for, but I had a hard time imagining an alternative. Who would pay me to do what I am passionate about?

When it came to finding my dream job, I had several counts against me. First, I owed a significant amount in school loans that I would have to start repaying after graduation. Second, the country was deep in the midst of a recession, and every day I heard more and more news on the growing unemployment rates of young professionals. Third, I wanted to return to Vermont to be closer to friends and family, but the small rural state has few opportunities for someone pursuing a career in international research. If I wanted a career in anthropology, I knew I would need to plan ahead.

My first decision was to delay my fieldwork until the fall (by taking independent research and study credits) and to use the summer to get an internship in a place I might want to work after graduation. I started by doing a Web search of areas of interest to me, but all I could find were a handful of small nonprofits who were either not hiring, would not pay enough for me to pay back my loans, or would not allow me to use the skills I learned in graduate school. Then, finally, I came across a company called ICF International, a research and consulting firm with an office in Burlington, Vermont. As a "do-gooder," I never considered working in the private sector, as I had the perception that doing so would somehow conflict with my overall goal of helping others. But after looking closely into the company, I found that they worked in the areas that I care passionately about: health, education, development, energy, and social justice. Although the company had no formal internship program or temporary positions available, I sent in my résumé and requested an interview. The company decided to give me a chance, and I found the opportunity I was looking for. At the end of the summer, they encouraged me to apply for a full-time position after graduation, and I did just that. I am now a Research Assistant/Analyst with ICF Macro International, and looking forward to building my career with the company.

There are several benefits to working for a large company in the private sector. I earn enough to slowly pay back my school loans, I know there is opportunity to move up in my career, and I am gaining the hands-on business and management experience that was previously lacking in my mostly academic résumé. Most importantly, the wide scope of ICF's work allows me to participate in a variety of interesting projects. I was even recently approached with the opportunity to assist with research on human trafficking, which was the topic of my M.A. thesis.

There are also some drawbacks to this work. It is not the career I originally imagined for myself. In my current position, "the field" is in my office, not in some remote village; data collection consists of hundreds of thousands of surveys completed by mail or by phone, not through years of establishing a relationship with a community; and analysis is completed by a team of statisticians, and not the intimate experience I had with my own MA thesis. But as the office anthropologist, I have found my supervisors to be incredibly supportive, encouraging me to bring my unique interests and skills to the company, and I know that eventually I will make my own way.

I would encourage anyone graduating with a B.A., M.A., or Ph.D. in anthropology to consider a career in the private sector. Companies like ICF are doing important work in areas of critical interest to anthropologists, and I believe the opportunity to work together in these areas is a mutually beneficial one.

Jennifer Cardew Kersey
Intrepid Consultants in Seattle, WA

Not too long ago, someone referred to me as a "practicing anthropologist," and I realized . . . I'm not a student anymore, I'm really an anthropologist! It sounds silly, but the question of "when am I an anthropologist versus a student of anthropology?" is one that is asked in departments across the country. My journey has been stressful at times, but it's been fun. And doing great research that benefits consumers makes it all worthwhile.

My graduate courses at the University of North Texas (UNT) really prepared me to use anthropology outside of academia by providing hands-on experience in the courses and in my practicum. I undertook my practicum with a small market research boutique, Intrepid Consultants in Seattle, WA, and I've worked there for two years now. I started conducting interviews after just a few months on the job, and I now lead multidisciplinary teams researching everything from physicians' perspectives on health and wellness, to what "local" means to children, to Web developers' habit and practices. A lot of my fieldwork consists of in-depth telephone interviews and focus groups in facilities and in homes. I have ventured into the world of virtual ethnography and social media monitoring in order to contextualize offline research and provide a more holistic view to our client.

The path I took to get to where I am now was untraditional at the time. I completed my degree in the UNT online Master's in Anthropology Program. I can honestly say that I got a great education and successfully entered into the anthropology community of praxis (CoP) by attending the Society for Applied Anthropology (SfAA) and American Anthropological Association (AAA) annual meetings, reaching out to others, and connecting with people online.

I actually found my practicum internship through a post on Twitter in 2006. It was an offer from an anthropologist working at Intrepid who had been following my Twitter feed. In the age of social networking, connecting with anthropologists is easier than ever. Being an anthropologist is wonderful because it means you're a part of a community, and it's a community that will support you throughout your career by giving you feedback or answers when you need them, connecting you with jobs, and giving you a sound body of theory to apply in your research.

The important thing to remember is to go into something you enjoy, with people you enjoy working with. If you don't, you'll only find frustration.

➳ *EXERCISE:* Where Can I Work?

In August 2010, the American Anthropological Association posted a PowerPoint presentation on their website, "Anthropology for Businesses," a slide show containing some very valuable information for those considering an applied career (AAA 2010a). Slide 2 asks, "Who Employs Anthropologists?" and goes on to list the following corporations: Intel, Citicorp, AT&T, Kodak, Sapient, Hauser Design, Boeing, Motorola, Walt Disney, Microsoft, General Mills, Hallmark, Travel One, Hanseatic Group, Manchester Memorial, Palisades Pharmaceuticals, and Celanese Corporation. You will find an even more expanded list of governmental agencies, companies, and organizations that have anthropologists on their payroll in Appendix 1. Your first task in this exercise is to identify ten for-profit, nonprofit, and governmental agencies that employ anthropologists with the background and training that you plan to have when you enter the job market. Second, look at the lists, check websites, search for the names of the anthropologists, and review their bios and qualifications. Note the results of your search in your journal and create a document listing relevant information that you can use for future reference. ◑

➳ *EXERCISE:* Comparing Careers

Read through the career stories in this chapter and in Appendix 2. Select three or four that are of interest to you. Then, for comparison purposes, create a table with four columns and enough rows to accommodate the number of career stories you are examining. In the first column of the table, list the individual's degrees, area of specialization, and areas of expertise. In the second column, list the agencies and organizations each person has worked for. In the third column, list the types of jobs they have held. In the last column, list the similarities and differences between the careers, based on areas of specialization and who they work for. Below the table, write a response to the question, "If I were going to follow the same path, what else would I need in order to do it?" ◑

SUMMARY

In this chapter, we covered in the most general terms the four fields of anthropology. We asked you to consider what got you interested in becoming an anthropologist and what you want to do with a degree in anthropology. We explored what jobs go with which degree, and discussed following an academic versus an applied track. And, we asked you to document when you got interested in anthropology and how you have fostered your interest over the intervening years. The exercises were to document (in your journal) where you could work within your field of interest, and to produce a table that listed agencies and organizations and types of jobs by comparing career stories.

FOR THE PORTFOLIO

Look back over your personal contract and modify it based on the new information provided in this chapter. Print a copy of the list of potential employers that you produced in your exercises.

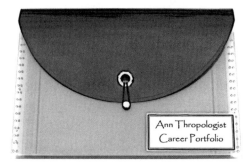

CHAPTER 4

PROFESSIONAL QUALIFICATIONS, STANDARDS, AND ETHICS

Anthropological researchers, teachers, and practitioners are members of many different communities, each with its own moral rules or codes of ethics. Anthropologists have moral obligations as members of other groups, such as the family, religion, and community, as well as the profession. They also have obligations to the scholarly discipline, to the wider society and culture, and to the human species, other species, and the environment. Furthermore, fieldworkers may develop close relationships with persons or animals with whom they work, generating an additional level of ethical considerations.

In a field of such complex involvements and obligations, it is inevitable that misunderstandings, conflicts, and the need to make choices among apparently incompatible values will arise.

Anthropologists are responsible for grappling with such difficulties and struggling to resolve them in ways compatible with the principles stated here.

—AAA Code of Ethics (2009), Excerpts from the Preamble

INTRODUCTION

In this chapter we present information on several interrelated topics, including member organizations, ethics, professional standards, and professionalism (not necessarily in that order). Sometimes the margins of these topics overlap and sometimes they go in opposite directions. Some of these matters are decided by outside entities, some by colleagues, and some by you alone. We start with the self, and personal professionalism, and how it can be achieved.

PROFESSIONALISM AND HOW TO ACHIEVE IT

Professionalism encompasses more than knowledge, skills, and strategies. It is how you package what you can do, along with your attitude and your behavior. The old adages "keep your nose clean" and "don't burn your bridges" are good ones to keep in mind. The field of anthropology is relatively small, and once you get down to the subfield level, there is no such thing as six degrees of separation. You're looking at one or two. It is a community in which everyone knows everyone else, or someone else who does. When you meet someone, you will be asked who you study with or who you work for.

If you stand out, for good or ill, people will know of you long before you walk into their door to apply for a job. If it's for good, then you not only stay employed, but potential employers will call you. If it's for negative reasons, then you may get known as someone who is difficult or doesn't get along well with others. Even simple problems can cause trouble, and this can take a lot of work to repair. Your reputation, good or bad, will precede you.

Building Your Reputation

As an anthropologist, you have been trained as an observer. You know about the concepts of ethnocentrism and cultural relativism. As such, you are entering the working culture somewhat more prepared than others. Teresa Tellechea says, in her career story, "anthropology had given me the main tools to connect with the world, which are to be engaged, open to many and different perspectives, connecting dots across disparate fields, to learn from others, and do something together to solve human problems." We recommend that you use these anthropological skills to your advantage. Watch those around you and the environment that they "inhabit." Note the spoken or unspoken hierarchy, the way people dress, attitudes, and behaviors.

Work hard and learn quickly. Take time to consider what is being said and ask questions. Your first job may not be your ideal job, but use it to your advantage, as a stepping-stone to your future. Develop a dependable work-ethic (see more in the section below). Employers and colleagues will notice if you don't care.

Keep your personal life at home and on your own time. Spending time on Facebook, Twitter, texting, emailing, or taking personal calls take time away from work. Limit these activities to lunchtime, breaks, or after work hours. And, by all means, even on your own time, be careful not to criticize your employer, colleagues, or job in public or on any social networks! People will notice.

You want to be remembered as the person who followed directions, showed up for work on time, stayed focused on the required tasks, did more than requested, had a positive attitude, worked well with others, learned new information or skills quickly, and was enthusiastic even under the most stressful conditions. Avoid gossip and rumors. Before you judge someone based on the word of another, verify your information. Who knows the basis for the rumor or what caused it? Just as you should be a connoisseur of information when doing research, you should consider the source and the context of information about colleagues.

When you walk in for an interview, present at a conference, or volunteer for an agency, you represent not only yourself, but your professors and instructors. Be aware that the person with whom you are talking may know your professors and that anything you say will most likely make its way back to them. Be positive and complimentary.

Remember back to Chapter 1. You are entering this field because you love it, not because it's a big money profession. Some of the worst problems can happen between colleagues by talking about salaries. Don't do it. Walk away. Don't be the one to take in that so-and-so makes more than you do and then compensate by slowing down so that your rate of productivity costs more. If you are unhappy, use direct communication skills (Chapter 11) and speak to your supervisor. Don't gripe to a colleague, as the conversation could make its way through the network and come back to bite you. If you don't want the job, find another. If you don't uphold the professional standards of the employer, you will be let go. "We are all replaceable," the president of one CRM company told Carol when she was considering taking a different type of job in a different location. "Whoever replaces you will not be you, but they will get the job done." During the conversation, he also said that knowing *her*, she would become quickly bored in a job that focused on only one thing. So, the advice worked in his favor; she stayed with the company for nearly ten more years.

MEMBER ORGANIZATIONS

Anthropological organizations are comprised of networks of professionals. Large organizations such as the American Anthropological Association have subdivisions that support programs relating to all four subfields. Other organizations support individual geographic areas and subdisciplines. Organizations are structured at the international, national, regional, state, and local levels. Each one has a specific mission and focus. The organizations are nonprofit entities comprised of officers and boards of directors. These individuals are elected from among the membership.

Most organizations host websites, publish journals and/or newsletters, and sponsor an annual meeting or conference where members can share current research. It is a good idea to research the organizations serving your field of study and join while you are a student. In her career story, Jennifer Cardew Kersey noted that attending annual meetings, reaching out to others, and connecting with people online were all important to her career (see Chapter 3). Student rates are generally less expensive than professional memberships. Joining an organization within your specialty will give you access to a network of professionals beyond those you could reach through your computer or by way of introduction from your professors.

In addition to professional anthropological associations, there are many avocational (non-professional) societies whose memberships include both amateurs and professionals. Anthropology, but archaeology in particular, draws interest from a broad cross section of the general public. Some of the oldest archaeological societies in the United States were started and continue to be sponsored by the interested public. It is important to belong to professional organizations, but it is also beneficial to the profession to belong to and participate with local avocational societies as well. The benefits of belonging go both ways; the amateurs gain from knowing you and receiving information from a professional, and you and the profession gain because these individuals will be better informed and less likely to do harm. Sharing information with the public is listed in the ethics statement, mission statement, or membership agreement of nearly every professional organization. Joining avocational associations provides you with an automatic audience, a network that will then inform others.

Ethics-based Organizations

The Register of Professional Archaeologists (*http://www.rpanet.org/*) is an organization whose purpose is to help develop standards and ethical responsibilities for archaeologists. Its code of conduct states that "Archaeology is a profession, and the privilege of professional practice requires professional morality and professional responsibility, as well as professional competence, on the part of each practitioner." The code goes on to describe an archaeologist's responsibility to the public; to colleagues, employees and students; and to employers and clients. In addition, its Standards of Research Performance are established to help ensure that the quality of information gained from archaeological practice is worth the impacts to the archaeological record.

☙ *EXERCISE:* RESEARCHING ORGANIZATIONS

Take some time to look into which professional organizations support your field of anthropology. Begin by conducting Internet research. Identify three professional organizations—one international, one national, and one regional or local organization. In your journal, note the following information for each organization that you select:

■ Name of organization

■ Address

■ Mission statement

■ Ethics statement

■ Student membership fee

■ Member benefits

■ Date and location of annual meeting (this can change from year to year)

■ Cost of attending annual meeting

To get you started, here is a selection Web addresses for professional organizations:

■ American Association of Physical Anthropologists (AAPA): *http://physanth.org/*.

■ Society for American Archaeology (SAA): *http://www.saa.org/*.

■ Society for Cultural Anthropology (SCA): *http://sca.culanth.org/*.

■ Society for Linguistic Anthropology (SLA): *http://linguisticanthropology.org/*.

- ■ Society for Applied Anthropology (SfAA): *http://www.sfaa.net/*.

- ■ National Association for the Practice of Anthropology (NAPA): *http://practicinganthropology.org/*.

Keep your data in your journal or create a document that contains all of the information. The exercise in Chapter 12 will be based on this research. ☙

As we mentioned earlier, it is a good idea to join at least one organization. Consider whether the international, national, regional, state, or local organization would be the most beneficial to you as you start your career. When making your decision, think about where you might be able to present a paper or publish an article. Local or regional meetings offer excellent opportunities for your initial foray into the professional world. If travel cost is an issue, check with your anthropology department. Many programs offer travel grants to their students who are presenting at a meeting or conference. Ed Jolie says that it is important to attend conferences; giving "papers and seeking funding, even if only small $$, are good practice for article and grant writing and only help you get better." He also thinks that "keeping busy in conferences, workshops, seminars, etc., helps advertise you and offers mini-job presentations whether you know it or not." And, "Eventually your name gets around and you start getting recruited for other projects, which is fun and feels rewarding." Additional information on membership organizations is located in Chapter 12.

PROFESSIONAL QUALIFICATIONS AND STANDARDS

Some agencies and employers have established professional qualifications and criteria. These qualifications set the standard for hiring for specific positions. For example, the Standards and Guidelines for Historic Preservation put out by the U.S. Secretary of the Interior "define minimum education and experience required to perform identification, evaluation, registration, and treatment activities." This document goes on to say that "in some cases, additional areas or levels of expertise may be needed, depending on the complexity of the task and the nature of the historic properties involved." It also defines what is considered "full-time professional experience" (*http://www.nps.gov/history/local-law/Prof_Qual_83.htm*).

An example of a listing from the Secretary of the Interior's Standards and Guidelines for Historic Preservation is as follows:

Archeology

The minimum professional qualifications in archeology are a graduate degree in archeology, anthropology, or closely related field plus:

1. At least one year of full-time professional experience or equivalent specialized training in archeological research, administration or management;

2. At least four months of supervised field and analytic experience in general North American archeology; and

3. Demonstrated ability to carry research to completion.

In addition to these minimum qualifications, a professional in prehistoric archeology shall have at least one year of full-time professional experience at a supervisory level in the study of archeological resources of the prehistoric period.

A professional in historic archeology shall have at least one year of full-time professional experience at a supervisory level in the study of archeological resources of the historic period.

The American Anthropological Association (AAA) and other professional societies and organizations have standards for professionalism embedded within their ethics statements. The AAA standards can be found online at *http://www.aaanet.org/issues/policy-advocacy/upload/AAA-Ethics-Code-2009.pdf.*

The concept of professionalism is also seen in the SAA Principles of Archaeological Ethics Principle No. 2: Accountability. This principle states that "responsible archaeological research, including all levels of professional activity, requires an acknowledgment of public accountability and a commitment to make every reasonable effort, in good faith, to consult actively with affected group(s), with the goal of establishing a working relationship that can be beneficial to all parties involved." The idea of professionalism is also embedded in SAA's other seven principles as well.

Job Announcements

An excellent place to get a feel for the professional qualifications necessary for your career is from job announcements. Job announcements list, in detail, the knowledge, skills, and abilities required for that position. More than likely, the job description has metamorphosed over time as the

knowledge of what that job takes has been refined. Most job announcements are divided into sections related to knowledge based on both formal and non-formal education, technological as well as other skills, and
abilities. The exercise in Chapter 5 will take you through the process of
examining job announcements and creating a list of the knowledge, skills,
and abilities required for the jobs that would interest you.

ETHICS

Joe likes to say that ethics are what you do when nobody is looking. It is
how you handle yourself in difficult situations. It is being above board,
doing no wrong, and doing no harm. It is following the law, even if no law
applies to your specific situation.

Ethics can be defined as the underlying thoughts, ideas, and philosophy that determine the ways you interact with people. Ethics influence
how you think about things, and the ways that you act in certain situations. There are different sorts of ethics and different levels of ethics. All
religions are based on ethical ideals: you shouldn't lie, you shouldn't steal,
you should treat everyone well. These same ethics should apply to your
professional life.

Students also have a code of ethics under which they should operate:
you shouldn't pass off someone else's work as your own (plagiarism), you
shouldn't cheat on tests, and so forth. Such codes are contained within
Student Codes of Conduct or similar documents, but they are codes of
ethics just the same. However, despite the fact that codes of ethics are a
part of our everyday lives, some are not always easily followed.

Should a law always be followed merely because it is the law? Should
we consider the "mitigating circumstances" that led to the breaking of the
law? As noted above, all the major professional anthropological organizations have codes of ethics or ethics statements that guide the actions and
activities of their membership. Some organizations (such as the Register of
Professional Archaeologists) can remove members who break the code of
ethics, while others use these codes as "guidelines." Regardless, ethics play
an important role in the practice of anthropology because our actions as
anthropologists can have far-reaching effects on the people we study.

Most professional codes of ethics outline your ethical responsibility
to your colleagues. It is important to recognize, however, that as you move
into your career, the relationships between you and your colleagues will
change. During your educational career, you have likely observed a student colleague or two who turned the educational process into a competition. Joe remembers a student who would check out all the required
readings as soon as possible as a means of gaining an edge on the other

students competing for funding. This student made good grades, but not many friends.

The particular ethical dilemmas you will face will vary depending on what career path you choose. Philip Young (2008: 62) notes, "Practitioners are likely to face ethical dilemmas that are different from those faced in conventional research, that are more frequent, more complex, and consequently more difficult to resolve." No single subdiscipline is free from ethical issues, and so you should be prepared to face them as your career grows. Jeanine Pfeiffer is an ethnoecologist. Earlier in her career, she accepted a position as a social science research director at a nonprofit, believing that this job had the most to offer her. But she resigned eighteen months later, when she perceived that her "core values were being compromised by the organization's policies and practices." She wished that she had "developed a list of core values before she began applying for positions, as it would have helped her ask more penetrating and insightful questions during the interview process, and to make better choices" (see Pfeiffer's career story in the Appendix 2).

As you become a professional, you will more than likely be asked to work with larger and larger groups of people. More often than not, you will find yourself in situations requiring cooperation rather than competition. If you work in a consulting firm, cooperation among all employees will be necessary to ensure successful completion of projects; if you become an academic anthropologist, while there might be some generalized competition among members of the department, cooperation toward a mutual goal is necessary for the department to flourish. Otherwise, the competition will fragment and destroy it. The best type of competition is within yourself, looking at what you've done before and pushing yourself to do better. Not all competition is bad, but most professionals will agree that cooperation is the key to being a respected and trusted colleague.

PROFESSIONAL IDENTITY

The development of your professional identity is an important facet of professionalism. This may be something you've never considered, but it's important, especially while you are in this transition between student and professional, to reflect on what you call yourself and how others refer to you.

Email

What is your email address? You might consider how a potential employer would view you if your email address read "*likes2party@...*" or "*digme@...*" or even "*arcy2be@...*." Even a cute email address is inappropriate in a professional context. For more information regarding writing and sending email, see Chapter 11.

Professional Name

Before you begin submitting documents, manuscripts, chapters, or papers to conferences, decide what name you plan to use in your byline. Once you begin publishing and people begin searching for your publications, it will be easier to find your work if your professional name stays the same. If your name is Matthew, do you want to publish under Matt or Matthew? Do you want to include your middle name or middle initial? If you are female and are on the verge of tying the knot, will you take your husband's last name, or will you keep your given name as your professional name? If you have already started publishing under your pre-married name, consider keeping it as your pen-name, as it will make it easier for those searching for your publications. As an example, we have a colleague who began publishing articles before she was married ("Jane Doe"). For a time, she kept her name but added her husband's behind a hyphen ("Jane Doe-Smith"). After settling into her domestic relationship, she decided to drop her maiden name and simply to go by her husband's surname ("Jane Smith"). If she divorced, she might go back to her original name ("Jane Doe") or retain her married name. All this presents problems, not only for someone searching for articles written by Jane, but also for those looking at or creating a bibliography. Her references end up being listed in three different places and looking like the work of three different individuals.

If you go by a nickname, should you use it professionally or go by your given name? The nickname might feel too informal, but what if you have always been known by your nickname or your middle name? Might it matter if no one recognized your authorship because no one knew you by your "professional" (given) name?

While you may not need to make a firm decision on this at the moment, it is a good idea to consider the possibilities and the potential ramifications. In other words, it's easier to do it right the first time than to try to undo it later on.

ಌ *EXERCISE:* Design Your Personal Professional Ethics Statement

We all have standards that we live by. We determine consciously or unconsciously the line that we will not or should not cross. In this exercise, you can develop your personal set of ethical standards that can (and should) guide you when making difficult professional decisions. It is important to think about these things before you encounter them.

Begin by researching ethics statements that have been drafted by various professional membership organizations. You can also review general ethics statements or instructions on composing ethics statements. Take a moment to Google "compose a personal ethics statement." Of course, you could start with simple, basic statements like "I will not lie, cheat, or steal." These should form the base of everyone's code of ethics. But what else would be important from a professional anthropological perspective? Here are a few questions to start your ethics development process:

- What is your professional responsibility to the communities you may work with?

- What is your responsibility to your employer, co-workers, employees, and colleagues?

- How should you treat the property of others?

- What should you do if you find yourself in questionable circumstances?

The ethics statement should be no longer than two double-spaced pages—short and to the point. Avoid the use of qualifiers. Use active verbs. Be realistic. The ethics statement will probably change over time, and there may be situations where you slip across the invisible line, but having a framework under which you work provides you just that—a framework. ဆ

Summary

In this chapter we focused on what to consider when developing your professional identity. The exercise on the professional organizations gave you some background on the sorts of anthropological networks out there, but it also helped you narrow your focus on where you should start your journey toward professionalism. And being a professional is more than just gaining the necessary skills required by particular job positions. Becoming a professional requires conscious effort and thought with regard to your display of professional attitude to everyone you might encounter, from the first moment you encounter them. At the conclusion of this chapter, you developed your personal professional ethics statement. This statement should provide a base that can be built upon as you learn from and continue in your career.

FOR THE PORTFOLIO

Your professional identity is the combination of how you present yourself, the portfolio, and its contents. This "package" is what makes you more or less employable than the others who are being considered for the job. To aid in building this professional package, you developed a personal professional ethics statement. This ethics statement should be placed into the Five-Year Plan and Ethics Statement section of your portfolio.

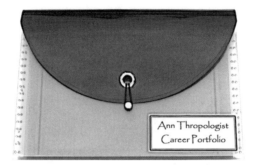

CHAPTER 5

PAST JOBS AND FUTURE CAREERS

"This class is helping me realize that I can combine real-world experiences with my degree and find a job"
—Gwen Mohr, journal comment, Avenues to Professionalism class

INTRODUCTION

This chapter is about transitions and possibilities. It is about trying to find the threads that can be pulled from everything that you've done up to this point and connecting them to what you want to do in the future. If you're feeling anxious and excited, that's good. This is what it's about—stepping up to the edge and knowing not only that the edge is solid, but that the step off is manageable because of the preparations you've made.

Linking Past to Present

How do the jobs that you've held so far help you land that first position of your career? Work experiences reflect more than one thing. They give you combinations of sets of knowledge, skills, and abilities (KSAs). *Knowledge* is the familiarity or understanding of information that you've gained from prior experience. For example, through taking an Introduction to Anthropology class, you have gained a basic knowledge of the subject. A *skill* is a developed talent or ability that comes naturally or easily. Nolan (2003: 35) divides this further into "self-management skills," "functional skills," and "technical skills." Self-management skills that would be useful to an employer might include being a good manager of time, being able to multi-task, or being organized. Good communication skills are an example of a functional skill. Technical skills might include the ability to draw. *Ability* is the competency by which you can perform your tasks. For example, by writing you increase your ability to write free of errors.

So, maybe you've never held a laboratory technician position, but have you ever had a job where you've had to accurately list information, count quantities, weigh, or measure? Maybe you've never conducted an interview. How are your listening skills? What about your ability to take accurate notes? Do you work well with others and take instructions easily? It is essential that you be able to look at what you've done in the context of what you will need to do, and build a bridge that will take you there.

The students in our Avenues to Professionalism class had held quite a range of non-anthropological jobs: personal trainer, babysitter, lab assistant, secretary, soldier, bartender, karate instructor, cleaner, lifeguard, camp counselor, landscaper, police officer, cook, retail salesperson, and computer teacher. What jobs have you had, and how can they help you? In this next exercise, you will identify previous jobs and consider the knowledge, skills, and abilities acquired in those positions.

☙ *EXERCISE:* Duties and Responsibilities

This exercise has two parts. The first is to develop a list of all previous jobs and delineate the tasks performed. The second is to analyze the anthropological skills that you've developed through your formal education.

Part 1: In your journal, or on a new document in your computer, list all of the jobs that you have previously held. (Do not exclude anything.)

After you have a complete list, take each job and list all of your duties and responsibilities—everything you were responsible for within that specific job. Next, identify the jobs that had tasks that might relate to jobs in anthropology. For example, if you worked as a secretary, some of the tasks might have included answering the phone, alphabetizing, filing, organizing, editing, typing, designing graphs and charts, and preparing manuscripts. Skills and abilities would include communicating well, working well with others, ability to follow instructions, and working independently. If you worked as a camp counselor, some of the tasks may have included supervising, teaching wilderness skills, scheduling, and organizing. Skills could have included communicating with different age groups, working with large groups of people, leadership, and patience. Using a highlighter, highlight the tasks and skills on your list that may be relevant to anthropology.

Part 2: After you have completed the job list, consider what skills you have acquired through your classes and labs. We're not talking about just the theoretical knowledge, but rather the directly applicable skill set that is specific to anthropology. How are your powers of observation and inference? Your ability to identify traits and attributes, to categorize, and communicate? Are you able to work independently, as part of a team, understand the "other," and deal with different cultures and beliefs even in uncomfortable situations? Are you patient and tolerant?

The task at hand is to parlay seemingly unrelated skills and abilities into a résumé that will earn you your first job. Save these lists. You will use the information to build your résumé and to begin your curriculum vita. ❧

Knowledge, Skills, and Abilities

"I know I will have to get myself as prepared as possible in terms of KSAs and set up a large contact network. Good fortune never hurts either."
—Ian Thompson, journal comment, Avenues to Professionalism class

Even if you've just completed a degree that would qualify you for a management position, we recommend you acquire some hands-on experience. School gives you a base of knowledge, but working in your chosen field will give you the skills and abilities you will need to successfully oversee a staff or teach a course. There are several knowledge and skill sets that you will need to achieve competency in your field.

Riall Nolan (2003: 78) mentions the advantages that come from a degree in anthropology: the ability to identify the major groups within your work; the ability to conduct and glean relevant information from research; ease in recognizing the "native language" of various domains; interviewing skills and deriving patterns from such interviews; the ability to comprehend the complexity of situations and the adaptability to deal with it.

Additionally, in a more general vein (2003: 119–120), he notes that anthropologists "look to culture for both answers and solutions"; we gain "understanding of a situation . . . by going out and talking to the people involved" rather than "imposing abstract theories, structures, or solutions on a situation"; anthropologists are "holistic in their approaches and perspectives"; we "look for similarities and differences between situations . . . are very good at comparing and contrasting cases, and building up a broad understanding of pattern that is ultimately more useful than single-instance learning." Finally, he notes that anthropologists are "interactive" and recognize that "people's informal contacts generate important structures and meanings of their own," thereby making anthropologists good administrators and managers.

In her career story (see Chapter 3), Robynne Locke talks about skills in terms of her current position with ICF International. She mentions that, as the "office anthropologist," she plies her trade within an office— not in the field—collecting surveys completed by mail or phone, which are then analyzed by others; yet still, she is able to bring her "unique interests and skills to the company." Maria Michalczk, registered nurse, says that she believes that her education in anthropology gave her "great tools to work on policy issues related to health and culture and could speak to cultural concerns and disparate health policies in our country." She goes on to say, "Although my nursing background gave me tools to actually take care of patients, it was the anthropology discipline that provided me the background to critically think about and apply anthropological principles to the work I now do." Michelle M. Carnes identifies what she calls "a giant toolbox of abilities" that includes "sharp writing skills, public speaking practice, course curriculum development, teaching experience (translating complex concepts for laypersons), self-directed learning/research capabilities, independent work styles requiring little supervision/guidance, strategies to manage multiple projects/priorities, interpersonal/group facilitation skills, ability to maintain records for long-term projects (if a dissertation isn't a "long-term project," I don't know what is!), knowledge of IRB requirements and responsible handling/protection of sensitive research information. We've dealt with customer service issues (irate students, complaining parents), created and enforced policies (classrooms need 'em). We've managed bosses (ahem, advisers) and taken sole responsibility for our work, stood by it, answered questions about it and been prepared to be criticized for it." She goes on to say, "When you start working in the applied field, I think you'll notice that these are skills that others will come to count on you for—and they are skills which make you a huge asset. These are skills which grad students must possess in order to successfully complete a graduate program, so ultimately, think of your experience as a job. In many ways, it is. This will help you translate your training for an employer if they ask you what you can do for them. Translating anthropology is important, but having been a doctoral grad student is a badge of honor all its own too! Don't sell yourself short—it's not just about your content knowledge. We have skills, we are valuable . . . and the world (desperately) needs us."

Do you recognize these skills within yourself? Has your degree path created these aspects in the way you look at the world?

WHAT EXACTLY
DO YOU WANT TO DO?

Now that you've identified the tasks that you've previously performed that might be useful to your future employment, it's time to consider particular jobs or specialties. If you are entering the field of linguistics, are you interested in working with Native American tribes on maintaining language? Are you entering linguistics but have a love of music? Have you considered ethnomusicology? If so, perhaps you'd enjoy working at a music library, on the humanities council, or in the Rock and Roll Hall of Fame. The possibilities of jobs and locations are beyond what one mind can imagine. In an attempt to assist you with brainstorming ideas, we've gathered career stories from professionals in the field and a list of agencies and organizations that employ anthropologists. These stories and the list represent a narrow view of what is out there, and they offer only some of the options in the United States. If you plan to live beyond the borders, your job search will have to tap into global networks.

The best way to consider the broad range of jobs and careers is to do a bit of research. In the next exercise, you will find career articles written by anthropologists. Good sources for articles on this topic are the newsletters or magazines of the professional organizations. As a base, you may want to start by looking at the career stories in Appendix 2 and at the list of employers who hire anthropologists in Appendix 1.

ᛒ *EXERCISE:* Career Article Search

Search for an article about a career, or an individual who is involved in a career, that you would be interested in pursuing. Read the article. On the odd page in your journal, write one paragraph that summarizes the article. On the even side (for thoughts and ideas), opposite the summary, write what you like about the career identified in the article, and list ideas that reading it inspired or that you had not thought of before. Some of the articles located by students in the Avenues to Professionalism class are listed in the Resources, Appendix 3. ᛇ

ᛒ *EXERCISE:* Reading Up on Careers and Reading between the Lines

Before continuing with this chapter, take some time to find another article about a career in a field that interests you. (You could use the same article, but that would defeat the purpose of looking at a range of career possibilities.) Read the article and use it as a basis for research. Address the following questions in your journal: Who was the article about? What is his or her background? Where does he or she currently work? What jobs, tasks, and responsibilities are described? How similar is your track to his or hers? Finally, if this is a job that you would like to have, what knowledge, skills, and abilities do you need before you could qualify for this position?

You might be able to answer some of these questions by reading the article; some might require more research. Look into who wrote it; it's always good to know your sources. Following up with an author search is a good way to practice tracking down information and to make sure it is valid before following the author's advice. ᛇ

Where Are Jobs Posted?

How and where are jobs posted? If you can't find openings, it is difficult to apply. As noted earlier, Jennifer Cardew Kersey found her internship through a Twitter post. More traditional places to start your search are websites of professional organizations, under their job, employment, or career pages. From the "Researching Organizations" Exercise in Chapter 4, you are already familiar with three organizations. Whether you plan to work inside academia or out, a couple of good general resources for job listings are the employment page of the Society for Applied Anthropology

(SfAA) website *(http://www.sfaa.net/sfaajobs.html)* and the National Association for the Practice of Anthropology (NAPA) website *(http://practicinganthropology.org/jobs/)*. For information on employers within academia, see Chapter 13.

Employers Outside of Academia

Identifying the agencies and organizations that hire anthropologists within your field of interest will help you find the jobs that interest you. The following list of potential agencies and organizations that hire anthropologists came out of a brainstorm session by the students in the Avenues to Professionalism class. To get you started, we've supplemented the list of places by identifying some of the specific jobs and providing some websites. A more complete list of agencies and organizations that hire anthropologists is included in Appendix 1.

Government Agencies
There are many agencies in federal, state, county, city, municipal, and local certified governments that hire anthropologists. "The federal government," writes Shirley Fiske (2008: 110), "is arguably the largest employer of anthropologists outside of universities." She goes on to say that Office of Personnel Management (OPM) data "show 144 general anthropologists and 1150 archaeologists working for the federal government" (Fiske 2008: 111).

Among the federal agencies that have positions are the Bureau of Land Management, Bureau of Indian Affairs, Bureau of Reclamation, Center for Disease Control, Department of Defense, Federal Highways Administration, Forest Service, National Park Service, U.S. Army Corps of Engineers (civil and military branches), U.S. Department of Agriculture, U.S. Department of Health and Human Services, U.S. Department of the Interior, and the U.S. Fish and Wildlife Service, to name a few. Jim McDonald notes that at the time he was graduating, "a few large departments were turning out way more Ph.D.s than there were decent openings. . . . On the other hand, it appeared that there would be quite a few federal job openings, so I firmed up my intention to take a terminal M.A. in Archaeological Resource Management and find a job with the feds." And he did, and he has stayed within the Forest Service, making it his career for 35 years.

If you are looking for a job in a federal agency, *http://www.usajobs.opm.gov/* is a good place to start.

A quick search on the USA Jobs website using the word "anthropology" just provided a list of 178 jobs that hire people with degrees in anthropology. Among the jobs listed in January 2010 were Archaeologist, Foreign Affairs Officer, Park Ranger, Historian, Cultural Anthropologist, Ecologist

(Quantitative) or Statistician, GIS Specialist, and Operations Research Analyst. You might also take a look at the career stories by Michelle M. Carnes, Jim McDonald, and Carolyn J. McClellan. These are all available in Appendix 2.

The governmental hiring process may be changing. On May 11, 2010, President Obama announced that the federal government needed to reform its hiring process. In the Presidential Memorandum titled "Improving the Federal Recruitment and Hiring Process," President Obama called on "executive departments and agencies (agencies) to overhaul the way they recruit and hire our civilian workforce. Americans must be able to apply for Federal jobs through a commonsense hiring process and agencies must be able to select high-quality candidates efficiently and quickly. Moreover, agency managers and supervisors must assume a leadership role in recruiting and selecting employees from all segments of our society." The full memorandum can be found online at *http://www.whitehouse.gov/the-press-office/presidential-memorandum-improving-federal-recruitment-and-hiring-process*.

What does this mean? In short, it supports the needs of prospective employees (like you) to build a network and get known by the people who are hiring or may be hiring in the future. An excellent way to get known is to begin working during your student years, either during the summer or as a student employee during the academic year.

Some federal agencies have employment opportunities for students whereby the agency will pay your college tuition in exchange for work. Generally, the agency hires you to work while you are in school; then, after you graduate, you owe them a year for every year of college they paid for. (It is sort of the civil service version of ROTC.) The Forest Service Student Career Experience Program (SCEP) provides entry-level jobs that relate directly to a student's career path. The Forest Service website states that "SCEP students may be non-competitively converted to career, term, or career-conditional appointments." Erin Hudson, Archaeologist for the Sandia Ranger District of the Cibola National Forest (and former student in Avenues to Professionalism) shares the following story of her involvement in the SCEP program.

> I started graduate school at the University of New Mexico in 2005. Shortly after the start of the semester, I learned that the Cibola National Forest was looking for a student archaeologist who could update their geographic information systems (GIS) heritage database. I submitted my résumé and shortly after received my first job with the federal government in the Student Temporary Employment Pro-

gram (STEP). Although my job was dependent on the budget, it was perfect; I worked part-time through the school year as my schedule allowed. In the spring of 2006, I was selected for jury duty and missed two weeks of work and school! My boss asked to meet with me shortly after I returned, and I thought, "Oh no, there's no more money and I'm going to be let go!" Instead, she offered me a Student Career Employment Program (SCEP) position.

I had never heard about the SCEP program before and could hardly believe my luck when my boss filled me in on the details. As a SCEP, I would receive all of the benefits of a full-time employee, including health insurance and retirement, but would continue to work part-time while in school. When I graduated, I would be converted to a full-time position as a District Archaeologist. With most SCEP positions, you are not required to take the job that is offered to you or to spend a certain amount of time working for the agency after you graduate. Neither is your agency required to give you a job upon graduation. They can also offer you a position at another location.

My boss told me to spend some time thinking about it, but I admit I was sold when she said "permanent job" and "health insurance." I became a SCEP in the summer of 2006 and was converted to a full-time career conditional position when I graduated in 2007.

Most of us go to college with a general idea of what we want to do when we graduate; however, we often don't act on our career choices until graduation is upon us or even after. By then, it can be difficult to find a job, particularly a full-time position, because you may be competing with people who have years of practical experience. Obtaining a SCEP while in school is a wonderful way to gain experience and training in archaeology that you may not receive in school. It provides a working environment that is geared around your education—the goal is to get you through school, not to work you like a full-time employee. And most importantly, it provides you with the chance to familiarize yourself with an agency without making a long-term commitment. You will know whether it is the right fit for you by the time you are ready to convert to a full-time job. And if it's not, you can always choose not to stay with the agency.

I cannot express how wonderful this program can be for students and encourage all who are interested in government archaeology to seek out employment before they graduate! Look for SCEP positions on USA Jobs, but more importantly, *be proactive!* Contact the federal agencies near you and send them a résumé, particularly right before the summer field season, and don't say no to a STEP; it may be temporary, but it is a foot in the door. You never know where it might lead you.

Summer and temporary student employment is also possible through the Student Temporary Employment Program (STEP). According to the Forest Service website, this program "provides an opportunity for students to earn money, continue their education, train with professionals, and combine academic study with on-the-job experience. Work does not have to be related to the student's academic or career goals." More information on the Forest Service SCEP and STEP programs can be found at *http://www.fs.fed.us/fsjobs/forestservice/scep.html*. If you are interested, you are encouraged to contact your local Forest Service Human Resource office. Check out the story in Chapter 10 for an example of how Carol's daughter's STEP parlayed into a post-graduation job.

State agencies generally mirror their federal counterparts in name and structure. In addition, each state has a State Historic Preservation Office, with a State Historic Preservation Officer (SHPO). State government officials carry out the national historic preservation program as delegates of the Secretary of the Interior pursuant to the National Historic Preservation Act of 1966, as amended. Contact information for the SHPOs can be found on the National Council for State Historic Preservation Officers website, *http://www.ncshpo.org/*.

The other state-based agencies that are part of a national program are the state departments of transportation. The full list of state departments of transportation can be found on the Federal Highways website, *http://www.fhwa.dot.gov/webstate.htm*.

Both of the above-listed state agencies hire anthropologists. In addition, some counties and cities have historic preservation ordinances and archaeological staff positions to enforce them.

Law Enforcement Agencies

The airing of television programs such as "CSI: Crime Scene Investigation," "CSI: Miami," "Bones," and "NCIS" has stimulated a new generation of students to enter the field of forensic anthropology and, to a lesser extent, behavioral anthropology—an influence called "the CSI effect." Donald Shelton, in the *National Institute of Justice Journal* (No. 259), says that one 2006 weekly Nielsen rating indicated that:

■   30 million people watched "CSI" on one night.

■   70 million watched at least one of the three "CSI" shows.

So many people spending so much time in front of the TV can make us forget that TV is not reality. The glamour and glitz we see there is mostly in the mind of the beholder. But some law enforcement agencies have taken advantage of the public's interest in modern crime-solving techniques by offering workshops or classes. If you are interested in working for a law enforcement agency in the field of forensics or behavioral profiling, take a class from an agency. In addition to basic anthropological training, behavioral anthropologists recommend that students considering the field take a course combined with psychology. Articles by Larry Sontag (2006) and Elaine Robbins (2006) offer examples of ways that anthropologists are used by law enforcement agencies.

All of these options will give you the opportunity to meet people in the field and to begin building your network. There are federal, state, county, and city agencies that hire forensic anthropologists. Smaller law enforcement agencies may share forensic teams with other agencies, or they may bring in specialists from the state or local medical examiner's office. Some of the agencies that hire forensic anthropologists include the Federal Bureau of Investigation, police departments, sheriff's departments, and offices of the medical examiner.

Current information about the forensic sciences, as well as job announcements, can be found in *Forensic Magazine* (*http://www.forensicmag.com*). Additional information about the field of forensic anthropology and the broader field of physical anthropology can be found on the American Association of Physical Anthropologists' web page, *http://physanth.org/career*. If you hope to do "real" forensic work, you should look into certification through the American Board of Forensic Anthropology (*http://www.theabfa.org*). On the page "For Students," they have a complete list of information and programs for those interested in pursuing this career.

Although forensics may be the first career that comes to mind in this day and age, it is not the only job for biological anthropologists. Biological anthropologists also work with archaeologists on field projects where human remains are often encountered. They may also work with investigators on Archaeological Resources Protection Act (ARPA) violations and on international antiquities trafficking cases with Immigrations and Customs Enforcement (ICE).

Museums
Museums hire professionals from each of the disciplines, but most look for people with master's degrees in museum studies first, and their area of

expertise second. N. Elizabeth Schlatter, in her book *Museum Careers: A Practical Guide for Students and Novices,* says, "There's no one direct route to a museum job" (2008:10). Who is hired at which museum is based on the specific focus of the museum. According to Larry Zimmerman, Professor of Anthropology and Museum Studies, Indiana University-Purdue University Indianapolis, "80% of jobs are in small museums such as historic houses, county historical societies, and the like" (personal communication). An excellent organization for information on historical museums is the American Association for State and Local History (AASLH), *http://www.aaslh.org.*

Museum jobs are broken down into categories such as curator, exhibits designer, and registrar. Schlatter provides an excellent list of museum positions by job focus. For example, if you were interested in jobs dealing with objects and/or exhibits, you would want to read her Chapter 3, which explains how the conservator, curator, designer, exhibition manager, librarian/archivist, photographer, preparatory/art handler, and registrar/collections manager each play a role. Interested in a public focus? Read Chapter 4. Each chapter includes job descriptions, educational requirements, and salary ranges. In Chapter 7, Schlatter goes on to clearly and concisely outline the most common majors among museum employees and explains what you can do with an undergraduate or graduate degree in each area.

Anthropology museums, art museums, natural history museums, and history museums all need qualified individuals to work within their departments and with their collections. Carolyn McClellan chose an applied path because it offered her "more potential." McClellan is now the Assistant Director for Community and Constituent Services at the National Museum of the American Indian. Her career story can be found in Appendix 2.

If you are interested in working in a museum setting, consider upping your value by taking a museum studies class or volunteering for your local museum. Volunteering or doing an internship (which we talk about more in Chapter 10) will not only build your knowledge and skills, it will introduce you to people working in the field who will be hiring when positions become available. And again, we cannot stress enough the importance of getting out there and building your network.

For more information on types of museums, the Virginia Association of Museums has a good list: *http://www.vamuseums.org/Resources/ ForMuseumStudiesStudents/TypesofMuseums/tabid/160/Default.aspx* .

Another good resource for exploring jobs in museums is the American Association of Museums website, *http://www.aam-us.org/aviso/index.cfm.* On the day we checked the AAM website, there were 48 jobs listed. Museums looking to hire included the Buffalo Bill Historical Center, Alaska State Museum, City of Manhattan (Kansas), Rock and Roll Hall of Fame, and multiple art museums throughout the country. Job openings included grants managers, curator positions, directors, assistant directors, educators, and a systems and digital collections librarian.

American Indian Tribes

American Indian tribes hire anthropologists to assist with a wide range of community projects. Linguistic and cultural anthropologists are hired by tribes for assistance with language documentation and retention, culture revitalization, and historic preservation programs. Many tribes also have museums that hire outside assistants. If you'd like to explore ideas for the types of things that anthropologists have studied with regard to Native Americans, take the time to look over the bibliography compiled by Peter N. Jones and Darby Stapp (2008) for the Society for Applied Anthropology. It is an incredible resource, listing all articles concerning Native Americans originally published in *Human Organization* (1941–2008) and *Practicing Anthropology* (1979–2008). The document can be accessed on the SfAA website at *http://www.sfaa.net/committees/indianissues/HOandPABiblio.pdf.*

Tribes hire archaeologists to analyze data and provide evidence that might support land claims as well as for cultural resources inventory and compliance issues. Ninety tribes (as of August 2010) have Tribal Historic Preservation Offices (THPO). These tribal offices have taken over the responsibilities for historic preservation on tribal lands that had previously been overseen by the SHPO. More information regarding THPOs can be found on the National Association of Tribal Preservation Officers web page: *http://www.nathpo.org/mainpage.html.*

Private Industry, Not-for-Profits, Non-Governmental Agencies (NGOs), and Other Realms

An anthropologist's broad base of training can offer significant contributions to almost any field and almost any employer. Anthropology takes whatever behavior is the subject of research and places it within the social and environmental context of the groups under study. It also considers the wide range of cultural beliefs and practices that influence human actions. The skills learned by the anthropologist fit well within the basics that drive industry and commerce, such as market research, advertising, human resources management, and many other industrial applications. Almost any industry that involves humans to any extent can (and probably should) use anthropologists.

Probably one of the best places to find insights into the many areas where anthropology is practiced and where anthropologists can find careers is within the American Anthropological Association's *Anthropology News*. Articles such as "Beyond the University: Teaching Ethnographic Methods in the Corporation" (Jordan and Yamauchi 2008: 35) and "Going Where No Anthropologist Has Gone Before" (Hahn 2009:31) give suggestions about how anthropology students can find non-academic positions. More specifically, the journal published a series of practitioner profiles under the title "Profiles of Practice." The series ran in the Career Development section of the *News* from March 2007 to May 2008. The people profiled included anthropologists working in financial services, industry, public health, non-profits, federal agencies, cultural resource management, and tribal cultural centers. Each of these stories enforces the idea that anthropologists can work just about anywhere!

More and more anthropologists are finding that private industry can use their skills. Genevieve Bell, for example, joined Intel Corporation (the computer chip giant) in 1998 as a researcher in its People and Practices research team. Her academic research focus on the intersection of technology and society made her especially suited for the job. With the growth of global economies, more and more businesses recognize the challenges that multicultural issues bring to commerce. Anthropological approaches to marketing (ensuring that slogans are appropriate to the local audience), cross-cultural communication (helping employees deal with stresses in new cultural locations), business management (providing employee training that fits the needs and style of the target audience being trained), and regional "cultures" of business help companies survive and flourish in a multitude of places.

In addition to private industry and nonprofits, two burgeoning realms where anthropologists are finding lots of work are with NGOs and international development organizations. Both of these are heavily involved in working with non-Western cultures in trying to provide services, development projects, economic programs, and other benefits. While there is no single all-encompassing definition of an NGO, generally they are organizations that are legally constituted to operate outside of formal governmental operation. Most often they have a wide social or economic aim but are not operated as a "business." A ready list of NGOs is available at the Worldwide NGO Directory (*http://www.wango.org/resources.aspx?section =ngodir*), and the wide range should make it clear that opportunities for anthropologists are far-reaching.

International development organizations, on the other hand, usually are focused on some aspect of economic, industrial, societal, or organizational development. The United States Agency for International Development (USAID), for example, works in close partnership with private voluntary organizations, indigenous groups, universities, American businesses, international organizations, other governments, trade and professional associations, faith-based organizations, and other U.S. government agencies (*http://www.usaid.gov/about_usaid/*), generally within developing countries. The Australian Agency for International Development (AusAID) serves a similar function (*http://www.ausaid.gov.au/about/ default.cfm*). Other development agencies include such groups as the World Bank (*http://www.worldbank.org/*) and the International Monetary Fund (*http:// www.imf.org/external/index.htm*).

The agencies, organizations, and employers of anthropologists we've noted in this chapter are but a small sample of the potential employment opportunities. Another lower-tech way to go about searching is to "let your fingers do the walking through the Yellow Pages." Check for likely offices in the government listings (usually blue pages, not yellow) and under headings such as Archaeology or Environmental Consultants.

ঙ *EXERCISE:* ANALYZE THE JOB ANNOUNCEMENT

Now that you've looked at some of the jobs and careers that others hold and the paths that they've taken, it's time to examine actual job announcements. Reviewing job announcements is a good way to gain a better understanding of what may help you obtain that, or a similar, position. If you make a habit of looking at job postings, you will learn what the market is actually seeking and what knowledge, skills, and abilities are needed to accomplish the tasks and responsibilities of the jobs being advertised.

Begin by finding a job announcement for a position that interests you. For the purposes of this exercise, the announcement need not be current—back issues of professional organization newsletters work well. If you are interested in what is currently available, check the job listings on professional organizations' websites.

Read through the job announcement once before analyzing its parts. After you have familiarized yourself with the information, set up a page in your journal or on a computer document.

■ Identify the reference

■ List the educational requirements

■ List the KSAs required for this job

■ Identify the skills you currently possess

■ Detail how you will get the other skills and satisfy the requirements for this job

Note any comments or thoughts about this job or a similar position

Example:

The SAA Archaeological Record, March 2005, Vol. 5, No. 2

Associate Curator, Royal Ontario Museum (entry level comparable
to Asst. Professor)

Education required: Ph.D. in Anthropology

Required KSAs: Background in New World archaeology, research
interest in Central/So. America, publications in peer-reviewed
journals, eligibility for research grant funding, teaching, museum
experience preferred

Skills I possess: Field experience in New World archaeology

How will I acquire these skills? Receive my Ph.D., develop an
interest in Central/So. America, write/get published, apply for
grants

Comments/thoughts: I have three years of museum curatorial
and administrative experience—how does that apply to this position? The museum experience is sort of glanced over; should that
not be much more important for this job as a museum curator
than research interests? ❧

Summary

In this chapter, we took you through the process of looking at how the
jobs you've held to date are relevant to the jobs you would like to have in
the future. By looking at the jobs and their duties and responsibilities, you
were able to construct a list of the knowledge, skills, and abilities (KSAs)
gained in each position. These KSAs provide the basis for your transition
from student to the first jobs of your career.

The second part of the chapter presented information to help you
identify what you want to do and then went on to offer guidance about
where to look for jobs. And finally, we suggested that you look at a career
description and a job announcement in a professional journal and identify the KSAs required for these positions. Together, these steps were designed to tie together your past and your future.

FOR THE PORTFOLIO

The research conducted through the exercises in this chapter resulted in lists and journal entries. If you want to maintain a complete paper-trail, we recommend that you type up the lists you created in your journal, print copies of the career articles and job announcements that you reviewed, and place them in the "Other" section at the back of your portfolio.

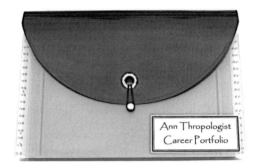

Ann Thropologist
Career Portfolio

SECTION II
DEVELOPMENT

The chapters in Section I took you through a series of exercises to build a base of knowledge. The second section is dedicated to the development of the job application components. Unlike the earlier chapters whose exercises required you to write in your journal and sometimes create an item for your portfolio, Section II focuses on the production of components directly related to your job search. These components and products will be kept in your portfolio, updated as needed, and proffered to potential employers during the application process.

In Chapter 6, you will formalize your plan and design the path by laying out your goals and objectives in one-, three-, and five-year plans. Chapter 7 provides instructions for creating your résumé and curriculum vita and for developing your biographical statement. Chapter 8 details how to create cover letters, letters of introduction, and letters of recommendation. And Chapter 9 gives you some practical techniques to help you apply and interview for jobs.

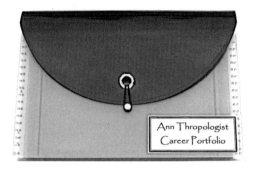

Ann Thropologist
Career Portfolio

CHAPTER 6

THE ROAD MAP

"Avenues to Professionalism is one of the most useful, practical and memorable anthropology courses that I have taken. It supplemented more traditional academic courses by causing me to think in a very specific manner about the jobs available within anthropology and the skills that are necessary to be successful in them. Today, a year after graduation and into my dream job, I still find myself using formats for the letter drafts and the five-year plan that we developed in that class, but more importantly, the basic tools and evaluative procedures that it introduced will be helpful over a lifetime."

—Ian Thompson, Choctaw Nation Tribal Archaeologist

INTRODUCTION

In 2006, Ian Thompson wrote in his journal, "How awesome it would be to build my KSA in traditional Choctaw ceramics manufacture for a couple of years, and then teach a class at the Choctaw Nation, taking students from clay-digging through cooking in finished pots." In July 2010, Joe and Carol took a class from Ian at the Oklahoma City Choctaw Center. He had a plan, and as the Choctaw Nation Tribal Archaeologist, he's made it come true.

Of all the suggested exercises and activities provided within this book, writing a five-year plan may seem either the most absurd or the most daunting. But writing a five-year plan means the difference between designing a path for yourself and knowing where you are going versus letting life take you where it wants. Granted, sometimes simply letting fate take its course is nice, but part of what we are trying to do in this book is provide a process for you to establish your career. If you want to be in control, you need a plan.

TRANSITIONS, MORE THAN CHANCE

If your goal is to transition from your life as a student to a life as a professional anthropologist, it is important that you lay out a road map for your career. Right now, a career in anthropology may seem no more than a pipe dream. Some (your parents?) may contend that pipe dreams are just that: unobtainable dreams. We beg to differ. If you really want an anthropology career, then you should go for it. The key to reaching your dream is advance planning and small steps. This chapter will assist you in laying out that plan and those steps.

Why write a plan? It's boring, it's time consuming—it may even seem like a waste of paper. But if you actually draft one, and use it to measure yourself against what you believe it will take to succeed, it will work like a charm. It will keep you focused on your dream while preventing you from trying to achieve everything all at once. Go back and think about why you've wanted to be what it is you want to be. The five-year plan is one way to make your dream a reality.

Where Are You and Where Do You Want to Be?

What do you plan to do this year? Where do you plan to be next year? How will you build the skills to obtain your ideal job within the next five years? Through the information and activities in this chapter, you will develop your one-, three-, and five-year plans. Having an outline of your career path will help reduce stress. It can be modified as time goes on, but it gives you a starting point. As the wise Larry Zimmerman once told us, "Remember: serendipity happens. The importance of this can't be overemphasized. I've seen too many folks develop life or research plans and feel somehow they are cast in stone, using it as an excuse for not taking advantage of potential life-altering experiences. The flip side of this is not feeling guilty or like a failure if something prevents you from meeting your goal." Patricia Sachs, owner of Social Solutions, Inc., says, "There was not an abrupt transition from being a student to having a career for me. It took me many years to complete my doctorate (from B.A. to Ph.D. took eleven years), because I needed to work the entire time, and I also had two children during that time." She said she overheard a couple of her professors talking during her first year of graduate school "about how there would be fewer academic jobs for us due to the demographics of departments"; they said "there simply were lots of people in departments who had fairly long careers ahead of them." This made her realize that she would need to think more broadly about a career. She said that it didn't affect anything specific; it just made her more conscious. Dr. Sachs says, "The process of becoming a practitioner was, in fact, practical." She needed to support her kids and stay in one geographical area. She said she was "opportunistic, if aided by awareness."

The other useful aspect of creating a plan is that it provides a mechanism for formalizing your thoughts about where you currently are and where you want to be. Simply putting words on paper may also allow you to view things more realistically.

‽ *EXERCISE:* DEFINING AND DESIGNING THE DREAM

Define your dream. If you can articulate what you want to do and where you want to achieve it, that in itself will lead you to your destination. The plan will provide the steps toward your goal. Before we move on to the formal development of the plan, reflect on the following questions and then address them in your journal.

- ■ What do you want to do in anthropology?

- ■ How will what you do contribute to or change the world? (This is what makes applied anthropology, applied anthropology.)

When we asked these questions in the Professionalism Class brainstorm, we were met with silence. We reworded the "What do you want to do?" to "What or who do you want to be?" It took a few moments, but then quietly, one of our students said, "I want to be Brian Fagan." When asked to define this further, she said, "I want to publish books for the general public."

If we look at the goal, to publish books for the general public, then we can begin to identify the knowledge, skills, and abilities needed to develop this career. ‽

Erin's Dream Career

To produce public-oriented publications, overviews, archaeological questions, history, and to see the big picture requires the ability to write to the audience and present information as a readable story. Knowledge would be accumulated over time through research. The skills needed include becoming proficient as a writer and developing a positive reputation.

The next step of the process is to take each of the components listed under the knowledge, skills, and abilities and develop the plan for acquiring them.

Let's dissect writing. For most people, writing doesn't just happen. It takes practice and a commitment. The more you worry about how to start or which words to use, the harder it gets. So how do you break the cycle and get it done? Here are Fagan's tips for writing.

- Get up every day and put 1,000 words on paper. Don't worry about editing or spell-checking. Don't stop—just write the first draft.

- When it is done, let go of it and don't worry that "it's not perfect." Get it to the editor. He or she will read it and provide recommendations to improve it.

- Revise, revise, revise! This is perhaps the most difficult stage of writing, but the most important.

- Let go of it emotionally and keep your ego on the back burner. Yep, you've just birthed it, but you have to let it go. Your work is only as good as you and your editor make it.

Some of the items on the list come with practice, but others can only be accomplished (or assisted) by learning more through research or taking a class. If your path is archaeological, we highly recommend reading Fagan's *Writing Archaeology,* which is now in its second edition (Left Coast Press, 2010).

Now, back to your career. In the following exercise, you will identify the knowledge, skills, and abilities that will be needed for you to reach your career goals.

๛ *EXERCISE:* Knowledge, Skills, and Abilities (KSAs)

Using either your journal or a new document on your computer, write a sentence stating your ideal career, the one that you would like to build. Set up a table with three categories, one each for knowledge, skills, and

abilities. Brainstorming with yourself does not work very well, so bring
in a friend or colleague. Jot down everything you can think of in relation
to the KSAs needed to achieve your career. (If you've missed the information on KSAs, refer back to Chapter 5.) Identifying the jobs that you
might hold along the way would be of great benefit here, as it would help
define the progression of skill and knowledge building.

Note that many of the skills and abilities we've mentioned so far extend into other professions in the field of anthropology, so feel free to incorporate them into your list when you develop it. If you want a prompt
to help identify KSAs, select a few job announcements for jobs that you
would like to have. Read through the job descriptions, experience
needed, and the educational background required, as you did in the "Analyze the Job Announcement" Exercise in Chapter 5. Build your list beginning with these items.

Example

Carol's dream career was to create high-quality archaeologically based
educational materials for teachers and students. To achieve this goal,
Carol needed to develop the following KSAs.

Knowledge	Skills	Abilities
M.A. in education	Writing	Patience
Classroom teaching experience	Analytical thinking	Translate technical information for the layperson
Curriculum development	General computer competency	Relate cultural information and archaeological methods to educational requirements
Learning styles	Typing	Correlate data
Teaching styles	Graphic design	Think laterally
Archaeological methods	Communication	
Field experience	Facilitating	
Cultural history	Teaching	
	Leadership	

Once you have completed this exercise, keep it handy, as the information will be used in the creation of your one-, three-, and five-year plans.

80

༄ *EXERCISE:* Relating the KSAs, Reality to Dream

Begin by looking at look what you've described as your dream career and the list of the KSAs you will need to accomplish that dream. Next, look at the list of your past jobs, and the KSAs that you developed in the exercise in Chapter 5. Compare and contrast the two lists and develop a list of the knowledge, skills, and abilities that you still need to acquire to reach your dream.

Third, look at the job descriptions you found during the exercise in Chapter 5. During this exploration, you saw what was available and what employers were looking for from candidates. How many applicants do you think will apply to any one job advertisement? What makes the person who gets that job stand out from the others? We'll look at other ways of gaining experience, extra qualifications, and so forth, throughout the book, but right now we need to focus on setting up a plan to chart your progress.

List the KSAs required for one of these job announcements. List the skills you currently possess. Compare and contrast the two lists and deduce what KSAs you would need to acquire to get that particular job. Add this list of KSAs you still need to the list you've already started.

To simplify:

■ Dream Career KSAs – Your Current KSAs = KSAs Needed1

■ Job Announcement KSAs – Your Current KSAs = KSAs Needed2

■ KSAs Needed1 + KSAs Needed2 = KSAs to acquire ༀ

Your next project is to detail how you plan to gain these skills and how long it will take you to do that. And, for now, don't think (or obsess) about the end; think about the practical everyday matters.

Identify a Goal

While your ultimate goal may be to become a writer of high-quality educational materials, attempting to do it today, without the background, experience, and contacts, would probably doom you to failure. Don't give up. Remember, *gaining your dream takes steps and time*. Use the time to not only to study and build your knowledge, skills, and abilities, but also to build your human network. For more information on networking, see the section on "Networks and Mentors" in Chapter 12.

Start developing your plan by identifying where you are right now. Jeanine Pfeiffer, in her career story, says that she knew she would face stiff competition when she graduated so she worked hard to augment her curriculum vita with teaching, scholarship, and grants. She goes on to say, "I also set a goal for myself to have at least five publications either published or submitted by my final academic year, and I formatted the chapters of my Ph.D. thesis as publishable units. For example, one chapter was published as a book chapter in an anthropological anthology on communities in Southeast Asia, another as a gender review article for an ethnobiology journal, and a third chapter as a scientific article in a special issue of *Environment, Development, and Sustainability.*" If you are in graduate school, use the experience and expertise at hand to gain the base of what you need to get done. Many people will help you with the requirements of graduation—the number of classes required, the prerequisites, and so forth—but here we are talking about the nuts and bolts of getting through the rigors of research and writing. Use this time to gain skills you will need in the workforce. Give yourself rewards for accomplishing your goals. Michelle M. Carnes says that she had to come up with her own reward system to acknowledge and celebrate her successes on her own terms: "I had to stop seeking approval from my committee; they did not have time to clap their hands about my latest breakthrough. Their job was to seek out and point out the weaknesses, omissions, and gaps—so that I may fill them. Thus, I had to throw my own 'little parties' when I finished a chapter, started a new one, when I wrote 25 pages in a single day, when I finished the bibliography. I learned to reward and congratulate myself (and to no longer wait for my committee to acknowledge or value it). Not only was this important for finishing my degree, it was an important lesson personally—and one that translated into a healthy workplace presence as well."

Try to think about the long-term—the M.A., the Ph.D., the academic position, the research lab—and how each thing you do can help you accomplish that goal. Look at the classes you have taken and ask yourself how those classes can be woven together to give you the results you need.

Means to the End

Perhaps your dream is to be a cultural anthropologist and to obtain a tenure-track appointment in a large university, but at the moment you are just completing your bachelor's degree. What are the steps that would put you in a position to apply for and get that position? The first and most obvious step is to complete the educational requirements and begin building the KSAs that would put your qualifications ahead of others applying for the professorship.

Now it's time to get real, look at concrete information, and get experience. You can look back and you can look forward. Reexamine what you want to be when you grow up.

℣ EXERCISE: WRITE THE PLANS

The background has been built, so it's time to develop the plan. Take your seat at your computer and begin a document, "My Five-Year Plan." You may want to format your document as a series of tables, or as an outline, or in paragraphs. Do whatever is most comfortable to your organizational style. Feel free to check out the two partial five-year plans written by Avenues to Professionalism students, in Appendix 4, Samples and Examples.

Initial Statement

At the top of the page, begin by stating your dream job. This clear statement will provide guidance. It declares what you want to spend your career doing. No need to get elaborate; simply name the job or type of job you aspire to, the one that represents what you want to pursue in your career and where you would like to pursue it.

Below that, note today's date and a description of where you currently are: location, level of education, job description, and your KSAs. Take a good hard look at what you have to offer.

Write the One-Year Plan

Where do you want to be emotionally, physically, and intellectually one, three, and five years from now? Begin the one-year plan by identifying exactly what you would like to be doing at this time. For example, "I plan to start graduate school."

Once you've identified the "what," add the details by addressing the location, job description, or course of study, KSAs that you expect to accumulate during this time, and what you plan to accomplish during this phase.

Location

Consider where you would like to be located and how much it will cost to get there. How much will it cost you to live in this location? Have you been to this place before, or is it just some place you'd like to be? If you've never actually spent any time there, you might explore online to get an idea about the neighborhoods, schools (if you have kids), cost of living, availability of a community that supports your hobbies, and crime rates. If you have the chance, take a break and visit the place. If this is where you want to attend a graduate program or get hired, will you have to have two jobs in order to support yourself in the manner to which you've become accustomed? Don't be too narrow. Keep your options open to unfamiliar places if a good job arises there.

Job Description

What do you see yourself doing during this phase of your career? Think about it realistically. Review the job listings that you looked at previously or do a new search. If you have your mind set on "the job," how open are you to a different physical location? The five-year plan gives you the opportunity to try out different jobs, to see exactly what you want to do. If the job of your dreams turns out to be your worst nightmare, modify and adjust. Use the opportunity to redefine your goals based on the experience.

KSAs

Are there any special certificates that would add to your KSAs? Is there a professional development workshop that would provide information and the opportunity to build your network?

We also recommend that you identify and join professional organizations in the state or region you live in, and nationally, as these will provide opportunities to meet people and build networks. Also, start presenting papers and publishing. These are important skills that often get overlooked. List what you plan to do to build these skills.

Now is also the time to think about the self-management, functional, and technical skills we mentioned in Chapter 5. Are there gaps there that you can strengthen? Can you take a course that will help improve your word processing and other computer skills?

Write the Three- and Five-Year Plans

After writing your one-year plan, it's time to attack the three-year plan. The three-year plan represents the midpoint of your plan. Your goals should place you partway between where you started and where you want to be. With this in mind, follow the same process you used in writing your one-year plan, but for each section consider the following information.

Location

You don't have to be in your ideal place immediately. This midpoint provides you the chance to think laterally and see if there are any alternatives. Consider locations with positions that would provide the stepping-stone to where you want to be in five to ten years. You think that you would like to be in Boulder, Colorado? Would you consider spending time in Fort Collins? You think Berkeley is "it"? How would it be to spend time at San Francisco Community College or UC Santa Cruz? Consider, is it the place, the general location, or the status of being at a particular job site? Is the paycheck associated with a status job worth the potential hassles?

Job Description

Think about how to work toward the position and what would make you the ideal choice. The middle of your plan is the best place to see not only where you've been, but also where you are going. Use the time in between to "practice" the job you want to do. Think you might want to teach but can't get a job at a university? Then try a community college or even volunteer to teach an evening or weekend class at a high school or other location. Want to work in museums? Volunteer to work in processing collections, helping to hang shows, working with the curator or educator, taking tickets, or helping at an opening. Each of these situations provides the opportunity to meet people, get known for who you are and what you can do, and to use contacts as references for the next step, whatever that might be.

KSAs

The three-year plan is your mechanism for thinking about being halfway to your goal. What do you need to accomplish to learn how to program that Total Station? How much GIS do you need to be a more-than-adequate geographic information specialist? How much experience do you need to acquire to be a crew chief or project director? What certificates do you need to be an assistant curator or educator? Will membership in the American Association of Museums help you gain an edge? Check to see if you can get a student rate now, and then carry it forward after you get out of school.

Remember that this plan is a road map to help you get where you think you want to be. By outlining the various "legs" of the journey, you stand a better chance of not getting lost along the way. You also develop your job experiences, KSAs, and networks incrementally rather than trying to gain them all at once.

The five-year plan uses the same general categories as the one- and three- year plans, but it is more than just a cumulative version of the others. It is important that it be either your ultimate goal or one of the "plateaus" on your career pathway. It should be your "best guess" at the time of its writing, and it should be based on your research, your knowledge, and your educational attainment. Just as you shouldn't plan on having your Ph.D. within five years of entering college, you shouldn't plan to earn a tenure-track position at a top-tier research university with only an M.A. Still, it is important to dream a little, because dreaming will help you identify what you want to be, and then help you discover what it will take to get there.

As you outline these final stages of your goal, continue to research. Are there job openings for your general areas of interest? If not, why? Are there particular areas of the country where demand for your dream position seems higher or lower? Again, why? What do you need to add to your KSAs to be at the same level of achievement as others who have landed positions like those you wish to attain? Are those KSAs achievable by you, or are they totally off-the-wall?

Research will help answer some of these questions, but none of us can really predict the future. International development and natural resource exploration might suddenly grind to a halt; future jobs may be found in computer simulation and game theory, not to mention in work focusing on the impact of tourism on renewable resources within the Antarctic!
ಣ

Despite these uncertainties, try to focus on the things that will make you a solid candidate in the areas where you want to excel, based on the information you have today. Look at what is available to work with, and then brainstorm about what it would take to get you there if you had the time, money, and drive to do so. And then develop the drive and tenacity to strengthen your experience and education to get you there.

It is also important to remember that, if at the end of five years you haven't found your dream job, don't be discouraged. Think about alternatives and other opportunities. Think about varying your search by location or job type. Think about what it is you really want to do, and whether there are other ways of getting there. Set the dream and the small steps to make gaining your dream possible.

SUMMARY

We hope that the exercise of creating your five-year plan was not too stressful. If it was, we understand. At this point in our careers, we often talk about creating our own new five-year plans. Of course, the ideal would be that five years would place us on a beach or mountain in the happy state of retirement. Like we said, it doesn't hurt to dream!

Remember, the five-year plan is not set in concrete. It should be flexible, able to change and grow as new things happen in your life, new jobs are taken, and new goals are set.

FOR THE PORTFOLIO

The product that you will add to your portfolio from the exercise in this chapter is your five-year plan. Or, more accurately, your one-, three-, and five-year plans. Your plans should be filed in the eighth section of your portfolio, along with the personal professional ethics statement you created back in Chapter 4.

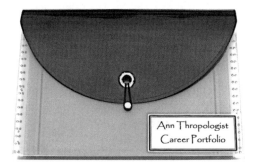

CHAPTER 7

THE RÉSUMÉ, CURRICULUM VITA, AND BIOGRAPHICAL STATEMENT

"What I have used and has impacted me the most was learning about CV, résumés, and cover letters, and not just me either. I would say it has affected at least ten other people who I have given my templates to, because they didn't how know to make one. No one I know knows how to write résumés and most don't even know what a CV is."
—James Douglas Rocks-Macqueen, undergraduate in the class,
current graduate student

INTRODUCTION

The job is looming and you have no idea what they are asking for when they request a cover letter and a curriculum vita (CV). You've applied to jobs before, but in the past, all you've ever done is fill out the standardized employment application.

At this point of your life and career, building experience means working at jobs within the field of anthropology and, unless you are applying for a government position requiring an SF-171 form, there are two products, minimum, that you must have to apply for any position: a résumé or curriculum vita, and a cover letter. Even the SF-171 form is about to become obsolete as the government transitions to new hiring regulations (see Chapter 5 for more information on government hiring).

The information in this chapter explains what a résumé and a curriculum vita are and provides information that will help you decide which should be used and under what circumstances. It also takes you through the process of producing your own résumé. (Since CVs are predominately used in academic settings, the CV exercise is presented in Chapter 14.) Chapter 8 will provide the background necessary to create the cover letter that should be included with a résumé or vita at the time of application.

This chapter also covers some basic information about biographical statements and how to create them. While "bios" are not submitted at the time of your job application, they are required under other circumstances when you submit your CV, such as with a grant application or proposal. Bios are a shorthand way of selling yourself to a prospective employer, but employers also use them to sell the company and its employees to potential clients.

RÉSUMÉ

A résumé is not a static document. It morphs over time as you change jobs or acquire new skills. A résumé outlines your previous experience (jobs worked) and the knowledge, skills, and abilities that you've acquired. Most importantly, the content of a résumé can and should be tailored to fit the needs of each position and employer. Pick and choose from all of your past employment, training, and volunteer experience the things that would work best to meet the qualifications of the position. When composing a résumé, you *do not* list every single job you have ever held. The résumé should showcase your abilities to the employer. The main point of a cover letter (see Chapter 8) and résumé (or CV) is to get you an interview. What can you say about yourself that shows you have the KSAs for this job *and* sets you apart from the others? Perhaps most importantly, a résumé should be only one to two pages long.

Think carefully when developing your résumé and consider your choice of words. Use action verbs and active tenses. Action verbs are verbs that can be used alone as the main verb of a sentence. The Evergreen State College provides an excellent online resource for résumé writing: *http:// www.evergreen.edu/career/resume/home.htm*. It also contains a list of Power Verbs: *http://www.evergreen.edu/career/resume/verbs.htm*. If you are a college or university student, you might consider taking advantage of the career center at your institution.

There is no one standard format for a résumé, but there are various standardized ways to organize your information. Three of the more common methods for organizing information are chronologically, functionally, and targeted. Some professions prefer one of these styles over the others, so you should consider asking people you know in similar jobs what style they used.

Résumé Versions

A *chronological* résumé lists your jobs in order, from the most recent to the ones held longer ago. It focuses on a logical job history and is the most common format used when applying for anthropological jobs. The *functional* version allows you to focus on your qualifications and accomplishments first, and then simply lists your employers after. A *targeted* résumé lists information in order of importance, with the less relevant experience placed at the bottom of the page.

Stockpile the Information

Since you will have to hand-pick your past experiences for different résumés, you need to stockpile all of the details relating to each of your previous jobs in a master file. Lucky for you, you live in the computer era. Imagine having to type your résumé each time it was needed, updating from top to bottom like we did! We recommend that you create a master file of all of your previous jobs. You've already started this task in previous journal exercises. It's now time to formalize it as a computer file. Describe the tasks for which you were responsible, and the knowledge and skills you gained in each position. Be as detailed as you can, because this is the "closet" from which you will pick your "work clothes." Also, make sure that you check the spelling, grammar, and punctuation in your master list. Ask someone else to proofread your information as well, because your familiarity with the information makes it difficult to see mistakes.

If the information is correct on the master list, then you won't perpetuate errors each time you create a new résumé.

ℰ *EXERCISE:* CREATE THE STOCKPILE DATABASE

Create this master file now, and update it regularly. Don't wait until you are ready to apply for a job to think back on what you did last. If ever there was a time to be obsessive-compulsive, this is it.

■ Write down the date you were hired and the date you left the job.

■ List your rate of pay when you started and the rate that you were paid when you left.

■ Note the name of the company that employed you, their address, phone number, web address, and the name of your direct supervisor.

■ State your job title and describe your duties and responsibilities.

Use minimal formatting, because you never know how you will need to access this information in the future. Save the file to your hard drive and save a backup copy onto a disk, backup drive, or thumb drive. Each time you update your information, update your backup. Perfecting the skill of updating information will come in handy later; you can apply the same strategies once you're employed to keep track of the information that you need for your annual reports and reviews.

If you are ever required to list every job you've worked (as on an SF-171, Application for Federal Employment form), you will have that information to copy and paste. Also, while no one really wants to think or talk about money, be certain to keep track of the beginning and ending salary for each job. Some employers ask for this information, while others will only be interested in what they want to pay you. ℰ

Résumé Format

As mentioned above, there is no single style or format for a résumé. Look at as many sample résumés as you can find, and pick one that seems right for you. But before you select a format that you like, check around to see if one style is more common within the subdiscipline you have chosen.

Visually, we recommend that you keep the layout simple. Avoid fancy elements like double-columns and formatted headings. A clean, simple résumé will be easier to transfer from computer to computer and from one word processing system to another. Don't reduce the size of the font to fit more on the page. Select a font, such as Times New Roman, that is easier for the eye to track and read. Keep the fonts used on your résumé, CV, and cover letters the same.

Watch your punctuation. Select a punctuation style and stick with it. Make sure that all of your listings under a particular category have the same series of commas and periods. If your brain is just not detail oriented, or if you've looked at your résumé so many times that it all blurs together, give it to someone to proofread. The more detail oriented your proofreader is, the better your résumé will look.

If you want your résumé to stand out from the others, select a paper stock that is slightly heavier than the multipurpose paper you use for everyday print jobs. Keep it clean and elegant.

Writing Your Résumé

Working on your résumé will give you the opportunity to take stock of the current point of your career. It will also give you the opportunity to plan for gaining the experience you still need for your dream job.

Because of the space limitations on the résumé, be certain to pick and choose carefully the jobs you want to highlight, the skills and abilities gained in those jobs that are directly relevant to the job you are seeking, and the professional expertise you have that will make you the most likely candidate for the job. Remember, while certain jobs will give you experience, they are not all relevant for every job search.

Be certain to include the information in the appropriate order for the version of résumé you are using. While the order of information will vary according to résumé type, all of the information should be available within your master file.

Sequence of Information

When looking at a résumé, we prefer to see the applicant's name, address, phone number, and email address at the top of the page. Carol prefers this information to be centered so that it is visually obvious at a glance. (Joe is not as picky.)

When reviewing résumés, we like to see a goal statement—but not everyone does. If you choose to include a goal statement, this should summarize your dream career and how this particular job will help make that happen. Remember to target the employer: look at the job announcement and construct your statement using key phrases from their listing. Take that sentence and connect it to your ultimate goal within the field of anthropology.

What comes next on the résumé? You may feel that your education is your biggest accomplishment, and as such, believe it should be highlighted early on. From an employer's perspective, however, your job history is most important. After you delineate your previous paid positions, list any relevant volunteer positions you have held. The résumé format allows for a *short* summary of duties and responsibilities under each job listing.

List the "Education" section next, followed by any honors or awards you have received and any organizations you belong to. If you have hobbies or special interests that might increase your chances of getting hired, they should be included at this point. You never know when the line about being passionate about opera will reverberate with a potential employer.

The last section of you résumé is for your references. You may either write "References upon request" or list two or three names along with their contact information. Before you name someone as a reference, make sure you've obtained his or her permission to do so. If an employer plans to offer you a job, they will contact some or all of your references. They may also contact several of your past employers (especially if they know people in that business, agency, or organization).

Before you list someone as a reference, consider whether this person will be able to speak highly about your KSAs and your work ethic. (More on ethics can be found in Chapter 4.) Be thoughtful about who you include as a reference. Should you list the person who supervised you on a day-to-day basis, or someone higher up in the hierarchy who knows you less well but has more prestige in the eyes of the future employer? Your references will not be contacted by everyone that receives your résumé, only by those who consider offering you a job.

Keep a list of potential references. When you add people to your list, make sure that their names are spelled correctly and that you have correctly listed their address, phone number, and email address. It is a good idea to maintain contact with these individuals at least once every six months or so. Keeping in contact with them ensures that you will have their most current contact information. Sending them an occasional email also keeps you active in their network. For more information on requesting letters of reference, see Chapter 8.

Personal Information

Never include a picture of yourself. Also, do not include too much personal information. Equal opportunity employment regulations stipulate that employers cannot ask for or use such information. Personal information that does not belong on a résumé includes the year you graduated from high school, marital status, number of children, age, or religion. If you are hired, you will be required to provide your social security number for tax purposes, but the other information is personal and is, as one of our reviewers puts it, "none of their beeswax."

◌ *EXERCISE:* Create Your Résumé

Begin by finding a job announcement for a position that you'd like and that you would qualify for at this time. You can use the job announcement that you dissected in the exercise in Chapter 5, if you prefer. If you are using a new job announcement, begin by highlighting the specific job and application requirements.

Create a new document on your computer and save it on your hard drive. Give it a file name that you can relocate easily and that an employer would recognize as yours, if you submit it via email. Something along the lines of "Resume_Watkins_7–15–10" declares what the document is and the date that it was created or updated.

In this exercise, you are to create a chronological résumé, with the jobs listed from most recent to longest ago. Use the résumé example provided in this chapter (pages 100-101) as a foundation. We also suggest that you search for and examine images of chronological résumés online for additional formatting ideas. Use the details described in the "Writing your Résumé" section listed above and the job details from your Stockpile Database to create your chronological résumé.

The product should be a fully usable one- to two-page résumé that can be included with your cover letter when applying for a job. ◌

The Curriculum Vita

The curriculum vita or CV is a comprehensive listing of your professional jobs, professional accomplishments, and professional relationships. (Note: *Vita* is singular, *vitae* is plural.) Loosely translated as "the course of [my] life," it allows you to highlight the aspects of your employment history and experience that relate to the job you are seeking. Unlike a résumé, your CV includes only those jobs relating to anthropology or, more specifically, the jobs that you've held within your subdivision of anthropology. Like the résumé, your CV needs to be continuously updated.

Generally, CVs are the required method of application for academic and research positions. They may also be required when applying for

Ann Thropologist
1234 Culture Cross Rd., Indiana, OK 76543
(123) 456–7890
ann.thropologist@gmail.com

GOAL STATEMENT:

My career goal is to use my anthropological training to work with indigenous communities and to assist them with achieving benefits as defined by the community itself.

RELEVANT EXPERIENCE:

June 2010–Present: Anthropological Assistant, Southwest Native Council, NSW, Australia

Assisted the Council's Senior Anthropologist with research relating to native title. Did ethnographic, archival, and genealogical research.

June–September 2009:   Assistant Researcher, Native for Native, Phoenix, AZ

Conducted community interviews. Assisted the staff anthropologists with data input and produced a descriptive report on the field procedures.

January–May 2009:   Research Assistant, Maxwell Museum of Anthropology, Albuquerque, NM

Helped inventory and catalog ethnographic collections. Used the inventory database to help create an online searchable catalog for public use.

June 2006–May 2008   Sales Person, East Coast Camping Outfitters, Alexandria, VA

Sold backpacking and camping equipment, advised customers on camping equipment based on need, helped lead backpacking adventures, maintained the rental equipment, took inventory and restocked shelves, and helped train new employees.

VOLUNTEER EXPERIENCE:

June–September 2008: Volunteer, For the People Foundation, Wilmington, DE

Helped create PR for the Foundation's website. Assisted with redesigning the Foundation's website to highlight their mission and reach more people. Did data entry on the mailing list. Worked on a team to help design an "infomercial" for public television.

Ann Thropologist / Résumé -2

EDUCATION:
M.A., University of New Mexico, Anthropology, with a Socio-Cultural specialization, 2010
B.A., American University, *Magna Cum Laude* in Anthropology, 2008

PROFESSIONAL ORGANIZATIONS:
2008–Present   American Anthropological Association.
2008–Present   Plains Anthropological Society, Student Board Representative.

SKILLS:
Proficient with Dreamweaver web design tools and Microsoft Office programs, for both Mac and PC. I am logical, efficient, and organized, and I work well as a member of a team or independently. Hold current American Red Cross Basic First Aid and American Heart Association CPR certification.

HOBBIES AND INTERESTS:
Reading, international travel, backpacking, wilderness camping, personal fitness, and drawing.

REFERENCES:
Upon Request

---

some jobs in the private sector and for grants and fellowships. Unlike the résumé, CVs are as long as your job history. For example, after 30 years of working in the field of anthropology, Carol's CV is eleven pages long. Keep in mind that the CV should only be submitted when specifically requested. In all other cases, use your résumé. If you are unsure whether to submit your résumé or CV, ask!

Since a CV is primarily used when applying for academic jobs, information about creating a CV and the exercise for creating your base CV can be found in Chapter 14.

BIOGRAPHICAL STATEMENT

In this last section of Chapter 7, we introduce you to the uses of biographical statements (bios). Bios are not usually submitted as part of an application package, and so maybe they don't really fit in this chapter, or even in this book. However, they are often included in grant applications and proposals. More importantly, though, employers often use them for marketing purposes and include them on company websites.

Bios highlight your professional experience, and they are written in the third person. It seems strange to talk about oneself as an outsider. It's also slightly uncomfortable to write positively about your abilities without feeling you are bragging or exaggerating the truth. Think about what someone would want to say if they were introducing you. Within two to three paragraphs, just say what's true and what you'd like someone else to know about you.

Bios generally begin with your name and title. This information is followed by where you are currently employed, a narrative listing of the colleges or universities where you finished your degrees, and the year that the degrees were completed. The few sentences should summarize your specialties and achievements, followed by top awards and publications. Bios are tailored to fit the need, so a bio submitted to help publicize a book will be different from one included in a grant application.

As we were completing this book, the publisher requested a bio from each of us for use in promoting the book.

Carol Ellick is founder of Archaeological and Cultural Education Consultants (ACEcs) and an adjunct faculty member in the Native American Studies Program at the University of Oklahoma. Ms. Ellick has a B.A. in anthropology from The Evergreen State College and an M.A. in education from Chapman University. She has worked in cultural resource management (CRM) for over 30 years, starting the first full-time public outreach program in 1995. She is one of the leading experts in archaeological education in the United States. Ms. Ellick's publications include articles in professional journals such as the National Park Service's publication, *Common Ground,* and the Society for American Archaeology magazine, *The SAA Archaeological Record.* She also has chapters in *The Archaeology Education Handbook: Sharing the Past with Kids* (2000) and *Past Meets Present: Archaeologists Partnering with Museum Curators, Teachers, and Community Groups* (2007).

Joe Watkins is the Director of the Native American Studies Program and Associate Professor of Anthropology at the University of Oklahoma. Dr. Watkins received his B.A. in anthropology from the University of Oklahoma and his M.A. and Ph.D. from Southern Methodist University. He has been doing archaeology for more than

40 years and has published extensively on his research interests—the ethical practice of anthropology and anthropology's relationships with descendant communities and aboriginal populations. His book *Indigenous Archaeology: American Indian Values and Scientific Practice* (2000) is a seminal work in indigenous archaeology. His second book, *Reclaiming Physical Heritage: Repatriation and Sacred Sites* (2005), written for high school and early college students, draws attention to important Native American issues.

☞ *EXERCISE:* CREATE A BIO

Before creating your bio, look at a sample of anthropologists' bios from various websites. Look online for information about people at the places where you'd like to work. You should also look at your departmental website. Each faculty member should have a brief bio listed there. Don't let the level of information or achievements scare you! Even your professors had to start somewhere. Part of the reason we encourage you to join professional membership organizations, present papers, write articles, and volunteer is to help you build your professional self. Use these experiences and note them in your bio as well as your résumé and CV. Read our bios. Look at your Stockpile Database, résumé, and CV and write a paragraph about yourself. Be positive. Let your professional self shine. And, have someone proofread your work. ☜

SUMMARY

Hopefully, after reading this chapter, you now understand the important role that your résumé and CV play in the context of the overall job application. There are no more important employment tools than your résumé and the network you build within the profession. Used in conjunction with cover letters and letters of reference, they will help you achieve your goals. In this chapter, we outlined the differences between a résumé and a CV, illustrated the importance of creating a database of your previous employment history, and described how to write a résumé. Through the exercises, you researched résumé styles and formats and developed a draft document.

In addition, we provided information on writing a biographical statement. Although the bio is not a component of a job application, it is used in grants and proposals, public relations documents, and company websites.

FOR THE PORTFOLIO

If you've done the work, this has been a very productive chapter. Through the exercises in this chapter, two have contributed to your portfolio and one will make tracking information easier from this point forward. Finish your draft résumé and bio. Have someone proofread them, make the corrections, and then print them on good bond paper. Place each in its appropriate section of your portfolio. If you really want to be prepared, include a good photo of yourself with your bio.

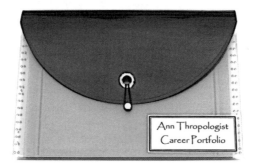

Ann Thropologist
Career Portfolio

CHAPTER 8
LETTERS THAT WILL GET YOU THE JOB

"The ability to write a cover letter has by far put me above my peers in terms of attempting to get a job."
—James Douglas Rocks-Macqueen, graduate student

INTRODUCTION

Sometimes in this day and age, being literate has more to do with one's ability to use technology and keep up with correspondence than with the ability to put together a well-written, grammatically correct, and coherent letter or document. Carol recently sat down with a pad of paper and a pen, thinking it would be nice to "write" a letter. As she started writing, she realized that she was so used to typing words that her brain and her hand didn't seem to know how to form letters and words. She laughed, put down the pen, and picked up the keyboard.

Correspondence has taken on new meaning. Cell phones, Twitter, texting, and chats have created a shorthand language that has replaced traditional forms of well-constructed words and sentences. We think in letter words and shorthand phrases, but, for the purpose of employment, "u nd 2 b" bilingual in your writing styles and further develop the basic letter-writing skills that your elementary schoolteachers, parents, and grandparents tried to teach you.

LETTERS OF APPLICATION

Traditionally, letters of application were typed, signed, and placed in an envelope with a résumé or vita. Email and the Internet have changed how we research, locate, and apply for jobs. While some employers still prefer receiving a physical copy of the application via the mail, more and more request electronic inquiries and applications. Even the federal government lists all job notifications online and utilizes a central application process (*www.usajobs.gov*).

The Email

Before anything else, we feel compelled to offer this advice: treat your email as you would any other written document. This is the *first* view that a potential employer will see, your *first* opportunity to make that first impression. Don't let the job go to someone else simply because you forgot to spell-check your note. Compose your email and send a draft of it to someone to review and edit, just as you would any other piece of writing.

We recommend against composing the body of your email in a word processing program for pasting into the email message. Most word processing programs have embedded codes that make things like apostrophes and quote marks look good in the document, but when pasted into an email may look something like <A@i> <A@e> when you really meant " ". If you still want to use a word processing program, you can reduce the chances of a problem by saving the file as a text file (.txt), or you can use the Word Pad accessory if it is available on your computer.

As we mentioned before, before you begin applying for jobs, set up an email address that will not raise eyebrows. It needs to be something professional and simple, such as your initials and last name, and not something cute like *digme2@aol.com*. You want potential employers to remember you and to take you seriously. You also need to consider the email provider. Some junk filters will automatically send emails with certain extensions directly to the spam email folder. Strange but true: when a user on the University of Oklahoma email system sends an email with a copy to him- or herself , the incoming email goes straight into the junk mail folder. According to the university's IT department, there was no way to fix the system so that the ou.edu address was considered okay, not spam.

Include a line toward the end of your email message requesting that the recipient acknowledge receipt of your message. If you have the option to send the email with a "Send receipt," you can do that, but often people will choose not to send the automated response. The key point here is that you want confirmation that the email actually reached the destination. If you do not receive a receipt, or if you have not received a response from the recipient, *do not assume* that your email arrived. Too often, emails do not reach their destination. Without being a pest, follow up on your initial contact, confirming that your first email was received.

Cover Letters

Résumés and CVs are generalized overviews of your previous employment and accomplishments. They are intended to get you the job interview so that you can demonstrate why you are the right person for the job. Everyone who applies for the job has the requisite résumé, but the person who gets the job has somehow stood out among the others. How do you show that you are the best person for a job? What puts you in a better position for that interview? It all comes down to the cover letter (and your references, but we will get to that later). The cover letter that accompanies your résumé or vita is where you get to introduce yourself and market your skills in direct relation to the employer's needs. Creating a good cover letter is an art that anyone can perfect through practice.

Nolan (2003: 109) breaks cover letters down into three categories: those sent in relation to a specific job announcement, those sent as a letter of introduction or at the suggestion of "a mutual friend," and those sent as a follow-up to an interview you have already had. Regardless of the type of cover letter, they all share similar attributes and elements.

ᴇᴏ *EXERCISE:* Collect and List the Information

You may be a novice at writing a cover letter, but the skills involved are not much different from others you've already accumulated, such as analyzing an assignment and completing it so that it fits the instructor's requirements. Begin by looking at the job advertisement. What are they looking for? Analyze the job summary, the list of desired skills, previous experience, and education requirements. Begin the process by creating a list of the knowledge, skills, and abilities required for this job. You may want to type the list or simply highlight the key phrases or keywords.

After listing what the employer is looking for, consider your past experience. Look at the list you created of previous jobs and the knowledge, skills, and abilities obtained there, as noted in your journal (Chapter 5). How do the two lists compare? What are your strong points? What have you done that would set you apart from other applicants? The answers to these questions will form the body of your letter. ᘓ

Drafting the Letter

The cover letter is a formal communication. In selecting stationery, we advise you not to use the letterhead or envelopes of your current employer. You are representing yourself in your job search, not your employer or your university.

Your address and the date should appear at the top of the page. You might consider creating your own letterhead in your word processing program and saving it as a template so that the only thing you need to change each time you write a letter is the date. Place the contact information in the header of the document.

The second section of the cover letter contains the employer's full name, company, and complete address. Be careful to get the name of the organization correct. One of our colleagues said she has received letters addressed to "University of Northern Arizona" instead of the correct name, Northern Arizona University. Another common problem results from reusing an existing cover letter. When you update a letter, make sure that you change everything that needs changing. If you are applying for a job at URS Corporation but in the middle of your letter you have a sentence saying you believe that SRI does the best research in the west, chances are your letter will be thrown in the reject pile.

The third component is the salutation. This is a formal situation. Even if you know the first name of the person to whom the letter is written, you should use the recipient's correct title—Dr., Mr., or Ms.—and last name. The proper punctuation following the name is a colon (:), not a comma. So, for example, if you were to address a letter to the authors of this book, the salutation would read "Dear Dr. Watkins and Ms. Ellick."

A word of caution: If you do not have the name of the person *or* if the name is not gender specific, do not simply write "Dear Sir." If there is a phone number, call and ask who will be reviewing the applications. If there is no way to know who will review your letter and vita, make the salutation gender neutral by using "To Whom it May Concern," "Dear Employer," or "Dear Search Committee." Only use "Dear Sir" if you are absolutely sure you are submitting your application to a man. Carol has been known to toss applications addressed to "Dear Sir" in the rejection pile because clearly the applicant (1) didn't take the time to change the salutation to meet the needs of the current application, (2) didn't read the job announcement well enough to see that the letters should be directed to a woman, or (3) didn't follow directions well. In any case, this is not someone she wants working for her. As they say, the devil's in the details; so is successfully obtaining the job.

The introductory paragraph should state the job that you are applying for. Use the title as listed on the job announcement and, if there is one, the job reference number. This is particularly important in case the agency or the organization is hiring to fill more than one position. You should also state that you have enclosed the specific components required for the application. Depending on the situation, this may include your résumé or vita, writing samples, and a list of references or letters of recommendation.

The second paragraph should state your qualifications and detail any special skills and abilities that would be an advantage to the employer in relation to the job you would fill. It is essential that you accurately describe who you are, what you have done, and what you can do. Make yourself look good, but do not lie or exaggerate your qualifications, as this will only come back to bite you. Use a sufficient (but not excessive) number of adverbs and adjectives as you write. You want to take this opportunity to fill in the details of your experience in a way you can't do on a short résumé. Focus your information according to the requirements in the job description. If possible, list your abilities in the same order that the requirements were listed in the job announcement. This way, you know that you've covered everything they have asked for *and* you have given it to them in the way they have asked for it.

Your closing paragraph should thank them for the opportunity to apply for this position and should let them know that if they have any questions or require any additional information, they can contact you by phone (list the number) or by email (list the email address). Sign your letter "Sincerely," leave a couple lines of space for your signature, and type your full name. You will sign your letter in the two-line space between "Sincerely" and your name. *And*, don't forget to sign your letter in ink.

As with the email, if you do not hear back within a week or before the application deadline, pick up the phone and call to confirm the receipt of your application. This is also an opportune moment to ask the employer if they need any additional information or to request a meeting.

While your cover letter is not the place to detail your entire employment history, if you have a specific job that directly relates to the job for which you are applying, highlighting that job experience can help move your application into the pile for potential interviews.

Make It Stand Out

The final piece of advice we wish to impart before you start writing has to do with putting the finishing touches on the product. The employer will receive countless responses to their cry for help, and most of those responses will all look the same—a cover letter, résumé, and letters of reference, all printed on white, multipurpose, 96 bright, 20 lb., 8.5 × 11-inch paper. Some may have arrived in a 9 × 12-inch flat envelope, others folded in a No. 10 envelope, but in the employer's mind, they will all blend together.

Printing your application components on high-quality bond paper will set your application apart from all others. Select a paper that is easy on the eyes and is slightly thicker than the standard copy paper. The subtle textural difference and color will make your application memorable and may be a tie-breaker between two applicants. Above all, send clean copies. Make sure that there are no smudges or smears (or telltale evidence from a previous meal). If you make a mistake, print a clean copy. This is your only chance to make a first impression.

In addition, think about whether to justify the margins of the letter. Some people prefer left alignment because the spaces between the words are equal and it produces a "ragged edge"; others prefer full justification because they like the even margins all around the text. Joe has found it's usually easier to correct and read letters and documents that are left-aligned rather than fully justified. Regardless of which format you choose, be consistent throughout the document. Again, attention to detail and consistency are important to the employer, and your cover letter should not sabotage your application because of inconsistent spacing or justifications.

If you do your own printing, buy a ream of paper and matching envelopes. Don't let the investment of $20 stop you; consider what you will make back if it gets you that job. If you plan to use a copying service, you can still take your own paper or you can select carefully from their stock on-hand. If your application materials add up to more than four pieces of paper, consider sending them in a flat 9 × 12 inch-envelope rather than trying to fold them to fit within a standard letter envelope. And be sure to provide sufficient postage on the application packet so that it gets there and doesn't get returned by the post office.

ᴥ *EXERCISE:* Create the Template for Your Cover Letter

Select a job that you would like to apply for or choose one of the job announcements you have used in previous chapters. Following the advice in the sections above, create a draft cover letter for the advertised position. An example of a cover letter can be found in Appendix 4, Samples and Examples. ᥱ

LETTERS OF INTRODUCTION

A letter of introduction is another form of cover letter. The main difference is that it is not sent in application for a specific job. A letter of introduction can be written by you as a self-introduction, or it can be written by a professor or someone who knows of your background and abilities. (This is where the impression you made during your volunteer position or internship can be especially useful.)

Letters of introduction can be of use when you are moving to a new location. The letter can help you establish an acquaintance in the new location with someone from a colleague's network. Use this ice breaker to set an appointment to meet for coffee and share your background and learn what opportunities might be available.

When you request a letter of introduction or a letter of reference from someone you worked for, provide that person with the day you started your position and the date you left. Give him or her a list of tasks that you accomplished and the knowledge, skills, and abilities acquired while working there. Providing this information will make the writer's task easier and will help ensure that you will get a letter that you can use in the future.

LETTERS OF REFERENCE

Your résumé or CV shows a prospective employer that you have the qualifications needed for the job, but it is your letters of reference that will help get you an interview and ultimately will get you your job.

Requesting Letters of Reference

Several years ago, we gave a series of lectures and workshops at the Archaeological Research Facility, University of California at Berkeley. When we stopped by Dr. Meg Conkey's office, we spotted a table with a set of boxes containing notes addressed to "All Students." Curious people that we are, we took a closer look and discovered that the boxes contained instructions to "All Students" in the archaeology program on requesting letters of reference and letters of recommendations. Dr. Conkey states in the second paragraph of her instructions that "letters of reference are one of the most important parts of your application. They can highlight your strengths, explain your weaknesses, and give a sense of you as a living, breathing human being." Her instructions go on to say that "when considering which faculty member to request the reference from, consider who knows you. Only individuals with whom you have worked or studied will have the background to write a strong letter." If they don't know you, then the letter they write will be nothing more than "lukewarm" (Meg's word), and in this day and age, lukewarm will not get you where you want to be.

As with your letter of introduction, you need to provide the professor or previous employer with the information needed to write a glowing reference. If you are requesting a letter from a faculty member, Dr. Conkey suggests that you provide this individual with your résumé or vita, your overall grade point average (GPA), your GPA in your major, your personal statement, the grade in the class or classes you took with that faculty member, any glowing comments that the faculty member wrote on your exams or papers, copies of your papers, and your current address and phone number, as well as a permanent address and phone number of someone who will know how to reach you once you've moved. Assume that once the faculty member has written the letter that he or she will throw out (recycle) any papers that you have provided, so never send originals.

There are other ways to help faculty members or previous employers write a glowing letter of reference. Take advantage of their office hours or other "down times." There is no better way for your professors to get to know you than for you to make the time to talk with them about career options. If possible, provide a copy of your job application (or scholarship or graduate school application) so that your referee can write a letter that addresses specifics. While your faculty member or previous employer will likely remember you if your tenure with them has been recent or long-term, it's to your advantage to provide them with the opportunity to get to know you *before* you need a letter. Joe has received requests for letters from students who never spoke up in class or never participated beyond the minimum, and has wondered why they asked him for a letter. Such letters (if the person agrees to write one) are at best lukewarm and at worst impersonal, and rarely help the applicant stand out from other applicants.

In most cases, potential employers will request that letters of reference be sent to them directly from the person authoring the letter. Doing so allows the referee to be candid in his or her assessment of your abilities. Professors have information that may be considered sensitive, such as your ranking in class, so sending the letter blind (not to you as a copy) allows them the freedom to include this information. In the exercise below, we take you through the process of requesting a letter of reference—in this case, a generic letter rather than one geared to a specific position.

This letter should be filed in your portfolio for future reference, for submission in the future, or simply for you to read over the years as a reminder of what you have accomplished. Provide a stamped, self-addressed envelope along with your request if you want to make it easier for your referee to send you the copy.

ஐ EXERCISE: REQUEST A GENERIC LETTER OF REFERENCE

Choose a person to ask for a letter of reference, someone with whom you have worked or studied, or someone for whom you've volunteered. Create your letter of request, addressed specifically to that individual. Let him or her know that you are creating your career portfolio and that you would like a letter of reference to keep on file for future use and not for any specific application. Provide the information suggested in the "Requesting Letters of Reference" section above, to assist your referee in writing the letter. Be sure to send your current email address as well, in case questions arise. An example of a request for a letter of reference is in Appendix 4, Samples and Examples. If all goes well, you should receive a letter of reference, most likely addressed "To Whom It May Concern." ಆ

Writing Letters of Reference

To help you understand the amount of work involved in writing letters of reference, imagine that the roles were reversed. Think what sorts of questions you might have if you had been asked to write a letter of reference for a colleague, employee, or student. If that individual has performed at the highest level, writing the letter is easy. But what if the person did his or her job, did it adequately, but didn't shine? How do you compose a letter that reads well, shows what the person can do, but is not negative? How do you present the facts of a problem or issue in a benign fashion that will allow the reader to read between the lines? In writing letters, it is important to be honest, to not give undeserved praise or criticism. Doing so may threaten your future credibility as a reference. For more information on how to address these topics, go to Chapter 11, Communication.

SUMMARY

In this chapter, you created two or three very important components of the job portfolio: your cover letter, letter of introduction, and your request for a reference. In addition, you should have received one letter of reference that can be used in future job applications. Before finalizing your letters for the portfolio, give them to someone to review. The person you select for this task should be someone at the employer level or a faculty member, as they will have the knowledge to review and comment from the perspective of an employer. Consider their comments carefully before finalizing your letters.

FOR THE PORTFOLIO

Print copies of each of the letters produced through the activities of this chapter. File these in your portfolio. Chances are you will not be using these exact versions of your letter of introduction or cover letter in future job applications, but you should keep the paper record on hand in case the digital copy is misplaced.

You should also file the letter of reference or letters of introduction written by past employers, people you volunteer for, or professors in your portfolio at this time.

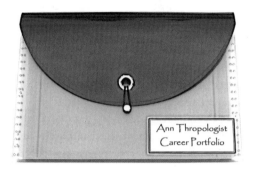

Ann Thropologist
Career Portfolio

CHAPTER 9

APPLYING FOR THE JOB

"He's one of your students? I couldn't believe it. He showed up for his interview in a shirt and tie. I was impressed, but it made the rest of us look like slackers."

—Richard Chapman, Director
Office of Contract Archaeology, University of New Mexico

(And, he got the job.)

INTRODUCTION

"You never get a second chance to make a first impression." While we're not sure if this was first stated by Oscar Wilde, Will Rogers, or Mark Twain, we can tell you that it is true. Don't minimize it—first impressions count. By the time you are selected for your interview, the total number of applicants has been narrowed down to, maybe, three. At this point, it's the little things that will give you a big advantage. (Now is not the time to try a Mohawk.) You want the employer to take you seriously. You want the job? This chapter provides some commonsense suggestions that may not be so common.

WHAT TO SEND IN YOUR APPLICATION PACKET

Read the application instructions carefully. We can't stress this simple advice enough. What are they asking for? Do they want a full curriculum vita or a résumé? How many references are they requesting? Do they want a list of people whom they can contact, or do they want people to submit letters on your behalf? If they are requesting a writing sample, do you have one handy, or do you need to request one from a professor or a previous employer?

You do not want to be facing an application deadline and realize that you lack a recent writing sample or that you have only two referees who are familiar with your current work, rather than the three being requested. Advance planning is essential: Joe says, "Luck is where preparation meets opportunity."

Written Submissions

Since you've already written a draft cover letter, open the document on your computer; rename it for this job application and save it in the folder. Consider how you want to organize your information. You may want to start a folder on your hard drive that holds all the materials submitted for this particular job, or you may want one "Jobs" folder that holds the files organized by job name and type. Review the job qualifications and requirements on the job announcement and the information on cover letters in Chapter 8; then revise your letter to best show your qualifications in relation to this position.

If you are using a letter you created previously as your template, be sure to use the correct date at the top of the letter and to type in the appropriate address, phone number, or email address. The person who reviews your application may put it in the circular file just for being addressed to the wrong person or company! Your own contact information on the letter should match the contact information on your résumé or CV. If you are submitting letters of reference from former employers and your contact information was different back then, don't worry about that. The employer will refer to the information on your CV or cover letter if they need to contact you.

Check your résumé or CV. If you have saved more than one version, make sure you have selected the correct version to include in your job application packet. Make sure it contains the most up-to-date information. Include any new jobs or any new tasks that have been added to your current position. If you have rotated off any committees or joined any new professional organizations, make sure that this information has been updated. If you update your résumé or CV regularly as suggested in Chapters 7 and 14, this should be relatively easy; otherwise, revise it now. It should go without saying, but make sure to check your spelling, grammar, and formatting before sending the material!

Organize the materials so that the cover letter is at the front of the packet, the CV or résumé follows, and the letters of reference and/or examples of your work are at the back. Double-check your materials against the application requirements. Address the envelope. Be sure to put your return address at the top left and affix the proper postage on the top right. Bear in mind that large flat envelopes take more postage than letters or card-sized envelopes. If you want to ensure that the application reaches the employer, play it safe. Take the envelope to the post office, have it weighed, and send it certified. If time is running short or if you want to have a tracking number and confirmation of delivery, you may want to overnight the application using FedEx or Express Mail, or similar service.

Digital Submissions

If the employer has requested the application via email, you should submit your documents as individual files attached to the email, not pasted into the body of the message. In addition, you should save your documents as PDFs prior to sending.

There are a number of reasons why you should save your documents as PDFs, but the most important is that by converting to this file type, the documents are secure; they cannot be modified once in PDF format. One minor complication with creating a PDF for submission is the problem of signing your letter. This can be easily overcome if you scan your signature and save it as a small JPG image. When you've finished your letter, you can then "insert" the image of your signature below "Sincerely" and above your typed name.

Another reason to save your documents as PDFs is that document formatting can change from computer to computer and from printer to printer. Your letter may look good and fit on one page on your screen with your settings, but when opened on another computer and printed from a different printer, it may end up on two pages with your signature hanging alone on that second page.

Any issues that the employer encounters when opening or saving your documents may lead to frustration on the employer's part and may result in your application being put in the "do not hire" pile. Don't let this happen to you.

A quick word about the structure of your email is warranted here. In addition to being sure you have a professional-sounding email address (see Chapters 4 and 11), be certain that the person to whom your email is addressed is the appropriate recipient. Joe has received emails addressed to what appeared to be one person but had been cc'd to a long list of people to whom letters of introduction had been sent. If you are sending the same body of the email to a list of people, make one last check before you hit "Send."

One more thing: your email should have a "signature block" at the bottom. This will say as much about you as your email itself. It should include your name and current contact information, especially telephone numbers that can be used to get in touch with you quickly, as well as your current position, if you are in a relevant job, or "MA/Ph.D. Candidate." If you include a quote as part of your signature, make certain it is appropriate as well. Or, if you want to err on the side of caution, set up a formal signature block without a quote and leave the quote for the informal emails.

Web Applications

Some employers (such as the United States government) use Web-based applications. Many of these applications allow you to "cut and paste" information from your documents into the Web application. Usually these are set up so that either the formatting problems are minimized, or the program allows you to save sections with the option of editing before submitting. Many Web-based application systems also allow you to enter some information, save it, and then come back at a later time to complete the application. Other applications allow the user to upload examples and supporting documents directly to the website.

Some organizations use Web-based applications because they allow for consistency among all applications. Others like the freedom from paper, opening and sorting incoming mail, and ease of handling. Web-based applications are not too common yet, but their popularity appears to be increasing.

Confirmation

Unless you have sent your application by certified mail, don't assume that the employer has received it. Keep track of the status of your application. Do not mail it and forget about it. Give the potential employer a few days to receive the packet, and then call for confirmation. If the letter made it, fine; if not, you might still have time to overnight another copy of your materials.

Likewise for an application sent by email, unless you receive confirmation of receipt, assume that it did not arrive. If you have the option of sending the email with an automated delivery and "read receipt," do it, but even this is not a guarantee that the employer has received and read your email. It's also good to be aware that, for security reasons, some systems or individuals do not respond to "return receipt" requests. The safest plan of action is to be assertive, within reason. Give the recipient a day or two to deal with his or her inbox, and then send a follow-up email, without attachments, asking if the original email arrived. If you still get no reply, and you are serious about this job, a telephone call is in order.

You can be assertive, but be polite. You just want to be assured that your application made it on time and in good shape. Thank the recipient for his or her time and provide your phone number in case additional information is needed.

INTERVIEWING

Fantastic! You've been selected to be interviewed from among the massive number of applicants. You've made the first cut. Usually, only the top three to five applicants are given the opportunity to interview. It's now time to shine.

Clothing Makes the Man (or Woman)

For most of us, today's lifestyle is quite casual. In Tucson, Arizona, it's not unheard of to see people show up for a symphony performance wearing jean shorts. While many of you may wonder why this would seem strange, we grew up in an era when people automatically dressed up for events, dinners out, and church or synagogue. Heaven forbid that the Sunday shoes were worn on any other day!

So, take a look in the mirror. Take a look around you. Become that observer you've been trained to be, and look carefully at what people are wearing in the type of office you are applying to work in. No doubt there will be a variety of styles. Our suggestion is to aim toward the lower end of the top or the upper-middle level in your clothing formality. Anthropologists, for the most part, are tolerant of human variation. If your appearance doesn't jibe with the traditional male or female image, that's fine. You probably don't need a three-piece suit, but a clean, pressed pair of chinos and oxford shirt will make the right impression. If you have footwear other than a pair of tennis shoes, consider wearing those. Select a shoe that fits well, stays tied if laced, and has a low heel.

Dress conservatively and comfortably. Wear clothing that is not too tight. Because the room may be too warm or too cool, have a layer that can be removed or put on so that you can stay comfortable. Avoid anything too revealing or too flashy. You want the employer to remember you for your intelligent answers, not your cleavage, legs, shoes, or "bling." Ruth Burgett Jolie, in her career story, advises interviewees to "Dress conservatively. Twinsets are good. As are knee-length skirts. No one wants to hire a woman with questionable attire. Ed actually irons his shirts. Shocking, I know. I'm not sure this should make it into the book, but I feel that cleavage ought to be kept out of the classroom!"

There are other issues that can also distract from an interview and potentially affect your chances of being hired. The following statements were shared with us while we were writing this book:

"It's not enough to just shower. Wear clean clothes. Once we interviewed someone for a job who we did not hire due to body odor."

"This (white) individual came to the interview with a scruffy appearance and dreadlocks. In retrospect, the faculty recalls him as the individual with 'the hygiene problem.'"

"While I have never turned anyone down due to tattoos or piercings, it's very difficult to have a serious conversation with someone whose tongue is visibly pierced and jeweled. It made me squeamish and unable to focus on the interview."

And what about your hair? Long or short, it doesn't matter. What does matter is whether it is clean and well kept. Earlier this year we were talking with a colleague while at a meeting in New York City. Since our last discussion, he'd taken a new job as a dean of a small college. Prior to the interview, he was told by someone familiar with the school that he should cut his hair. He was shocked. We were shocked. His hair, while quite long, is always clean and well groomed. It is part of his identity. He did not cut it, but did agree with my recommendations. If it is long, tie it back or at least get it out of your eyes and off your face so that you avoid the tendency to keep pushing it back in order to see.

I get bad interview anxiety and I think that by preparing for the interview—researching the company, and going over the list of interview questions that might be asked at the interview—I can alleviate some of the anxiety.

—Gwen Mohr, journal comment, Avenues to Professionalism class

How to Prepare and What to Bring to the Interview

Before the day of the interview, use the resources at your fingertips. Use the Internet and your network as resources to do some research on the agency, organization, or company. Get to know who they are and what they do so that you can better understand the type of individual they would hire. The better prepared you are, the less nervous you will be. Look at their website and answer the following questions in your journal:

■ Where are they located?

■ Do they have more than one office, branch, or campus?

■ How many people work there?

■ What area (geographically) do they work in?

■ What is their specialty?

■ Who currently works for them?

■ What are the backgrounds and specialties of the faculty or staff members?

This is where ethnographic interview skills really help. Use the information to help you develop some questions to ask during the interview. Don't be surprised if they ask you what you know about them. A little research pays off.

Interview Day

Before you leave for the interview, make sure you have everything with you. You know that job portfolio that we've had you keep—look in it. Take it with you or retrieve a copy of your résumé or CV, letters of reference, and any examples of your work that would give the employer a better idea of who you are and what you can do for them. Check yourself in the mirror. Remove the metal from your tongue. Take time to eat a good meal, not just a cup of coffee and a jelly donut. It's hard to sit still and calmly answer questions if you are hyped up on caffeine and sugar. Brush your teeth after you eat so that you don't have to wonder what your breath smells like or if there is a poppy seed stuck between your front teeth. Before you enter the building, take the gum out of your mouth, wrap it in paper, and deposit it in the trash.

Arrive at the interview a few minutes early. Arriving late may cost you points. As Murphy's law says, "Anything that can go wrong, will go wrong." If you are not familiar with the location of your interview, look it up on a map, GPS unit, or mapquest.com. Be prepared for traffic, trains sitting on the tracks, or detours. If you are being flown in for an interview, bring your interview materials and clothes *with you in your carry-on,* because if your luggage is going to take a trip without you, this would be when it happens. And, before you walk into the office, turn off your cell phone.

Interview Questions

Most people being interviewed are passive in their participation. They expect that the interviewer will read their cover letter and résumé or CV, and ask questions based on the job description and previous work experience. But a job interview should be more of a conversation, with questions going both ways. The process may not be a one-for-one volley of questions, back and forth. The interviewer may talk a bit about the office and then ask questions of you. Once you've responded to those questions, you may be asked if you have any questions. Use this time to find out more about the job, office or department structure, focus of research, or opportunities within the company. Use the research you did prior to the interview to demonstrate that you *are* interested in the type of work the organization does and that you are interested in more than just the paycheck.

There are websites with the "Most Commonly Asked Interview Questions" that can (and should) be looked at before you go to an interview. Carol's alma mater had what she considered an incredibly good set of resources which she has shared with countless people over the years. Of course, 30+ years ago those resources were typed on a typewriter and made available in printed format (a set of which Carol still has in her portfolio). You can now access similar resources on The Evergreen State College website, *http://www.evergreen.edu/career/interview/home.htm.* Evergreen's list of questions comes from the Northwestern Endicott Report by V. R. Lindquist. The original questions were available through the Northwestern University Placement Center in Evanston, Illinois, *http:// www.evergreen.edu/career/interview/interviewemployerquestions.htm.* Your university career center also may have resources that would assist you prior to interviewing for a job. Some even offer video-recording services that allow you to see and hear how you appear so that you can make conscious efforts to perform better.

Interview questions vary slightly by job and employer, so if you really want to prepare, look at a variety of lists and consider answering most, if not all. Scribd.com, *http://www.scribd.com/doc/239734/55-Most-Frequently-Asked-Interview-Questions,* lists 55 of the most frequently asked interview questions and advice on how to answer them. Collegegrad.com, *http:// wwwcollegegrad.com/jobsearch/Mastering-the-Interview/Fifty-Standard-Interview-Questions/,* lists 50 questions and suggests that you don't just read through the questions and consider what your answers would be, but that you set up a mock interview with someone you know so that you can practice your responses. In the Avenues to Professionalism class, we adapted a set of standard interview questions for our purposes and set up a mock application process and interviews for pairs of students. The first section of the evaluation tool included a set of statements that the interviewer addressed through observation during and after the interview:

■ The individual showed up to the interview on time.

■ The individual was neat in appearance.

■ The individual was at ease with the questions asked.

■ The individual took time to think about the questions before answering.

■ The individual asked questions regarding the position.

■ I would recommend this person for consideration.

These statements were answered "yes," "no," or "somewhat," and there was space available for comments below each statement. The second section included the questions asked of the potential employee:

■ What are your long-range career goals?

■ Why did you choose the career for which you are preparing?

■ Why should I hire you?

■ And, one other question based specifically on the résumé.

A copy of the interview form developed for the class has been included in Appendix 4, Samples and Examples.

In addition to standard questions, some interviewers might try asking an unrelated or seemingly off-the-wall question like, "What's the last novel you read?" Answering a question like this shows how well you can think on your feet and about your outside interests. If you get asked something like this, take a moment to process the question and come up with a succinct answer.

> *"I thought the mock interviews went real well. Matt, Debi, and I interviewed each other. We really got into a zone when we were being interviewed. We all answered the questions honestly and were also honestly impressed with each other's answers. We BS'ed a little, but when it came down to the actual interview, it was pretty serious—kind of cool."*
> —Joseph (Woody) Aguilar, journal comment
> Avenues to Professionalism class

ঌ *EXERCISE*: Interview Preparation

Take your interview preparation one step further. The more you prepare, the less nervous you will be and the more confident you will come across at the real interview. Copy the statements and questions above to create an interview evaluation form or download questions from the collegegrad.com web page or other comparable list onto a blank document and save it on your computer in the job file you have set up. Address each statement and answer each of the questions, incorporating details you gleaned from their website and from your previous experience. The process of reading, writing (or typing), and reviewing will help reinforce the information, so that when you are asked the question in an interview context, you will be able to calmly recall the information and provide a detailed and accurate response. Chances are that any one interviewer will ask only a selection of these questions, but since you never know what they are going to ask, you should be prepared for anything.

Next, draft a friend or colleague to take you through a mock interview. Provide your interviewer with the question sheet with spaces for comments. (You can use the sample provided in Appendix 4.) Set up an appointment to meet, and show up on time. Dress appropriately, bring your portfolio, and be prepared to address his or her questions as you would with a prospective employer. Have the interviewer take notes during the interview and complete them before conducting a debriefing. Review the interview together and discuss what you can do to make yourself a stronger candidate. ఔ

What to Ask at the Interview

Regarding what you should ask your interviewer, we advise you *not* to ask (at least not first) "How much does this job pay?" Remember, you decided on this profession because of your love for it, not on account of the money you could make. Your first questions should relate more to what your areas of interest are and how you might be able to pursue those interests within the context of this job. It is permissible to ask about health insurance and physical benefits, but don't focus entirely on such things. Ask about the things that are important to you beyond the benefits. The research you did before going to the interview should certainly offer suggestions for good, valid questions. If you don't have any questions, ask if you can call at a later date if questions arise.

Follow Up

Don't simply wait around to hear back from your interviewer. More than likely, that is what everyone else is doing. Believe us when we say that the employer will be impressed that you took the initiative. Remember that there is a fine line. You want to ask without coming across as pushy, because if you don't get this job, you want to be remembered positively when you apply for their next opening.

The Thank-You Note

When you get home from your interview, send a quick email to the employer, thanking him or her for the opportunity to meet with them. If there was anything in particular that impressed you about the organization, add that in as well, but don't try to suck up. The note can be composed and sent as an email, but before you hit the Send button, read through it for grammar, spelling, and punctuation. Keep the comments professional and relevant to the job interview. Do not comment on peripheral issues unless they were part of an intentional discussion during your interview.

Learn from Your Mistakes

If you do not get the job offer, find out what would have made the difference. Send an email thanking the employer for the opportunity of interviewing, and ask what you could do to increase the likelihood of being hired for this position should it come available again. Don't be surprised or disappointed, though, if you don't get a response. If this is the type of job you want, then the information that this employer provides could be invaluable and make the difference between being considered or not in the future. Perhaps you were not lacking an essential element at all, but maybe you simply needed to strengthen how the information was presented. Use any feedback as constructive criticism to make changes to your documents or your interview skills.

SUMMARY

The focus of this chapter was sending in your application, preparing for an interview, interviewing, and follow-up. We covered what to send, what to bring, what to wear, and what to ask. While some of this information may seem like common sense, we have learned how uncommon that sensibility can be. And, even though our moms or grandmothers have always reminded us to thank the person who gave us a gift, or to learn from our mistakes, it doesn't mean we actually did. So here's your chance, and what better reward for your thank-you than a job!

FOR THE PORTFOLIO

Though you had already completed the materials needed for your application packet in previous chapters, the process of interview preparation created components that you should hold onto for future reference. Review the information that you gathered about the agency, organization, or educational institution that you planned to apply to. Print a copy of the questions and answers and place them into the "Jobs Applied for" section of your portfolio. Print a copy of the interview questions with your answers and place that into the portfolio as well.

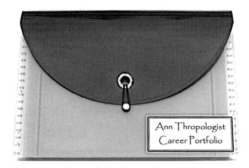

Ann Thropologist
Career Portfolio

SECTION III
SET YOURSELF APART

Consider your competition for a moment. You are entering the job market as the next generation of practicing professionals. Graduating from college means that you have completed a course curriculum designed to provide you with the basic "tools" of the trade. But, everyone else in your graduating class and in the graduating classes of every other anthropology department across the country essentially has the same baseline knowledge, and every one of those individuals is in competition for the same jobs you are considering. It is therefore essential to accumulate experiences that will build your knowledge, skills, and abilities beyond those of your competition. These last few chapters are intended to provide ideas and options for doing just that.

This final section of the book contains six chapters. Chapter 10 discusses the benefits of volunteering and internships. Chapter 11 focuses on communication—verbal, nonverbal, and written. Chapter 12 encourages your involvement with professional organizations and ways that you can start setting up your network. Chapters 13 and 14 provide information on academic employment options and how to apply for them, and Chapter 15 looks at the reasons why you should maintain the portfolio that you've created through the readings and exercises in this book and then sums everything all up.

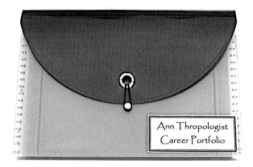

Ann Thropologist
Career Portfolio

CHAPTER 10

INTERNSHIPS AND VOLUNTEERING

"Most of the people who worked for me at AltaMira started as interns. It was a way of trying them out to see if I wanted to hire them; and a way of them trying out the company to see if they wanted to work there."

—Mitch Allen, Founder, Left Coast Press,
friend and publisher of this book

INTRODUCTION

Got a day, week, or month available? Although spending the time relaxing with a book (murder mystery or trashy romance) or the full set of DVDs of the last season of your favorite TV program may be what you really want to do with your well-earned time off, we recommend that you actually use it to your advantage. Volunteer! (Yes, this is a one-word sentence that can be read as a command.) While volunteering or interning at an agency or organization may not pay money, it does pay for itself ten times over when you begin applying for jobs. Money gets spent. It disappears out of your wallet and bank account faster than you can track it. The "payment" from volunteering is one that can pay dividends well into the future. Payment may be in the form of the experience and skills you gain, the additions to your professional network, or the letter of recommendation that you will request from your supervisor prior to your departure from the volunteer position. So, how do you find a place to intern or volunteer?

INTERNSHIPS

Internships, also known as *practicums*, can be arranged through your university, through your department, or sought out on your own. Some internship sponsors provide a stipend or honorarium, which is an added bonus. The advantage of arranging the internship through your university or department is that you can then arrange to receive college credit for the experience. If your college does not offer a formal internship program, speak to your adviser about the possibility of receiving credit as a directed reading or independent study.

Before arranging your internship schedule, talk to your adviser to find out how many hours of work are required per credit hour. It may seem like a lot compared with how many credits you earn per class, but class credit includes more than face-time with the instructor. Class or course credit also calculates in the learning you do when researching, writing papers, studying for exams, preparing presentations, and other class-related activities. The number of internship hours per class credit varies. Our limited online research found that most universities require approximately 15 hours per week during a 10-week semester to accumulate the 150 hours needed for a 3-credit-hour internship.

Internships are beneficial to both the intern and the sponsor. As an intern, you get hands-on experience you would not have access to in the classroom. Use your ethnographic skills to study the workplace and the organizational culture. The more you understand of the big picture, the more you will learn from the experience, and the more likely you will be hired to stay on. If you choose not to stay on, you can still use the experience gained during your internship in later job situations. Use your journal skills to build the lists of key informants—people you are close to, who you might use for references, job leads, or general information about the company and the industry. The people you work with can also help you network within the company or organization.

The sponsor has the benefit of training someone they might employ sometime in the future. If they do hire you, they have the added benefit of reducing the time it would take to familiarize you with their business or activities. Jennifer Carden Kersey conducted her practicum with a small market research boutique, Intrepid Consultants in Seattle, WA, and has worked there for two years now. (See her full career story in Appendix 2.) Robynne Locke looked and looked for a place to do an internship. Eventually she found a research and consulting firm that, while in the private sector (which she had presumed would not be in keeping with her personal philosophy), actually worked in areas she cared passionately about. Despite the fact that the company had no established intern program, she applied anyway and was given a chance—which led to an eventual job there. Carolyn J. McClellan, in her career story, related the following: "One of the biggest life-changing events of my college career was when I applied for and was accepted as an intern in the American Indian Program at the Smithsonian National Museum of Natural History the summer prior to my senior year. I worked for Dr. JoAllyn Archambault on the Mohave Tribal Catalog Project researching the Mojave collections, not only at their museum but across the country. Dr. Archambault then asked me to stay on for the fall semester of my senior year, and the University allowed me to earn credit for my research project which allowed me to graduate in the spring of 1996. This experience taught me the value of research, of the vast amount of data available at other repositories, and working with tribal communities other than my own." Dr. McClellan is now the Assistant Director of Community and Constituent Services at the National Museum of the American Indian. (To see more about Dr. McClellan, read her career story in Appendix 2.)

Bear in mind, however, that interns are not free labor. There is a cost to the employer. They must take time to supervise you when they could be doing something else. Instead of giving your tasks to someone who already knows the job and could complete it quickly, they are giving it to you as a learning experience, which means a slower turnaround for them. There is a chance that you might leave before the tasks are completed, so they might have to spend time training another person to complete the job. All of these things cost money. The cost-benefit ratio needs to be in balance because, if it is not, this employer may think twice about offering internships to students again in the future.

Scheduling an Internship

Don't wait to schedule an internship! Look back to your five-year plan. Perhaps you already planned to do an internship. Is the timing still good, or do you need to alter your plan to accommodate changes that have occurred since you originally laid out your plan? If you have not yet incorporated an internship in your five-year plan, where would it fit? Janet Chernela, professor at the University of Maryland, says, "While I was going for my M.S. (Hunter College 1970–73) and Ph.D. (Columbia University, 1975–83) in anthropology, I had a research assistantship at the American Museum of Natural History. I learned far more as a research assistant than I did in any class. It was the activity of scholarship-in-process rather than the reading of finished scholarship that was so useful."

If you are a planner, you might want to initiate a conversation with the intern sponsor so that you can get placed on the practicum schedule early. This is particularly important if there is a specific place you want to do your internship. Since most organizations accept only one or two interns per year, waiting until the semester you plan to do this internship might be risky: they may have already selected their student interns for that period of time.

Larry Zimmerman, in his review of this chapter, noted that "the best internships happen after a reasonable amount of classroom instruction so that students have at least some knowledge of a subject area. We recommend, for example, that our M.A. museum students wait at least until they have had the required intro class and at least two additional classes, which effectively means no earlier than their second semester. We really like to have them in the last half of their degree. With undergrads, we require that they have the intro class and the museum methods class before their required internship. This way, students have a framework on which to hang their on-the-job experience." Kelley Hays-Gilpin, in her comments, said that some museums sign up their interns as much as six months in advance, so it's best to think ahead.

Identifying Potential Intern Sponsors

If you want to do an internship but have no idea where to start your search for one, we have a few suggestions. Begin by identifying what you are looking for. Grab your journal and flip back through the pages. Look for any notes or comments you may have made that identified geographic locations where you would like to work, skills that you would like to build, and knowledge that you would like to gain. Check the list you generated of places that hire anthropologists within your discipline. Start a new list of the experiences you would like to gain from an internship. If you are taking classes during the same time frame as your internship, then you will probably need to stay fairly close to home. If you are planning an internship for a time when you are not in class, however, that may open you up to working in another geographic area.

If you don't have a specific agency or organization in mind, you can check the listings at your university career center for places seeking anthropology students.

■ Check the Yellow Pages telephone book. With the Web, we sometimes forget to use this useful reference.

■ Talk to your professors. There is a good chance that they have worked with students in internships in the past and may be able to recommend good sponsors to you.

■ Talk to the people in your network. Ask them about their internship experiences and recommendations for potential sponsors.

■ Check the Internet. Interested in working for the federal government? They now have one web page that can link you to all positions, *http:// www.usajobs.gov/studentjobs/*. Many of the government agencies offer a Student Temporary Employment Program (STEP) that bypasses the formal hiring process and allows them to select students directly for specific positions. To qualify for the STEP program, you must show that you are currently a student and that you are enrolled for the term following your internship.

Carol's daughter worked as a STEP employee for the Forest Service for five summers, and received college credit for two of those summers; one summer she worked as an interpreter and one as a member of an archaeological survey crew. She selected different geographic areas and different jobs based on the skills and knowledge she thought she would need when she graduated and was fortunate enough to work in Alaska, New Mexico, Utah, and Washington. (She also selected areas based on access to kayaking or rock climbing!) During her senior year, she started her job search (with a bit of prompting by mom) in February before graduating and was hired in a full-time temporary position in the location of her choice (close to prime rock climbing). Her five summers with the STEP program put her miles ahead of a student walking out of college with a degree and no job experience.

Before You Start

An internship is a learning situation. Like a regular job, internships require a scheduled commitment, but your payment is the knowledge you gain. Although an intern is not merely free labor, bear in mind that all jobs, especially entry-level ones, include some menial tasks that someone has to do. So, while you may take the internship with the intent of assisting with data collection and analysis, don't be surprised if you also have to put stamps on envelopes or answer the phone.

Contact the internship sponsor. Find out who your supervisor will be and make contact with this person either by phone or by email. Build your base of knowledge so that you can walk in feeling a bit more comfortable knowing what you will help with. Ask what books or other resources might broaden your knowledge about their programs or the work you will be doing. Find out what the normal work schedule will be. If you need to negotiate your schedule because of other obligations, now is the time to do it.

Before starting an internship, create a learning contract for yourself, similar to the contract that you made with yourself in Chapter 2. Share the draft with your adviser or departmental sponsor and with the person who will supervise your internship at the work location and finalize it once you have incorporated their comments. The learning contract will provide the framework for the internship, so make sure that you list the types of tasks you will be involved in and the knowledge you'd like to gain. Note in your contract how this internship relates to previous classes or work that you have done and how it will assist you in achieving your goals for getting future jobs.

During Your Internship

Use your journal skills during your internship. Note meetings, conversations, recommendations, and contacts. Ask questions and jot down the answers. You may also wish to use your journal to record time spent on various tasks. Tracking information in this way will help when it comes to writing your performance evaluation at the end of the internship.

Set regular meetings with your direct supervisor for the end of each week or every two weeks. Use the time to note what they would like you to do next and to discuss what you have just completed. If you are confused, speak up. Ask for clarification or additional background information. Midway through the term, talk with your on-campus sponsor. If you are having difficulties, speak up, ask for help. They are not going to know what is wrong unless you talk to them. Don't let this opportunity go to waste, even if you figure out partway through that this is not really what you want to do with your life. Find a way to end it positively. Anthropology is a small community, and people talk. You want to make sure that what they say when your name comes up is positive.

At the End

At the end of your internship, evaluate your own performance. Look at the contract you wrote before you started. How well did you do in relation to what you'd hoped to achieve? Also, ask your internship supervisor for a performance evaluation. If you have not done so already, show your contract to your supervisor so he or she has a base on which to build your evaluation. Set up a time to meet and discuss the evaluations of your performance. This is also the ideal time to request that all-so-important letter of reference or to ask if you can rely on your supervisor for a letter when you are applying for specific jobs in the future.

VOLUNTEERING

Do you have limited time but would still like some practical experience, networking, and letters of reference? Volunteer! While an internship is generally scheduled as a single quarter or a semester-long commitment, volunteering can be as short as a day, or a day here and there. We recommend, though, that regardless of the duration, you treat it as a serious commitment. Even though this is not a paid job, these people are counting on you and your time.

Scheduling When to Volunteer

Volunteering can be a less formal arrangement than an internship, and fitting it into your already crowded curriculum should be easier than designing a semester-long internship. There is no limit to how often or how many places you can and should volunteer, and the more you do it, the better known you will get within a community. Our recommendation is to start volunteering early in your educational career and continue doing so as you progress. You may want to try spending time with various agencies or organizations. If you find that you like one particular group, stick with it.

If you would like to contribute to your field of study, volunteer for the professional or avocational associations in your area. They are always looking for volunteers to assist with everything from annual meeting registrations to stuffing packets to monitoring sessions at meetings. One advantage of volunteering at conferences or events is that they are short-term annual events that occur at specific times of the year. You can build their schedule into yours and block out the time well in advance. Some professional organizations, like the Society for American Archaeology, offer waived or reduced registration fees in exchange for a specific amount of volunteer time. Thus, volunteering serves the purpose of getting you into the all-important national meeting where you can network (see Chapter 12 for more on the importance of national organizations and networking to your transition to professional life) at a cost far below what most other attendees have to shell out.

Identifying Places to Volunteer

Larry Zimmerman says, "Volunteering opportunities may be as close as down the hall in the archaeology laboratory or with a faculty member on a research project or helping out a graduate student who is doing a short dig on a site near campus. I always mention in letters of recommendation student participation in our anthropology or museum studies clubs where you can actually pick up lots of skills and sometimes rub shoulders with high roller speakers." Imagine the conversations you might have with Donald Johanson and Jane Goodall (or Joe Watkins or Carol Ellick) if you were to pick them up at the airport and drive them to the symposium on campus!

Many of the same places that you would work or intern also accept volunteers, but there are even more places that you may not have considered. As mentioned above, getting involved with the local archaeology, anthropology, or historical society can be very beneficial. Volunteering with local avocational societies helps them and helps you. You might also want to consider helping with the Boy Scout or Girl Scout troops in your area. Most groups could use a workshop, speaker, or badge sponsor. Many organizations depend on volunteers and will take as much time as you make available, but you can hold your commitments down by offering to give a presentation or help at an event or annual meeting.

Museums are another excellent venue for volunteering. They always have a backlog of projects and a lack of funds to pay to get them done. Back in 1977, between jobs and schools, Carol wandered down to her favorite high school hangout, the Cleveland Museum of Natural History. When she walked in, she just stood there, uncertain of what she wanted to do or where she wanted to go. The person at the information desk asked if she needed help. In an instant that changed her life forever, she said, "I'd like to volunteer." The information person asked her if she had a particular area of interest and she said, "Anthropology." The next thing she knew, she found herself being led down to the anthropology laboratory where she spent the next two months sorting through fossil hominid fragments and making molds and casts of Lucy. Other less tangible experiences included meeting Mary Leakey and listening to the sometimes heated debates on human origins. The tangible outcome was a letter of recommendation from Donald Johanson recommending her as an excellent addition to any project team.

If you are not sure where to start looking for a volunteer position or who to contact, start with the people you know. Ask other students, your faculty, and your mentors for suggestions and recommendations. They have the background and experience to help you identify a place to start and a person to contact.

Before You Start Your Volunteer Gig

Do your research. Within moments, a simple Google search can turn up more information than you could ever imagine. Look up the organization. Read through the mission statement. Find out who works there and what their specialties are. Develop some questions that you can pose to the people you will be helping. Think about how much time you can reasonably devote to volunteering. Be realistic in your plans, and try to remember that there are only 24 hours in a day and that school is the equivalent of a full-time, 40 hour a week job. Don't put yourself in a position where you might start feeling exploited. Most places will accept as much as you can give, so it is up to you to monitor what works. If you get overwhelmed, let someone know that you need to cut back.

During Your Volunteer Work

Don't be afraid to ask questions. Clarify your tasks with the person giving you the instructions. Working independently is a good thing, but make sure you are doing what the supervisor envisioned. If you are producing something, do the first one and then check to make sure it is what they wanted. If you are monitoring an event, run through the checklist before the event begins. Know where the light switches are if you will be turning down the lights. Try it without the audience in the room so you know which switches dim and which ones turn the lights off completely. Check that the extension cords are taped down or out of the way of people's feet. If you are operating a projector, make sure you know how to turn it on and cool it down before shutting it off, and where the spare bulb is.

   If you are volunteering at a public event, giving a talk to a classroom, or teaching a workshop for scouts, we recommend that you read through the chapter on communication (Chapter 11). In the past 20 years, public outreach and education have become recognized as an extremely important component of professionalization. The American Anthropological Association and the Society for American Archaeology both have extensive resources available on their websites for practicing professionals. Carol has chapters published in books that provide information on presenting in both informal and formal learning situations. (Check her bio in Chapter 7 for the titles of both books.)

At the End

Talk to the person who oversaw your work or participation. Thank him or her for the opportunity to volunteer. If you enjoyed it, offer to help again in the future. And, if you would like a letter of recommendation, now is the time to ask for it.

Summary

Internships and volunteering are what separate you from the person who simply takes classes. They can provide you with the first hands-on, practical experiences within your discipline, or they can give you alternative experiences to complement those you already have. They introduce you to the tasks and, more importantly, they provide you with the opportunity to meet practicing professionals and expand your network beyond the faculty at the university. The most important thing you walk away with is the experience itself.

For the Portfolio

If you set yourself up to apply for an internship, you should have drafted a learning contract. This should be finalized and added to your portfolio. Upon completing your internship, add your evaluation to the portfolio.

The other products that were created as outcomes of this chapter are less formal and include lists of ideas on what constitutes a good venue, what you might like to do that relates to your field of interest, and potential volunteer and internship locations. Each of these should have been noted in your journal. Don't discount these products; you may find them useful in the future.

If you received letters of introduction or letters of reference, put those safely into your portfolio. If you took digital photos, save those on your computer; if you maintain an e-portfolio, save images there. If you receive hard-copies and maintain an e-portfolio, scan the letters as PDF documents and upload them as well. Document your experiences and use the experiences and documentation to help pave the way to your first paid positions.

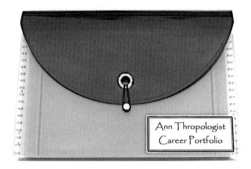

Ann Thropologist
Career Portfolio

CHAPTER 11
COMMUNICATION

"I know you think you understand what you thought I said, but I'm not sure you realize that what you heard is not what I meant."
—Alan Greenspan, Economist, Former Chair
United States Federal Reserve Board

INTRODUCTION

The above quote is one of Carol's favorites. The English language is complex and imprecise, and too often the information we take in is lacking some of what the speaker has tried to convey. Ever play the game "telephone" as a child? Everyone sits in a circle. One person whispers a phrase into the ear of the person next to her. That person whispers what she heard to the next, and so on around the circle. The last person in the circle says the phrase aloud. It is never the same as it started and results in uproarious laughter, at least from a group of five-year-olds. In most circumstances, though, difficulties arise in communication when what is said is not what is heard. There is an art to listening that goes beyond simply hearing what is being said.

In this chapter, we cover a wide range of topics relating to verbal, non-verbal, and written communication. Good communications skills lie at the heart of most things that go radically right or drastically wrong in your efforts to begin a career. Our goal in this chapter is to provide you with some basic information that will help you in moving toward your goals.

LEARNING STYLES

The saying "a picture is worth a thousand words" is true. If we could all be as verbally descriptive as a picture, then part of the issue concerning communication with others would be solved, at least for the auditory learners. The visual learners would still need that picture.

There are three primary learning styles—auditory, visual, and tactile. The majority of people process information best by listening, but we also take in information through sight and touch. In theory, a good teacher will teach to all learning styles, since all classes will have all types of learners. It's easy to envision teaching a tactile and visual math lesson on percentages at the elementary level if you consider what can be done with the number of each color of M&Ms in a bag. In middle school, high school, and college, teaching becomes oriented more toward auditory learners. But learning styles don't change. If you are a visual learner, you are not going to automatically become an auditory learner to accommodate a teacher whose only teaching method is to lecture. Those of us who are visual or tactile learners and who have made it through the system, have taught ourselves learning techniques to compensate for lecture-based teaching.

> "The discussions of learning styles gives us the information necessary to start being active in the professional world and pursuing our career choices. It also provides us with information necessary to interact in the professional world."
> —Gwen Mohr, journal comment, Avenues to Professionalism class

Types of Learners and Why the Differences Matter

As anthropologists, we are taught observation skills. Observation is a fundamental skill within every subdiscipline. The ability to take what you have seen and detail those observations as completely as possible—as if drawing them on the page, so that readers will feel as if they are having the experience themselves—is what is most important. These same skills—observation, inference, listing of data, and descriptive writing—can benefit you in your career. To some of us, observing and describing come easily; others struggle with converting observations to details on a page. How we best take in information is based on our learning style, and knowing how we learn can make the classroom or the job easier.

Visual Learners
Visual learners take in information by seeing it. There are two types of visual learning: graphic/image-based and text-based. The text-based visual learner can pick up information more easily from reading words. Graphic learners may also pick things up by reading, but sometimes they see words as a form or shape rather than as the individual letters that make up the words. As anthropologists, perhaps we all tend to be somewhat visually oriented.

Tactile Learners
See it; touch it; do it. Archaeologists study material culture. They must use their visual as well as their tactile senses in order to fully comprehend the material culture that they are analyzing. Tactile learners have the more hands-on style of learning. Once shown, they need to touch it, do it, and create it to learn it.

Auditory Learners
Auditory learners learn best by listening. Perhaps linguists lean more toward the auditory end of the spectrum. Auditory learners process lectures best and succeed well in "traditional" learning situations. Most of us who have survived or flourished in college and graduate school are auditory learners or have developed our auditory learning capacity. But mistakes and problems can arise if we automatically assume that everyone takes in information adequately by hearing it. If you want to make sure that the people you are talking to have understood what you said, ask them to repeat portions of it back to you. This is a simple technique that may help alleviate some frustrations.

It may seem strange to think about learning-styles at this point of your life, but to be a successful communicator, it is important to understand how people learn. Knowing how people learn is not only relevant to those going into academic fields of anthropology. If we supervise employees, interact with others, and present at professional conferences, understanding how people learn helps us gauge how best to communicate with them.

Cultural Influences on Communication

Cultural influences. Wah-hoo! We should be good at this! Cultural influences—isn't that what anthropology is all about, people, culture? Yes, but our involvement in culture is generally as the observer and annotator. As the scientist, we are the outsider looking in. Linguists might focus on the influences of culture on communication, but that doesn't mean that the interactions influence our speaking, hearing, or relating. And, we might examine the influences, but how deeply do we think about the consequences or make recommendations for reducing impact?

Communication among individuals is more than merely talking and listening. Our communication—beyond the words we speak—is influenced by the amount of shared experiences and cultural information we presume others to have. For example, most of us have friends that we know so well that a glance, word, or action can convey a whole series of thoughts or reactions. Conversely, there are some people who, no matter how hard we try, we just can't seem to comprehend (and we're not talking about accents here). Such shared information relates to the level of cultural (shared) context between individuals.

> "For me, being a Native American and trying to be an archaeologist I find myself in a little pickle. Being Native, I realize now, after Joe explained communication styles to us, that I am very indirect and require high context when communicating. As an archaeologist, I should have the opposite communication style. I need to find a way to communicate more directly. It's not that I have to change who I am, but I need to learn how to play the game."
> —Joseph (Woody) Aguilar, journal comment,
> Avenues to Professionalism class

High and Low Context

Archaeologically, context is the relationship of one artifact to its place and the other objects around it. When we communicate with others, our communication gets placed within the context of the situation. A broader generalization might be that our various cultures provide us the "context" with which we interpret and deliver communications.

"Low context" communication occurs when there is little shared cultural experience. Most of the information is fact filled and explicitly presented between individuals (or groups). College classrooms are perfect examples of a situation in which low context communication is required. The "culture" is varied; there is no cohesion within the group. To successfully communicate the content of the course, the instructor must explicitly communicate specific ideas and thoughts.

"High context" communication tends to occur when most of the information and background are shared. Families or groups of friends are good places to find high context communication. For example, communication at the completion of a two-month field season is different than at the start. The group, through time, has created its own shared culture. At the beginning of the field season, everything had to be explicitly stated. By the end, everyone has shared the same experiences and stories to the point that if someone were to mention that today there was another problem with shoelaces, everyone would understand the reference, and the new story could be told without explaining the previous experiences.

Direct and Indirect Communication

In conjunction with the level of shared cultural context, communication can also be direct or indirect. Direct communication is straightforward and explicit. It leaves no doubt as to what was said. Indirect communication is more subtle. Meaning may be conveyed through an action rather than voice. Indirect communication requires inference. You need to ask yourself, what did they mean? Were they trying to communicate something beyond telling me a story? Was there a moral to the story? When a supervisor tells you that he really liked the look of the lab yesterday, is he trying to simply praise you for cleaning the lab, or is he implying that you should try to keep it that way daily?

Understanding communication styles and the importance of cultural context will help you as you transition from school into your career. Ed Jolie, speaking of himself and his wife, says that communication is essential to survival in graduate school and beyond: "Both of us being in grad school, though difficult, made it easier in some ways. We each knew what the other was going through. We've been, I think, very good at communicating with each other in our relationship. Couples, whether one or both are nascent academics, need to make sure that they're communicating very well with their spouse/partner. You cannot do this alone, and that means leaning on your friends and loved ones as much, if not more, than on your academic advisors/mentors." Utilize the analytical skills gained through working with people. Become sensitive to the way that culture influences the ways humans communicate with one another. As you move into an organization, you will likely have to interact with people from many different backgrounds; being aware of the various culturally influenced communication styles will make your understanding of group dynamics (and your integration into the group) easier. More information on cultural context and communication can be found in the Peace Corps training guide, *Culture Matters* (see Appendix 3, Resources).

NONVERBAL COMMUNICATION

We communicate consciously and subconsciously in many different ways. In addition to the obvious spoken word, we communicate loudly by the way we stand, sit, and make eye contact. We transmit signals to those around us whether we are aware of it or not. As with other forms of communication, our "body language" is influenced by our culture. People in many European cultures stand close to one another during conversations, but people in the United States tend to stand farther apart while talking. Some cultures think nothing of people touching each other during conversations, but, in the United States, touching is usually reserved for close acquaintances. This is not the place to discuss the many cultural differences in the ways that body language is perceived or the protocol involved in presenting yourself to others. It is necessary, however, that you understand that people always gather information from the way you present yourself to them.

❧ *EXERCISE:* OBSERVING BODY LANGUAGE

Be an ethnographer. Grab your journal and go to a public place. Find a comfortable place to sit on the outskirts of the area you will watch so that you can observe people alone and in conversations. Begin by watching how people move and how close they stand or sit to each other. Do they have their arms crossed? Are they slouched? Do they look at each other when they talk?

Select an individual. On a clean right-hand (odd) page in your journal, describe his or her posture and body language. On the left-hand (even) page, describe what you believe the body posture means. Next, select a pair or group of people to observe. Repeat the process that you used for the individual on each member of the group, and then describe the interactions and the ways the body language changes among the different individuals in the group as the conversation evolves. Based on your observations and their body language, do you believe they are colleagues, friends, or strangers? Do they appear nervous, wary, or confident?

Consider your own body language. How have you been sitting while watching the others? Think about how others in this location would perceive you if they were observing your body language. ❧

As you enter the workforce, become aware of your body language, because what you say and how you are perceived by others includes more than the words that come out of your mouth. At your job interview, sit straight with your shoulders back and down. Practice keeping your legs uncrossed so that others will believe you are comfortable and accepting of them and their ideas. When sitting, keep your hands clasped together in your lap; when standing, keep them in front of you or at your sides. If you are in a formal situation, keep your legs together and feet on the floor. When you are asked a question, look at the person who asked it, but then also look at the others in the room, if there is more than one interviewer. Try to portray confidence, even if it is not quite what you are feeling.

WRITING AND WRITTEN COMMUNICATION

"The past belongs to everyone, not just anthropologists. That totally changes my attitude towards publishing! It's not just about colleagues showing off to one another, it's making the research available to everyone. It's not self-serving at all! It's for the benefit of everyone that is interested in the subject!"
—Gwen Mohr, journal comment, Avenues to Professionalism class

Just do it. There is no other way to get better at it. The first piece of advice for becoming a better writer: write, write, write (words from our editor and other wise individuals)! Writing is a skill, an art, and a craft. You can't dream yourself better at writing any more than you can dream yourself to fly (try as we might). The second-best advice for becoming a better writer is to read and analyze the writing of those you admire. The third piece of advice is to write descriptively, as if you are having a conversation.

Finally, be aware that the way you write should be focused on the audience you want to reach. If you are writing to specialists in your field, your writing can use jargon that presumes high context/shared knowledge; if the work is for the general public, throw the jargon out and write in such a way that anyone could read it and understand it.

Larry Zimmerman, in his book *Presenting the Past* (2003: 32), offers ten tips to help simplify writing. Many are commonsense suggestions. For instance, "1. Figure out who your audience is"; or "10. Read the work aloud. Normally, people don't speak in as complicated a way as they write. If the prose sounds complicated, it probably is." Others are more esoteric: "9. Every so often, calculate a readability index to see whether your writing meets what you think the appropriate reading level is for your audience. If it doesn't, then rewrite." Applying these suggestions will help you improve your writing.

Learn to Write

You may think this section doesn't apply to you, but at some level it does. You may not be following an academic "publish or perish" path or planning to write a book, but your career will probably entail writing something. One of the biggest complaints we've heard from employers across the profession is that students graduating from college cannot write. Professors complain that students arrive at college with the inability to write proper sentences, format papers, cite sources, and/or construct the list of references. It takes time to learn to read and write, and the only way to get better is to do it.

We highly recommend that you write and submit articles to newsletters and journals. Take every opportunity that is offered that will help develop your writing skills, build your résumé, and get you noticed by potential employers.

If you know your writing is deficient, get help. Your journal editors, employers, and clients will thank you for it later! Most campuses have a writing center where you can get help on particular papers, but most of the time these centers do not actually "teach" you how to write. Read and study some basic writing books such as Turabian's *A Manual for Writers of Research Papers, Theses, and Dissertations*. This advice is especially important if you are a graduate student.

Find a good editor, or two. Technical editors will look for spelling, grammar, and punctuation errors. They will check word choice to make sure that you have not used "there" when you actually meant "their." They will look at your hyphens and recommend when to use an "en-dash" or "em-dash."

Content editors will look to see how the thoughts you have developed are connected. They will identify where you may have wandered off topic or where you need more information. They will be able to see if point A leads to point B, and then arrives at point C, which in turn leads to the conclusion, and if your conclusion relates to your introduction. Content editing involves linear and lateral thinking, and a good content editor will make recommendations on how to broaden or focus your argument.

As a writer, you should carefully consider the recommendations from your editors and reviewers. Good editors will provide constructive criticism and will make recommendations they think will improve your document. It is up to you as the author to consider their recommendations and decide whether to incorporate them or not. Read what they recommend, and do not be frightened by the red ink. If you do not understand what they have said, ask. It may be that they did not understand what you wrote in the first place, in which case you need to fix the sentence to alleviate confusion. One of the most important pieces of advice we have ever heard about writing was also from Brian Fagan. He said that writers should "lose the ego" and not take criticism about writing personally. It will get in the way of your ability to improve your writing.

In the workplace, your writing should improve as you learn from your mistakes. As it improves, you will reduce the amount of time it takes you to write, the amount of time it takes for someone to edit your writing, and the amount of time it takes to incorporate the recommended fixes into your document. But having a good basic writing ability to begin with ensures that you can more quickly become a more valued member of the team. And, in order to become an even better writer, check out such "how-to" books as *Writing for Social Scientists: How to Start and Finish Your Thesis, Book, or Article* (Becker 2007). A more comprehensive list of writing resources is included in Appendix 3, Resources.

Deadlines

As educators, writers, editors, and publication managers (we've worn a lot of hats), we can't stress enough the importance of holding to a schedule. Establish a writing routine and chart out the plan. If you have the habit of procrastinating, break it early in your professional life and you will be a much more productive and a much less stressed individual. Stop thinking "I can't." Remove the excuses that allow you to push writing aside.

Deadlines are important. If you're writing a grant or turning in a report, meeting the deadline may mean the difference between keeping your job, or not. If you are contributing to an edited volume, you are just one of several writers who will be submitting work to the editor. If you are late, your actions affect everyone. Don't fall into the trap of thinking, "Well, the editor has everyone else's work to look at, so it won't matter if mine is late." Set a deadline for the completion of your project. If someone has set a deadline for you, establish your own personal completion deadline a week before the actual due date. If your project has sections or chapters, chart out a course for competing each. Create a schedule and post it on your wall. Physically mark off each task as you complete it. A visual reminder that reinforces what you are accomplishing is positive reinforcement. Reward yourself when you complete the project. Too often, we finish something and move on to the next task without congratulating ourselves for getting it done. Think of extrinsic rewards (bribes) for a job well done. Small accomplishments deserve small rewards. Bribe yourself: "When I finish writing 1,000 words, I will allow myself 15 minutes of reading in the novel before I have to move on to the next task of the day." Submitting the completed chapter or book deserves a much larger reward.

Technical Writing

Most anthropological jobs require you to contribute financially to your own employment in some way. Even university professors must conduct research, which means they must procure grants that will fund their research *and* provide a healthy percentage of the overhead costs to the university. Learning the strategies (and tricks) to technical writing early in your career can mean the difference between continued employment and the unemployment lines.

In our Avenues to Professionalism class, we provided copies of a request for proposal (RFP) and grant applications to help students understand some of the basic techniques of writing proposals. We covered important information about the proposal, submission requirements and deadlines, and ways of "parroting" back information within the proposal. We also discussed how to develop associated cost proposals and justifications, and helped students understand what was required within each document. However, for this book, we are simply going to encourage you to seek out sources, look at RFPs and grant applications, and familiarize yourself with the types of writing that will be required in your dream job or jobs.

OTHER COMMUNICATION CAVEATS

This section is a catch-all, to cover other communications topics that don't fall under any particular category. Some of these relate directly to your job search and your interview and some to employment. Our reason for including them here is to build your awareness of these issues.

Emails

If you are like us, email rules your life. It can be an extremely efficient means of communicating with others, but it can also be extremely vulnerable to miscommunication. All the discussion about context and directness applies to email communication. As you compose a letter or email, remember that what you are producing is a written document that will be read once or more by the recipient. It is not just what you say, but also how you say it that matters.

Don't be drawn into the "web" of immediacy! Email can eat up your entire morning; it can become a long, drawn-out conversation composed of one-sentence responses. If something takes a series of emails to explain, pick up the telephone and call. A "New message" indicator in your in-box doesn't mean that you should stop work to read and answer it.

There are also rules about email etiquette that are important to know.

■ ALL CAPS IS AKIN TO SHOUTING! (Please don't yell.)

■ If you receive an email from a list-serve, but only want to reply to the author of the note, do not simply hit "Reply."

■ Don't forward jokes, no matter how cute, to everyone in your email directory.

■ Reread and spell-check your email before you send it.

Probably the most important rule, however, is to never write anything in an email that you might regret. Email communications, once sent, stick around forever. Email communications, taken out of context, can make a saint appear to be satanic or an angel agnostic.

■ Never write an email in the heat of the moment.

■ If you are angry, turn off your machine and walk away or throw a pencil across the room (providing there is no one across the room who could get hurt).

■ Do not write a snappy, vitriolic response intending to delete it; what happens if you accidentally hit Send instead? You can't take it back.

If you find that your email tends to get the better of you, check your emails only at specific times of the day: when you first get to work, sometime during mid-morning, after lunch and mid-afternoon. Scan for High Priority emails if something is pending, but don't open emails from friends.

It's amazing that even as recently as 20 years ago, it used to take messages weeks or even months to arrive, and we were content to send a response and wait for an answer. Now the immediacy of it all seems to drive our need to respond at a moment's notice.

Email Etiquette

Bear in mind that anything you write can go anywhere and to anyone. There is nothing private about an email unless you specifically request that it not be forwarded by the receiver. If you are having a private email discussion, do not send a blind copy (blind carbon copy—BCC) to someone outside the conversation. If this were a face-to-face private meeting, you would not bring colleagues with you to support your side of the discussion.

Too Much Information

Just because you think it, it doesn't mean you have to say it! This is especially true for oral communication, but it applies equally well to written communication. Learn to think before you disclose. Do you need to tell the entire story? "…I was on my way out the door when I realized that there was something wrong with the cat and I had to take her to the vet, but when I went to start the car, the car battery was dead so I had to call my friend, but she wasn't available for an hour, so I had to wait for her, then we had to wait at the vet because we didn't have a scheduled appointment." You could simply say, "I'm sorry, an emergency arose and I am going to be two hours late. I will make it up this week."

Wait Time

Another communication technique that can be quite valuable is "wait time." Sometimes, we reply to a statement or question without actually processing what was said. We respond to what we thought we heard. Stopping for a moment and fully processing the information before responding can reduce the potential for misunderstanding. You can also give yourself processing time by repeating or paraphrasing what the other person has said by stating, "I think I heard you say. . . ."

Once again, culture can play an important part in the conversations we have with others. In consultations with Native American groups, it is often considered respectful to wait an appropriate amount of time (often unstated) between speakers to let the information "soak in."

Eye Contact

In the United States, many of us are taught as children to "look people in the eye" when you talk to them. We may have been told that "honest" people will look you in the eye during a conversation. However, many American Indian cultures believe it is an insult to look directly into the eyes of a speaker. Avoiding direct eye-contact is a sign of respect. If you are working with people from cultures not your own, it is important that you conduct additional research on intercultural communication beforehand so that you can be a better communicator during your work with them.

SUMMARY

In this chapter we covered topics relating to communication—verbal, nonverbal, and written. We discussed some of the issues that can be encountered when communicating with those outside our culture and recommended using your anthropological skill set to better relate to or blend in with the community.

Each form of writing has its own style and purpose. In this chapter, we've touched on some of the problems pointed out to us by colleagues and friends, and we've made recommendations for how to learn from your mistakes and become a more valuable employee.

However, only so much can be said in a short chapter. In the case of learning how to write, we highly recommend that you not only read, but critically evaluate how what you enjoy reading was written. Work with your editors to improve your writing and consult additional sources that delineate the writing process. We recommend *Writing Archaeology: Telling Stories about the Past* by Brian Fagan (Left Coast Press, 2010) and *Presenting the Past* by Larry Zimmerman (AltaMira Press, 2003).

FOR THE PORTFOLIO

No new content was produced for your portfolio in this chapter. We would recommend, however, that, given your new insights on writing, you reexamine the documents in your portfolio and make sure that they actually communicate what you intended to say. We also recommend that you place a copy of your best written work into your portfolio to use as an example of your writing, should a potential employer request one. This document should be traded out for newer work as time goes by and your writing skills improve.

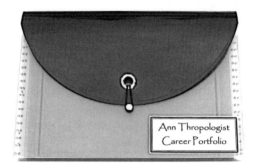

CHAPTER 12

PAYING YOUR DUES: ORGANIZATIONS AND CONFERENCES

INTRODUCTION

Although membership to professional organizations is not mandatory, we highly recommend it. An anthropological organization is its membership. Generally, within major national organizations, everyone except the executive director and the office staff is a volunteer. Smaller state and local organizations are managed entirely by volunteers. It is the membership (professional anthropologists) that gives guidance and direction not only to the organization, but to the decisions and directions of the profession.

In Chapter 3, you located and identified one local, one national, and one international organization associated with your discipline. In the exercise, you identified specific requirements and costs for each organization. In Chapter 10, we recommended conferences and meetings as excellent venues for volunteering. In this chapter, we discuss in more detail the advantages of membership, service to the profession, networking, and contributing and participating at conferences.

MEMBERSHIP

Don't like how things are done within your profession? Join the professional association and change it. Want to meet others interested in ceramics, feminist anthropology, DNA analysis, indigenous archaeology, or some other subspecialty of anthropology? Join a committee, task force, or interest group. Want to know the direction of your subdiscipline in a way that you can't in a classroom? Go to conferences. Want current research, not information that is 10+ years old from your textbook? Sit in on a few sessions and listen to the people who are practicing the profession. Want excellent cutting-edge books focused on relevant topics? Check out the Left Coast Press table or the displays of some of the other publishers in the exhibit hall.

The main point here is: get involved. It is important that you maintain your identity as an anthropologist, and attending anthropology meetings can help you do that. Membership is not and should not be limited to academic anthropologists. The field of anthropology extends beyond the confines of the ivory tower, and if it is to mature properly, input into its development should be balanced between applied and academic anthropologists.

The advantages of membership go both ways. The organization gets funding, board members, committee members, and other volunteers (without which it could not function). The members have a voice, colleagues, networks, and opportunities to bring their research to light through publications and presentation.

Dues

Membership dues are paid annually and vary from organization to organization. Generally, the local and state dues are fairly inexpensive, ranging from $10 to $50 per year. National dues are higher. Dues are fixed by individual organizations and are based on various criteria. All professional organizations have a student membership rate—generally half the cost of a "regular" membership—and can range from $35 to $70 depending on the organization. Most organizations have a fixed-price scale for students, regular members, associate members, spousal members, and members from other countries. The one exception to the fixed pricing fee structure is offered by the American Anthropological Association. Their regular membership is on a sliding fee scale, based on income, except for students, who are charged a low fixed rate based on their status as an undergraduate or graduate student. Graduate students making more than $20,000 pay on the sliding fee scale, same as professionals.

Somewhere in between the state organizations and the national ones are the regional organizations. Many professionals regularly attend regional meetings yet shy away from national conferences. The reasons are as varied as the members, but most cite preferences for "smaller," "cozier," or "more personal." Regional meetings also allow you to interact with people more likely to be interested in your particular subject. Topics of the Plains Anthropological Society meetings cover all the major subfields of anthropology generally circumscribed by boundaries of the Great Plains, and dues are generally less than those of the national organizations.

When you join at the student membership level, organizations usually require that you submit a copy of your valid student ID with your membership application. Of course, there are no "dues police," but everyone expects you to be honest and professional in dealings with your professional organization.

Member Benefits

Joining an organization doesn't commit you to anything other than identifying yourself as part of the group and agreeing to abide by the rules and codes of that organization (remember the discussion of the codes of ethics in Chapter 4). The most basic benefits of membership include a publication of some sort, access to an organization membership list, invitations to conferences, and voting rights in the organization's elections.

Another important benefit offered by organizations that will help you on your road to becoming a professional is the opportunity to present your research in sessions at the annual meeting. Most (if not all) organizations require that you be a member in good standing in order to present at the annual conference or pay a significantly higher registration fee if you are not a member. Some organizations do not allow you to present unless you join the organization. In the following sections, we offer some basics on preparing a submission and putting together a presentation. There are other excellent resources available that focus more specifically on this topic; one that we recommend is *Presenting the Past* by Larry J. Zimmerman (AltaMira, 2003).

If you want to participate and want to start networking beyond your university, join a professional organization. By joining, you will have access to member directories, workshops, and services not available to non-members. In addition, presenting papers at conferences and publishing in their newsletter or peer-reviewed journal will help you get that professional position more quickly. Elizabeth Briody begins her career story with, "I was in my last year of my anthropology Ph.D. program at The University of Texas at Austin. A friend of mine came back from the ASA (American Sociological Association) Meetings and said she had met a guy there from General Motors (GM) who was looking to hire an anthropologist. She told me that she thought I should apply for the job." Briody told her friend she was going to be a professor, so she didn't need to apply. But her friend persisted, so she applied; and by the end of her interview day, she'd done a complete 180-degree turn and took the job. Based on her experiences, her advice is to

> network as much as possible. Building and maintaining social and professional networks inside your group or organization is an excellent way to help others learn from you, and to help you learn from them. Knowing the key roles, those with influence and control, and the extent of alignment and division among individuals and groups enhance any applied effort. Networking with anthropologists—whether locally or through a professional association—helps you, your anthropology colleagues, and anthropology as a discipline. In addition to sharing knowledge and applications, such networks can be valuable sources of internship placements, consulting arrangements, research collaborations, and hiring opportunities.

Jennifer Cardew Kersey concurs. She "got a great education and successfully entered into the anthropology community of praxis (CoP)" by attending national meetings, reaching out to others, and connecting with people online.

PRESENTING

Annual meetings and conferences usually offer several different ways to get involved and present research findings. Most meetings are organized around topics or themes. Individuals can submit a paper or poster, organize a symposium, or develop a poster session.

If you are just starting out and have an idea for a presentation but haven't been invited to present as part of a larger session, you can submit a proposal for a paper or poster as an individual. The program manager for the meeting will review your proposal (usually called an "abstract") and place you in a session of similar topics. If it is a smaller meeting, chances are that your participation will be in a session with other individual "papers," and there may be no commonality other than that you all submitted an abstract.

The Title and Abstract

The title of your paper may be the most important set of words you can come up with. The title is what will grab people's attention so that they read your abstract, which in turn will draw them into the session to listen to you speak.

Your title should be clever, short, and relate to the content of your presentation. Some people like to build their title in two parts separated by a colon, such as was done with the title of this book, *The Anthropology Graduate's Guide: From Student to a Career.*

In the context of advertising your presentation, the abstract is the second most important self-promotional writing you can do. At its most basic, the abstract is an abbreviated description of the presentation you would like to give at the conference. Be succinct. State what your research project is and what makes it of interest to the people attending the conference. Tell them what you plan to talk about. It's okay to say, "In this presentation. . . ." You don't have to keep that opening phrase in the abstract, but it's a great way to start putting words on paper. Besides summarizing what you will talk about for 10–20 minutes in 100–200 words, abstracts should be written to entice people to come and hear what you have to say. Don't give it all away in the abstract. If you do, people will have no reason to attend.

Abstracts are submitted well in advance of the meeting. It is not unusual for a national organization to put out the call for papers a year before the actual conference and for the closing date to be six months in advance. Smaller conferences have shorter deadlines and turnaround time.

Papers

Above, we noted "paper" in quotes because a paper is something you write. Unfortunately, too many times at professional meetings, a paper is what is read. This, in our joint opinion, is just plain wrong. At a conference, you have a rare opportunity to interact with a group of professionals. Instead of reading a paper, give a talk. Be animated. If you plan to apply for academic jobs, use your presentation to polish your delivery skills. (For more on academic job talks, see Chapter 14.)

Most presentations are time restricted. Don't waste precious time on analytical details; your presentation should summarize your research. Another fatal mistake is saying at the opening that because of time limitations, you are going summarize your findings or that you are going to be brief. By doing this, you've already wasted time. Just get to it.

We also recommend thinking through your presentation and writing out the information in a paper format; this will help you keep within the time limits. If you want your paper length to match the time restrictions, write a few pages and then, with a stopwatch in hand (or in the hand of a partner), read aloud for one timed minute. When the time is up, mark the stopping point on the page and count the number of words read. Remember to read slowly and enunciate as you would when talking to a group. When we tried this, we read approximately 150–160 words within a minute. A double-spaced page written in a 12-point font will contain 300–350 words, depending on the number of paragraphs and the word length. So, it should take approximately two minutes, give or take 30 seconds, to read one page of text. Multiply that out, and you'll find that a 15-minute presentation should be 2,250–2,400 words.

It is important to remember that your presentation is much more than the written content. A successful presentation involves knowing your audience, preparing in advance, and providing the information verbally, visually, and if possible, tactilely.

Know Your Audience

Chances are that regardless of the venue, the audience will be mixed. Avoid jargon and technical terms. People know that you had to learn them to prove yourself worthy of the college degree, but they will respect you more for your ability to say the same thing using words that everyone can understand.

Avoid opening with a joke unless you are someone who jokes easily. Never tell a joke about another person or group. Chances are good that a percentage of your audience won't get it. Do you really want them to spend the entire session trying to figure out the joke instead of listening to the presentation?

You are the specialist. It's your presentation. Your job as the speaker is to communicate your knowledge to your audience.

Preparation Is the Key to Success

As with writing a paper, composing a presentation takes time. Do not wait until the last moment. (Yes, we sound like your parents, but you should listen to us.) Write your "paper" not as a paper to publish, but as if you were carrying on a conversation.

There are three parts to a presentation: introduction, body, and conclusion. And it is okay to say, "In conclusion. . . ." People will know where you are (but hopefully not sigh with relief).

Read through the "paper,"out loud, ahead of time, to get a better feel for how it will flow. Develop a detailed outline to act as a key that will get you through the presentation. Know the information inside and out. Practice the first couple of minutes of your presentation, over and over, and over again, not just reading, but saying it. It's all right if you do it differently each time. It will make the actual introduction much more comfortable. Time the whole presentation at least once to be sure that you will keep within the time limits.

Body Language and Clothing

Like it or not, you will be judged on your appearance. This does not mean that you need to run out and spend the month's food allowance on a new suit. Dress simply, professionally, and comfortably. Google "business casual" and aim for that. For more information on clothing and appearance, see the "Clothing Makes the Man (or Woman)" section in Chapter 9.

Prior to your session, check yourself in front of the mirror. Is everything buttoned and zipped? There really is nothing worse than finding out that you forgot to zip a zipper. Carol can say this from personal experience. She thanks her lucky stars (and the person behind her) that the zipper problem was discovered in the cashier line when buying morning coffee, and not as she was walking to the podium.

Wear comfortable shoes, as you'll be standing for at least 10 minutes. If you have laced shoes, make certain the laces are tied.

Faux Pas and Annoying Habits

Avoid playing with your hair, rocking back and forth, sighing audibly, and mispronouncing names of people and places. If you are unsure of a pronunciation, ask someone who has worked with these people or in these places for the proper pronunciation. Practice the pronunciation and write it out phonetically in a way that will make sense to you when you read it.

Technology

Bring backup copies of everything. Bring a copy of your presentation on paper, on a memory stick, and on a CD. Bring a copy of your PowerPoint in every conceivable way as well. Make sure that your digital presentation is in a compatible format. This is particularly important if you are using a Mac and the session computer is a PC or if you are using the most recent version or a very old version of a program that is not on the session computer. If something can go wrong, it will.

Some session organizers will want to receive presentations ahead of time. Make their life easier. Send it to them (another reason not to wait until the last minute). The deadline for submitting your paper is not the date and time of your presentation. It should be one to two weeks *prior* to the scheduled presentation.

Create PowerPoint slides that support what you are saying. People cannot read one thing and listen to another. Do not simply say what is on the slides: that is just plain boring. Make one verbal point per slide. Plan to show one slide every one to two minutes. If you have a fifteen-minute presentation, use a total of ten to fifteen slides.

Graphics should be clean and crisp. Before inserting your images into PowerPoint, reduce their size by compressing them and lowering their resolution; they should be saved at less than 150 dots per square inch (dpi). Higher resolution is unnecessary, as most projectors project at 72 dpi. Select the compression options that will compress all images and will do it automatically every time the presentation is saved. Compressing the images reduces the overall file size, thereby making it easier to save to a thumb drive or send via email.

Fonts should be plain, easy to read, and no smaller than 18 point. Use a maximum of three font styles, and use them consistently in each slide. For example, all the captions should be in the same font. All the headings should use the same font. Use short phrases; avoid content that actually has to be read by the audience. Designing the slides with PowerPoint's templates is easy, but these standard styles can get tiresome. Before you settle on a specific background or slide design, take time to see what is available and experiment with color choices. For additional information on color, color choices, and accommodating color-blindness, see the "Preparing Your Poster" section in this chapter (pp. 163–164).

If you can, practice with the machines and equipment that will be used in the session room. Some conferences have practice rooms, but chances are you will have to practice in a session room during a lunch break or after the last session in a room. Even the little things count. If you will be using a laser pointer, try it before you need it. Point it and move it slowly, or your audience may never see what you are trying to highlight. If you are using a microphone, make sure it is on and adjusted to your height.

Knowing that things will work when you want them to will reduce your stress during the presentation. Make life easier on yourself by taking a few minutes to become familiar with your surroundings before you have an audience watching you.

Timing

An American Anthropological Association session provides 15 minutes per speaker. You cannot present an entire thesis in 15 minutes, nor would you want to. It will be your responsibility to keep your presentation under 15 minutes. Focus on just a few key points and provide information that supports those points. The moderator will warn you as you get close to your time limit. Respect these limits. Respect others (a lot of other people don't). Practice your presentation. Know the essential points you want to make. Be ready to modify your presentation if you are running out of time. If you leave something out, it's okay. No one will know but you, and everyone will appreciate it if you are on time. Larry Zimmerman says, don't worry: "Almost everyone will run overtime or not make it through a paper at some time in their career, so if it happens to you, don't beat yourself up for it afterward. It happens to the best!"

> *"It went average. Problem I ran into is that how I practiced is not how it turned out. I need to have a written plan about what I am going to do. Second, I need to practice in front of someone, instead of the mirror. That way, I can figure out if what I am saying matches what they hear. In other words, it may make sense in my head, but does it make sense to other people?"*
>
> —Doug Rocks-Macqueen, journal comment,
> Avenues to Professionalism class

Presenting

Carry only what you need to the podium. Do not feel bound by the podium or the microphone. Depending on the room size, people may be able to hear you without the microphone. It is okay to move and talk.

As you speak, look at your audience. Make eye contact with occasional individuals whom you know, or pick out a face in the crowd back left, front left, middle, right. The audience is there to hear what you have to say, so speak slowly and clearly. Pause occasionally.

Avoid using words to take up the time between thoughts. A paused silence is better than "um," "and," "so," "OK"—or, heaven forbid, "like." We get into bad habits of incorporating these verbal tics into our daily conversations. Start by trying to be conscious of using them with peers; then try to remove them, or they will sneak into your presentation. Be confident when you talk, or at least try to portray confidence. If you tend to vocalize sentences such that your voice (pitch) goes up at the end, as you might when asking a question, practice speaking in a declarative way. Keep your tone level at the end of the sentences, and keep your volume constant.

Keep your hands in front of you when they are not busy pointing out a detail on your graphics or changing a slide. Clasping them will help you keep track of them so that they do not inadvertently wind up in your pocket jingling the change. Wear a watch. Keep track of time, so you know that you are where you should be in your presentation, when you should be. If you have a chance, note the time you start and the time you should finish. It is no crime to finish a little early, but don't talk fast just so you can fit it all in. If you get a chance, comment positively or refer to points in previous presentations as they relate to what you have to say.

Look at the audience and say "thank you" at the end of your presentation. Pick up your notes and step down. If there is time for questions, stay to respond. People cannot always hear the question asked, so it is important for you to take a moment and restate it. This also gives you the chance to think of an appropriate response. Be concise. If someone asks a question that is beyond your research, say so. Don't try to make something up. If it is a forum that provides for other comments, open it up to the room: "Does anyone else have experience with...?" When all is complete, say "thank you" again and return to your chair.

If Something Goes Wrong

It happens to all of us. At one SAA Public Session, Brian Fagan got up to the podium and announced that the slides for his presentation were lost in his luggage. He proceeded to give a very animated presentation, occasionally pointing at the blank screen and saying, "In this slide, you can see. ..." If something like this happens to you, roll your eyes, throw up your hands, act disgusted. Relax. Make a joke about it and move forward with the presentation. Of course, if it's a technical problem, don't be afraid to ask for assistance from the room monitor.

Poster Presentations

"I prefer poster presentations, as there is some anxiety relief in that you are not the sole focus of a large group of people."
—Monica Mondragon, journal comment, Avenues to Professionalism class

Poster presentations are growing in popularity at many meetings. In the past, poster presentations might have been considered second-rate, but there are some distinct advantages that make poster presentations preferable. Posters

■ Make it easier to present complex graphics that simply cannot be easily comprehended in an oral format;

■ Provide the visual background for dialogue and interaction between presenters and attendees (unlike a session, where the dialogue is limited to post-session comments in the hall);

■ Provide an easy, more relaxed opportunity for presenting research at professional meetings;

■ Can be used for educational purposes well after a meeting, especially if displayed in academic hallways or other public places.

Posters also have drawbacks. They take more effort than a "typical" oral presentation, and they can cost anywhere from $1 to more than $3 per square foot to produce. The "typical" space for a poster is approximately 4 feet by 8 feet. But before you start laying out your poster, find out the width of the plotter printer paper you'll be using. Most rolls are 36 inches wide, so the more critical poster measurement is length. PowerPoint and access to high-resolution plotter printers make it easier than ever to produce a high-quality poster, and once printed, the poster can be used for additional venues.

Preparing Your Poster

The two biggest mistakes most people make in designing posters are (1) trying to cram too much information into a poster, and (2) failing to openly and concisely state the purpose, methods, and conclusions of the poster. Keep the text to an absolute minimum by creating some basic sections. Using a format that has a brief introduction, clear research objectives or hypotheses, methods, results, conclusions, and references will make the poster cleaner and more understandable. A good poster has all the elements of a written paper, but uses bullets or short paragraphs for the research objectives, methods, and conclusions to help emphasize the main points without extra words. Remember, the poster is the backdrop for your conversations with the people who come to see it.

Use figure captions to explain a few charts, diagrams, photographs, and simple statistical summaries. Concentrate on just two or three main points, and highlight major trends and comparisons. Choose images carefully, because images are crucial for getting and holding your audience's attention. Don't use abbreviations and acronyms unless necessary, and try not to use too many numbers or complicated graphs.

Place the poster title, author(s), and sponsoring institution's information at the top of the poster. (If appropriate, sponsor information may be put on the bottom of the poster instead.) Organize the content on the poster to start in the upper left corner as you look at it and move from left to right and from top to bottom. Your background color or texture, along with contrasting colors, should complement the text and images and make the poster easy to read. Avoid making the poster too busy. Consider the possibility that some of your viewers may be color-blind and avoid using red with green; someone who is color-blind will see them both as the same color or hue. Another poor color combination is gray and green. These colors could be problematical for you if one of the judges is color-blind. (For more information on visual accessibility, check *http://www.stc-sig.org/ usability/newsletter/9910-color-blindness.html.*)

Lettering must be easy to read from a distance of at least 2 meters (6 feet). You should also consider contrasting the font colors and the background—white on a dark background or black type on a light background work quite well, especially in captions. When choosing colors, consider color saturation. A full black or solid color background could totally empty an ink cartridge! Before printing your final poster, print a small draft version of your poster that can be checked and edited.

Presenting Your Poster

Bring a few supplies in case the surface of the presentation venue is different from what you envisioned. Poster panes can be fabric-covered or cork. Most posters can be attached to the fabric poster panels using the hook-end side of Velcro tape (which is readily available at most office or craft supply stores). You should have your own pushpins and Velcro available, instead of counting on borrowing from other presenters.

Be prepared to answer questions about your research results and interpretations. Engage your audience in dialogue at every point possible. Bring supporting information appropriate for readers who have more than a casual interest in your research—publication reprints, handouts, or small versions of your poster work well. The small printouts of your poster should have black text, with all or most of the background colors in your full-size poster removed.

Get some business cards made prior to the conference so you can give them out or exchange them with others; even computer-generated cards are better than your name scribbled on a piece of paper that might get lost or accidentally thrown away. A pad of paper for recording the names and addresses of individuals seeking additional information or for jotting down interesting comments and ideas is also more convenient than trying to remember numerous conversations.

Forums

A forum, sometimes called a *roundtable*, is a fairly recent addition to professional meetings. Structured differently than a symposium, a forum has no formal papers. It consists of a moderator and a group of individuals who have been selected to participate based on their expertise in a particular subject. The moderator usually introduces the session and the members of the forum. Then, each will speak briefly on a specific topic, generally no more than five to ten minutes each, depending on the number of panelists and the overall length of the session.

The idea is that after this brief introductory presentation, the session is opened up to a conversation with the audience. The moderator may structure the session interaction by asking specific questions to get the conversation going, or he or she may ask the panelists to involve the audience. Forums are excellent opportunities for interaction and conversation.

ಬಿ *EXERCISE:* Compose a Submission

In Chapter 4, you researched organizations that appealed to you and were related to your field of anthropology. It's now time to get more serious about your commitment to your career. Refer back to the list of professional organizations you created through the exercise in Chapter 4. Select the annual meeting of the organization that you would most like to attend. In making your choice, consider the realities of attending, such as schedule and cost. Before committing to it, make sure you will be able to take the time off from school or work and will have the funds to attend. (You don't actually have to submit your participation form during this activity, but we would like you to consider making this activity more than an exercise.)

Access the organization's website and find the "Meetings" page. This should contain information about the next annual meeting and the submission instructions if a call for papers has been issued. Read the instructions and start a document in your word processing program that will contain the information required on the submission. Pay particular attention to the rules regarding the word length for the abstract. Some organizations simply cut off the abstract at the required length. This may mean that if your abstract is 105 words and the maximum is 100, you will lose the last 5 words of your statement! Create your submission by including the following information:

■ Your name, as you would like it to appear on your name tag and in the program

■ The full name of the place you work or the university you attend

■ The title of your presentation

■ The abstract

After you've composed your draft abstract, show it to a professor, adviser, or colleague (or all three). Revise the abstract based on their recommendations and file it for future reference. ☞

NETWORKING AND MENTORS

We casually mention building and maintaining your network here and there throughout the book, but perhaps we haven't really reinforced its importance strongly enough. Network, network, network! Your immediate network is that of your family, friends, peer group—your cohort, classmates, and graduate class—professors, advisers, employers, and mentors. All of these people know you and what you can do. They also know other people. When the organizers of the anthropology graduate student symposium wanted to get Brian Fagan as the keynote speaker, they came to us because they knew we knew him (we'd mentioned it in class). And the network worked. Dr. Fagan agreed not only to give the keynote, but to give an informal lunch presentation, and to provide office hours.

Mentors and mentoring is another topic that is so important that it should have its own section. In your graduate career, you will get assigned professors and advisers. It's your job to seek out a mentor. Who do you look up to? Whose work do you admire? In her career story, Erica Gibson, biomedical anthropologist, recommends that "anyone pursuing a career in anthropology [should] find a mentor in the type of job you think you would like to have as early as possible in your education. This way you can go to them for help or answers to questions about their duties, likes and dislikes, and general help in choosing how to proceed through your career." Mentors can also be found through member associations. The National Association for the Practice of Anthropology (NAPA) has a program called Mentor Match that been set up to assist students and individuals contemplating a career move. Help is as close as the completion of the web form (*http://practicinganthropology.org/mentor-match/*). Also, don't discount the idea of being a mentor.

Networking, in Carol's opinion, is the best (and most important) part of attending a conference. She spends most of her time in committee meetings, meeting with colleagues, and getting excited about ideas. Annual conferences are where she touches base with other professional archaeological educators. They are her network, a network that cannot be found anywhere else. She can't even remember when she went to a session that she wasn't participating in. We both participate in committee activities and social events, present papers, posters, wander through the exhibit hall, and catch up on what colleagues are doing.

Everywhere we go, we carry a stock of business cards, and we recommend you do as well. As mentioned above, if you are not provided business cards by your employer or university, ask about getting some made. It can probably be easily done; and even if you have to pay for them yourself, it's worth the $50. You want people to remember you? Hand them a card and scribble something on the back about wanting to talk about [something] in the future, or to email for more information about a poster.

Ask people for their business card, and note where you received it (e.g., 2010 AAA meeting), as well as something important about the individual so that you can remember who this person is. You may need to contact him or her in the future, and if you've made notations on the card, it will make it easier to figure out who is who, two years after the event.

Volunteering

We talked about volunteering in Chapter 10, but as you get more and more involved in your professional organizations, think about giving back to them in a way beyond your membership dues. Most of the miscellaneous jobs and needs are met by volunteers, especially at meetings when there are so many chores to be done and needs to be filled. You need not be a student to volunteer. When we are in Washington, DC, we often stop by the Society for American Archaeology office and donate a couple of hours on whatever project they need help on.

Volunteering at the meeting or conference itself can be of financial benefit. Many, if not most, organizations waive the conference registration fee for those who volunteer at the meeting, and some even provide a small stipend for each shift worked (about enough to buy a soda or bottle of water).

Volunteers do a variety of jobs, including working at the registration desk, sitting at the message center, and monitoring sessions. Most organizations require about twelve hours of time spread out over the duration of the conference. Most split the time in three- to four-hour shifts and take your interests into consideration when scheduling, if you speak up. Let them know if you have a particular interest in hearing a session; perhaps you could be assigned as the volunteer to monitor that room. It would be a win-win situation for both of you.

Some publishers use student volunteers to help them show and sell books at these conferences, in exchange for free books. We do this regularly. Our library has benefited greatly, and it offers us a fixed location to find people we wouldn't otherwise encounter.

Another area where volunteers are needed is in relation to the discipline of anthropology—namely, in the various professional committees and subcommittees within anthropological organizations. The Society for American Archaeology, for example, has created a student member position on every one of its various committees so that students can participate in organization governance at the national level. The World Archaeological Congress actually has a student committee to consider student issues, and students serve on numerous other committees as well.

While volunteering in and of itself is good for you as an anthropologist, it strengthens those all-important networks that will help you as you move forward in your career. Be cautious in the amount of volunteering that you do, however. Don't agree to do more than you can handle; try to volunteer for things that really interest you or things you can devote the time to in order to do it right.

SUMMARY

Paying your dues has multiple meanings, but in the context of this chapter, we are talking about joining and participating in professional organizations. These are your organizations. The people who manage them are selected from the membership, and the views and directions come from all paid members. This should include you. In this chapter, we discussed the importance of membership, the submission process, and each of the usual session types. We pointed out the importance of networking within the context of the professional meetings and volunteering, and we provided an exercise that involved creating a draft abstract submission.

FOR THE PORTFOLIO

In this chapter, you created a draft submission for an upcoming professional meeting. Print a copy of this document and place it in the "Other" section of your portfolio, or if your portfolio has additional sections, label one "Professional Organizations" and place your document there.

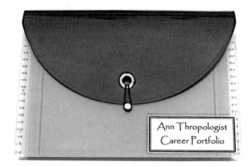

CHAPTER 13

ACADEMIC OPTIONS

"The starving of public higher ed means we are now hiring more part-timers, as adjuncts and lecturers. The audit culture associated with neoliberalist 'reform' means my students and younger colleagues need thicker vitas, more publications, more grants to climb the rungs of the academic ladder. And most who have attained tenure-track jobs have also had years of postdocs, CRM work, and adjuncting between completion of their Ph.D. and a tenure-track job."
—Robert Paynter, Professor, University of Massachusetts

INTRODUCTION

Because applying for academic jobs differs so much from applying for jobs in the private sector, government, and nonprofits, we give this topic two chapters of its own. This chapter discusses the different academic institutions and career possibilities, the types of positions available, and the options open to academic anthropologists. Chapter 14 delves into the details of applying for academic positions. Like the chapters covering jobs in applied anthropology, this chapter includes career stories and words of wisdom written by current anthropology professors.

EMPLOYERS INSIDE OF ACADEMIA

By our definition, institutions of higher education include community colleges, colleges, and universities, in small communities and major cities. The choices are numerous, but bear in mind that where you attend graduate school (geographically) and your research focus (thesis or dissertation) automatically put you on a particular track, not only for the positions available to you, but where you might get a job.

An excellent resource that will assist with locating academic jobs is the Career Center on the American Anthropological Association (AAA) website: *http://careercenter.aaanet.org*. The "Jobs" tab on the Professional Development page organizes jobs by category, state or province, and by country. At the time of writing this chapter, there were three jobs in archaeology, three jobs in linguistics, one in medical anthropology, one in physical/biological, and thirteen in social/cultural anthropology listed on the AAA website. Fifteen jobs were in the United States. One was in Hong Kong, China, and one was in Taiwan. All of the positions were in college or university settings.

INSTITUTIONS OF HIGHER EDUCATION

"Teaching at the community college gives you the opportunity to work with students one-on-one in shaping their perspectives and their future."
—Shereen Lerner, Ph.D.
Chair, Cultural Science Department, Mesa Community College

Community College

A community college is a post–high school institution that offers a two-year associate's degree as well as some of the basic courses required for post-secondary instruction. Community colleges attract three major audiences: students desiring post–high school education to fill more technically oriented positions, those wishing to transition from high school to a four-year college or university, and older students returning to obtain a post–high school degree. Unlike four-year colleges and universities, most community colleges have a generally open enrollment policy. This means that they accept nearly everyone with a high school degree or equivalent general education degree (GED).

Qualifications to teach at the community college level are generally equivalent to those required to teach at the high school level; but unlike teaching at the pre-college level, many community colleges do not require their instructors to have completed any specific classes in education. However, because of the increase in the number of graduates seeking employment, you should expect to find that many community college instructors have M.A. degrees and some have doctorates. Mesa Community College has four full-time and six to ten part-time anthropology faculty (depending on the semester) and offers more than 30 sections of anthropology each semester. And, before you turn your nose up at the idea of working at a community college, know that, like their counterparts at four-year academic institutions, community college instructors do get the opportunity to do research.

While community colleges might be considered a lower rung of the academic job ladder, they provide fulfilling career options. Dr. Shereen Lerner, Cultural Science Department Chair, Mesa Community College, notes that teaching at the community college is an opportunity to teach to a diversity of students in terms of ethnicity, economic status, age, and more. Many of the students she encounters are returning to school for re-careering, students who are simply interested in the class topic, and students just out of high school. She says, "It is a challenge to teach to such diversity, but also offers the students and faculty a chance to learn from each other. It is great to watch an eighteen-year-old student work with a retiree on the same project, and see the respect grow between the two— they often become fast friends, crossing generational lines."

College

A college is an academic institution structured to provide a four-year course of study that concludes with a bachelor's degree in arts or sciences. Colleges aren't necessarily limited to undergraduate programs; some offer limited graduate programs or degrees. A college can be a stand-alone institution or it can be part of a university, private or public. Bowdoin College, Brunswick, Maine, is an example of a private liberal arts college, whereas The Evergreen State College, Olympia, Washington, is an example of a public (state) liberal arts college. Bowdoin offers bachelor's degrees only, while Evergreen offers both bachelor's and master's degrees.

Stand-alone colleges are generally smaller than universities. For those interested in teaching at the post-secondary level, but not wanting to work within the larger university setting, a college can provide an excellent teaching opportunity.

To teach at the college level, you must generally have a Ph.D. within a specialization. While this is a general rule, programs that offer only un-dergraduate programs may hire instructors with an M.A., or those who have completed all the requirements for a Ph.D. except for the dissertation (known as "ABD" or "All But Dissertation").

Job notices will specify the nature of the position: that is, whether the college is looking for a cultural anthropologist, archaeologist, physical an-thropologist, or other specialization. In addition, the department may be looking to fill a specific niche—for example, a specialist within a geo-graphic region or culture.

> "We were lucky—yes, we worked really hard, but let's not ignore luck. Mercyhurst happened to be expanding their program, we hap-pened to fit their requirements (including willing to work in Erie. Honestly)."
>
> —Ruth Burgett Jolie
> Assistant Professor, Mercyhurst College

University

A university is an academic institution that offers both undergraduate and graduate programs. Universities generally house one or more colleges or schools, such as the College of Law, the College of Medicine, or the College of Arts and Sciences. Departments of anthropology are generally housed within the College of Arts and Sciences or College of Social and Behavioral Sciences. Anthropology programs within universities can be in different colleges, depending on the organizational structure of the university. At the University of Oklahoma, the Anthropology Department is housed within the College of Arts and Sciences, whereas the University of Arizona now has the School of Anthropology. Programs range in size and breadth, based on the overall focus of the college and size of the university.

Job qualifications for university positions are generally the same as for colleges, but because programs may have specific areas of study, the positions may require more focus in their specialization. Larger programs may have multiple anthropologists within each subfield, each specializing in a specific culture or geographical area.

In addition, colleges and universities also operate within a somewhat poorly defined "tier" structure. Some ranking systems (*U.S. News & World Report*, for example) rank schools by various factors such as student academic achievement, amount of federal funding, number of Ph.D. degrees awarded per year, and other "measures" of success. Although more and more colleges see these "tiers" as artificial, competition for positions at the "first-tier schools" is more intense. Regardless of the purported ranking, the basic amount of education received at each university is generally felt to be equivalent.

Universities hire individuals to teach their courses through a variety of positions—by the course, on annual contracts, and for tenure- and non-tenure-track positions. University positions, especially tenure-track positions, are highly sought after and highly competitive.

RANKS OF ACADEMIC POSITIONS

Within the academy, there are various "ranks" of positions based primarily on levels of experience and productivity within the discipline. Each rank carries with it associated rights, responsibilities, and salary ranges, and are usually attained through a combination of teaching and administrative experience, publications, and other measures of productivity, including obtaining grants, service to the department and university, and other types of contributions to the department.

Instructor

Just about anyone can be an instructor, in terms of academic settings. More often, however, they are people who have not yet completed the "terminal" degree in the program. They usually have a degree "higher" than the majority of the students they will be teaching and evaluating for grades. However, some instructors have specialized knowledge obtained outside of the classroom (Native American language instructors, for example) that give them qualifications beyond the academic degree.

Being an instructor gives individuals the opportunity to see whether they like teaching and whether they can deal with the administrative and technical demands of that profession. Many departments use graduate students as instructors, but also use other qualified individuals to fill specific needs within the program.

There is a great deal of flexibility in the university's use of instructors. Since the need for instructors is driven by student demand, the department can hire or discontinue instructors on relatively short notice. Departments usually hire instructors from their internal ranks, but qualified individuals who are able to step in with minimal advance notice are also used. Also, since instructors are generally paid by the class, and based on student enrollment, they usually do not receive fringe benefits such as health care, retirement, or paid leave.

The Postdoc

While not a "rank" or an official academic position, a postdoctoral research appointment (postdoc) is a prized opportunity that many people pursue to increase their marketability. A postdoc position (sometimes a fellowship) lets you work with established research professors to gain experience, sharpen skills, develop contacts, and get known (network) within your field. It also affords you the ability to expand your research focus or to work with a specific professor on a pointed research problem and to publish. It is a transitional stepping-stone in your career.

Erica Gibson found herself defending her dissertation in the summer, putting her off schedule for applying for academic positions that fall. So she began looking for other options.

> [I was] told about a postdoctoral fellowship in an NIH program focused on pain research at the University of Florida. My dissertation focused on birth practitioner choice and stress during pregnancy; however, one of the main themes that emerged was that of pain during labor. Although it was not my main research focus, I was able to use this experience to gain a two-year fellowship as a postdoctoral researcher. . . . This experience helped me focus on what I truly wanted—getting back into an anthropological teaching setting in a university rather than being a token anthropologist on a multidisciplinary project. During my first year as a postdoc, I applied for many academic positions in anthropology departments, and I was ultimately hired in a tenure-track position by the University of South Carolina.

Darna Dufour, professor at the University of Colorado at Boulder, explained her transition from student through postdoc to assistant professor and professor in biological anthropology as follows: "I took a postdoctoral fellowship in the UK (London School of Hygiene and Tropical Medicine, and Glasgow University) to gain depth in research methods, and then a position as an assistant professor at the University of Colorado. I am still at Colorado, and am now a full professor in anthropology and an Associate Dean for Faculty Affairs."

Assistant Professor

The rank of assistant professor is usually the lowest in the professor series. Assistant professors are usually just beginning their career and often have minimal experience in teaching or publications. Most of the time, assistant professors have recently completed their Ph.D. or are just breaking into the academic world.

Taking a position as an assistant professor allows you to learn how the academic world works. Responsibilities usually include a combination of research, teaching, and service. The assistant professor usually continues the research that formed the basis of his or her dissertation, and it is generally expected that research opportunities will be given to students within the department. Teaching loads per year can vary, but generally it is expected that assistant professors learn how to teach in this stage of their career. Service to the department includes mentoring students as well as serving on departmental committees that relate to the department's continued functioning.

Departments and universities usually hire assistant professors at lower salaries and benefits than at other ranks. Assistant professors, in some ways, are unknown quantities in that they often lack a proven track record. Ideally, the department can take the time to groom the assistant professor to meet the needs of both the individual and the department. And the assistant professor can use this time to determine whether the university is a good fit for the himself or herself as well.

Associate Professor

Associate professors are usually at the middle rank of the professorial system. Once they have proven themselves as assistant professors and have met other requirements (particular requirements depend on the university or department), assistant professors can be promoted to associate professors (with tenure; see below for what that means). Along with increased salary and benefits come increased responsibilities and expectations. More attention is paid to the quality and quantity of publications as well as the continued productivity associated with department needs.

In some situations, newcomers to the academic world may be hired as an associate professor. Some individuals demonstrate high levels of productivity in publications or grants (or both) outside of the academic realm and are highly sought after by departments. In such situations, their experience in the outside world is weighed in relation to the levels of experience expected of associate professors.

Full Professor

Full professors are those who have demonstrated that their abilities and skills are generally of the highest levels. Full professors are generally seen as having reached the highest level of academic achievement, and promotion to such levels generally requires excellence in teaching, productivity, and service to the university, department, and discipline.

TYPES OF ACADEMIC FACULTY

When looking at academic positions, don't limit yourself. In addition to the assistant, associate, and full profession positions, most departments employ people in adjunct, term, and research positions.

Adjunct

Adjunct faculty members are people who have an arrangement to work with the department as a convenience to both the person and the department. Usually the adjunct faculty member is a part-time professor hired on a contractual basis. However, some adjunct faculty members only want an affiliation with the department for research privileges or other reasons and do not teach classes.

Many university departments hire large numbers of adjunct faculty because such faculty members are more flexible in teaching schedules and cost less to the department than traditional full-time faculty members. Like regular faculty, an adjunct professor usually must fulfill basic educational requirements before being allowed to teach college or university courses.

For a university, there are a number of advantages to hiring adjunct professors. Because adjunct professors are viewed as temporary, departments can hire them to expand course offerings or to meet student demand for a program that has an insufficient number of regular staff. Because adjunct professors lack tenure, those who fail to perform to departmental standards can be more easily removed—simply by having their contract or affiliation to the department or program lapse. Adjunct faculty members are also much less costly to hire because they are usually not entitled to personnel benefits such as health care and retirement plans. Most adjunct professors are paid by the class, and their teaching loads vary.

From the point of view of an adjunct professor, there are both benefits and disadvantages to this kind of work. The flexibility allows adjunct professors to leave after a term if they are offered better work, they usually do not have administrative duties, and most are not required to perform research or to publish work unless they are interested in seeking full-time work. Some people actually prefer working as adjunct faculty because they enjoy teaching, but dislike the academic or administrative rat race associated with tenure and full-time responsibilities.

Kelley Hays-Gilpin noted in her comments on this chapter that when she was an adjunct professor, "some of the students told me they liked to take classes from adjuncts like me because we 'weren't tired all the time' like full-time faculty. We adjuncts taught because we enjoyed teaching, and could groom students for jobs in our fields (my full-time job was working as a ceramic analyst for the Navajo Nation Archaeology Department). I think the students also appreciated our 'real-world' perspectives that complemented the knowledge and experience of the full-time faculty."

Term

"Term" faculty members are hired by the university or college for a fixed length of time. The length of the contract of employment can vary, but the faculty members generally have similar rights and responsibilities as tenured or tenure-track employees, including administrative duties, publication requirements, and requirements for service to the department.

The term faculty member signs a contract with the university that define the services each will provide to the other. The university usually provides benefits to the faculty member in addition to a salary, and the faculty member agrees to provide service to the department and the university. The contract delineates the rights and responsibilities of each party in the agreement and requires "cause" for termination by either party.

Teaching loads (the number of courses the faculty member will teach per semester or academic year) for term faculty can vary, depending on departmental needs. Some term faculty may teach more classes than tenured or tenure-track faculty, but some may be called upon to fill administrative needs such as student advising, recurring instructional demands, or other things that require specialized skills or knowledge.

Term faculty members generally have more job and financial security than adjunct faculty, but less than tenured or tenure-track faculty. Because the term of service is stipulated in advance, the faculty member can gain valuable experience in teaching and other duties associated with academic programs. The faculty member also has a measure of financial security for a known length of time. On the negative side, there is no guarantee that the position will continue beyond the term of the contract, even though contracts are often extended for more than one term.

For the department, term faculty provide the flexibility often needed to fill student need and demand without long-term obligation. Term faculty also provide a level of consistency for students and departments and can help develop programmatic options. Since the contract is for a fixed length of time, the department can better budget to accommodate fluctuations in demand or student numbers. On the negative side, term faculty often provide a short-term solution to long-term problems.

Researcher

There are research positions at certain universities or within certain areas of particular departments where teaching is not a major requirement. These positions may be filled at various levels, depending on experience. Even though these individuals work within academic institutions, their primary responsibilities are aligned more toward research and publication of that research than toward teaching and administrative duties. Research positions virtually always require that position holders obtain their own funding through grants and contracts. The university provides lab space, for example, but salary, benefits, and expenses come out of the money the researcher raises from outside the university.

There is also a trend within universities to combine the traditional academic position with the research position. Lori L. Jervis, a sociocultural anthropologist at the University of Oklahoma, says this of her career:

> After eleven years, I took a position at the University of Oklahoma, where I now have appointments in Anthropology and the Center for Applied Social Research. In the end, I am not sure whether I chose an "applied" career or whether it chose me. I guess I must have chosen it, albeit unconsciously, by selecting topics of study with a practical dimension. Working with American Indians provides a further impetus for research with potential to shed light on real-world problems, as in most cases the acquisition of knowledge for knowledge's sake is simply no longer enough of a compelling motivation for engaging in further research—communities want action!

TENURED AND TENURE-TRACK POSITIONS

The teaching positions described above are generally viewed as "temporary" in one way or another. Even term faculty positions are viewed as temporary, since the term of the contract is known. Even though both the individual and the institution have obligations to each other, those obligations do not extend for an indefinite period of time.

Tenured and tenure-track positions, however, are generally viewed as permanent, lifelong, positions. The hiring of a faculty member in a tenure-track position is a long-term commitment by both the university and the applicant. Once an individual meets all the requirements set forth by the department and the university, that individual usually cannot be fired without "just cause." While "just cause" has a myriad of meanings, it is usually difficult for a university to terminate the contract of a tenured professor for anything other than the gravest of misdeeds. The faculty member, however, can resign from the university department with much fewer problems, should it become necessary.

Tenure and What It Means

Tenure is a process whereby a faculty member demonstrates he or she is capable of meeting and surpassing expected levels of productivity in the three main areas of academic life: research, teaching, and service. Faculty members usually are given a specific period of time to develop a body of work that demonstrates their abilities in the areas of the position description under which they were hired. They develop teaching skills and classes and are evaluated by their students and colleagues. They conduct research and publish the results of their research in journal articles and books. They serve on departmental and university committees and mentor students. They participate within their broader discipline by giving conference papers and public presentations, and by participating in their discipline's professional organizations.

"Tenure" literally means "time held in office," but for people in academic positions it means career security. Tenured professors are expected to continue producing and participating in departmental business, but knowing that their job is secure, they can experiment with new research ideas or with controversial topics. Tenure often gives marginalized faculty members the freedom of speech that allows them to draw attention to situations they perceive to be problematic. Tenured faculty are also expected to become more involved in departmental and university service, as well as to take on more responsibilities at national levels in their disciplinary focus.

To departments, tenure means consistency. Once a faculty member has completed the requirements for tenure, the department can count on that faculty member to contribute to the continued growth of the department and its students. The department can also distribute its administrative chores among those who are assured of continued employment, rather than relying on those who may not be around four or five years ahead.

To some outsiders, however, tenure has often been misinterpreted as giving rise to complacency. Some believe that tenure creates professors who no longer have to "work" at their craft since they can't easily be fired. Some see this system as giving lifetime jobs to those who meet only minimal standards and whose levels of accomplishments dwindle later in their careers. There have been proposals to abolish tenure, but, as Rob Jenkins (2009) has written, "Faculty members can only speak their minds, however, if they are confident that doing so won't place their jobs at risk should a dean find their remarks offensive." Tenure, therefore, should be seen as a process that allows freedom and consistency in a program rife with uncertainty and growth; the idea is not that professors are free to do as they please, but that colleges are better able to plan for the sometimes uncertain economic future.

ॐ *EXERCISE:* WHERE TO WORK?

Use the information in this chapter to help define the type of academic position you would like and the positions you would need to hold to obtain your dream job. Next, identify the locations where you might be interested in working, and conduct a search for the colleges and universities in that general region.

List a minimum of three colleges or universities and then initiate a search of each institution's website. For each, note the following:

■ The total number of faculty positions within the anthropology department;

■ The number of full professors, associate professors, assistant professors, lecturers, instructors, and adjuncts.

Note the results of your search in your journal, and create a document listing the relevant information for future reference. ॐ

ॐ *EXERCISE:* COMPARING CAREERS

Read through several of the academic and academic/applied career stories provided in this book. Select two or three that are of interest.

Go to the websites for the faculty you identified in the previous activity. Find the biographies, curriculum vitae, and profiles for at least three individuals. Read through the information, paying particular attention to their graduate degrees, employment history, grants, and awards. Create a table with four columns for each person. In the first column, list the individual's degrees and where those degrees were obtained. In the second column, list his or her employment history. In the third column, list the individual's grants and awards. In the last column, compare the information in the previous three columns and address the following questions:

■ How much time passed between receiving their Ph.D. and gaining their current position?

■ What academic positions have they held?

■ What non-academic positions have they held?

■ How many grants and awards did they receive during the course of each position?

On a separate piece of paper, do a cross comparison of the individuals researched. What are the similarities and differences between the careers? Complete the exercise by writing a response to the question: If I were going to follow the same path, what else would I need to do? ∾

Summary

The academic career path is one that most graduate anthropology students aspire to because it is often seen as easier and more secure. People generally believe professors only work nine months out of the year, and only for three to ten hours a week. The academic career path, however, requires a long-term commitment to helping create the next group of learners, researchers, and instructors. When not teaching, professors are developing course materials, refining their readings and lecture notes, struggling to find time to get their own research completed, writing articles for publication in order to expand the knowledge base, and serving on student and departmental committees—all the things that make up the minimal job descriptions of the academic life. Kelley Hays-Gilpin says, "I work 70 hours a week during the school year, mostly on teaching and service. Research mostly gets done on weekends, during breaks between semesters, and on sabbatical leave. This isn't atypical. Most full-time faculty I know try to set aside one day a week for research, but it rarely happens that way!"

Some new faculty members find that they do not like teaching and turn away from academic careers; others find they love the teaching but not the research or administrative aspects of academic careers. The increasingly shrinking number of academic positions will continue to guarantee many more applicants for each academic position than there ever will be positions available; as such, the next chapter should help to increase your likelihood of gaining one of those positions.

FOR THE PORTFOLIO

Look back over your personal contract and your five-year plan and modify them based on the new information provided in this chapter. Print a copy of the results of the exercises and file them in the back of your portfolio.

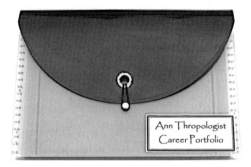

Ann Thropologist
Career Portfolio

CHAPTER 14
GETTING AN ACADEMIC POSITION

"I started applying for academic positions while preparing for my dissertation defense at Columbia University. I applied for every job and postdoc that I could possibly connect to my interests and training. This required reframing my application materials for every position, which is time-consuming but necessary. I was fortunate to get an offer relatively quickly for a tenure-track position in the Honors College at the University of Oklahoma."

—Amanda Minks, Honors College, University of Oklahoma

INTRODUCTION

For some, colleges and universities—academia, the Ivory Tower—are the end-all, be-all of careers possibilities. Academic careers can be great, but remember, you've only seen them from the student side. Before you commit to the academic path, do your research. Find out what being a professor is really like from the professor's perspective. Talk to your professors and others in your department. Talk to those in academic positions at professional conferences and ask them about the realities of their jobs. Network, network, network.

In Chapter 13, we discussed academic employment options. In this chapter, we cover the application process, from the analysis of the job description to negotiating the terms of your contract.

FINDING THE JOBS

Academic job announcements are posted in any number of places, in print and online. The easiest place to locate current openings is on the websites of professional organizations. In Chapters 4 and 12, we offer information and exercises designed to familiarize you with a variety of regional, national, and international professional organizations, and we list some of their websites. If you haven't read those chapters and completed those activities, we recommend that you do so prior to proceeding with this chapter.

When exploring the professional organizations' websites, look in their jobs or career area for current job announcements. Professional organizations also publish monthly or quarterly newsletters or magazines, which usually have a section for current job announcements.

Job announcements can also be found on the websites of individual academic institutions, so if there are specific universities where you would like to work, searching their websites may be an option. If you want to broaden your search, you can always go to Google or your favorite search engine.

RESEARCH THE EMPLOYER

Before you start pulling together your curriculum vita and cover letter, check out the institution doing the hiring. Find out as much as you can about the school, the department, the teaching load, research opportunities, and service requirements. Use your anthropological skills to delve into the departmental website and read through the departmental information, the bios, and the curriculum vitae of the faculty.

---

෨ *EXERCISE:* RESEARCHING AN EMPLOYER

Do you have an anthropology department in mind where you might find your dream job? What do you really know about the department, programs, practices, and faculty members? In preparation for the potential of obtaining that dream, take the time to do some basic background research. Look at the information as a potential colleague, not as a student looking for a degree program. Look beyond the name and the reputation. Do your own research, dig below the surface, and get to know who you'd be working for and who you'd be working with. Kelley Hays-Gilpin says, "Some things to look at are balance of gender and ethnicity. Do you want to be the only woman or the only ethnic minority on the faculty? Some do! I know a professor who really wanted to be the 'only Indian' and resented younger Native Americans trying to make their way up. But many of us would feel isolated. Likewise, you probably don't want to be the only assistant professor in a department of full professors. You will get stuck with all the work nobody else wants to do, and they will call it paying your dues." So, when looking at where you want to be, look for a balance.

In this exercise, you should research and answer the following questions for two or more anthropology departments where you'd consider working. Go ahead and pick your dream school, but then research another possibility that you may have never considered before.

Some of the questions that you should answer are:

■ Which college within the university is the department housed in?

■ How is the department structured?

■ What fields are represented?

■ How many faculty are there representing each subdiscipline?

■ How many students are enrolled in the undergraduate and graduate programs?

■ How would your qualifications benefit this program?

■ And, based on Kelley Hays-Gilpin's wisdom, would this be a faculty to which you would like to belong?

After completing research on each department, compare and contrast the similarities and differences between the departments. If you want a more complete picture of the department and its statistics, look through the current *American Anthropological Association Guide*. These can usually be used in (but not borrowed from) an anthropology department.

It is always best to know what you would be jumping into, before you apply. This background preparation is not wasted time; the information recovered will assist you in developing your cover letter or forming responses during your interview. ❧

JOB ANNOUNCEMENTS

The ability to decipher a job description is the first important step toward applying for and ultimately landing the job. Academic job descriptions usually provide detailed information about the position the department wishes to fill. The advertisement will generally list the minimal levels of education and experience an applicant must have to be considered qualified, as well as the area of research expertise, the expected duties, and the application procedures.

In Chapter 5, Past Jobs and Future Careers, we offer a number of helpful exercises, including one titled "Analyze the Job Announcement." If you have completed this activity, refer back to your results. If you have not completed this (or the other preparatory activities), we recommend that you take time to look at the information contained Chapter 5 prior to continuing forward in the book.

COMPONENTS OF AN APPLICATION

There are multiple components to any job application. For academic jobs, the application requirements usually include a cover letter, curriculum vita, writing samples, and letters of reference (although in some cases, the letters of reference may be requested by the hiring institution after the first cut and before the initial interview). Some applications require a teaching portfolio. According to Kelley Hays-Gilpin, "minimally, this includes some syllabi that you have developed (whether or not you have actually had the opportunity to teach the class), a statement of teaching philosophy, and teaching reviews from students or peers (have a faculty member sit in on one of your classes and write a letter of evaluation). If you haven't taught a class yourself, you can include TA reviews and/or evaluations."

More than likely, you will be submitting multiple applications at the same time, over time, until you land the job. In preparing each application packet, check and recheck that you have addressed the letter to the right person at the right institution. Make sure that the CV you selected is formatted according to their style and that you have included the required components in the packet.

Cover Letter

The cover letter should make you shine. It can be the tie-breaker that gets you the interview. A good cover letter serves to highlight your experience and your qualifications and allows the prospective employer to get a glimpse of the skills and abilities you might bring to the program. We discussed cover letters at length in Chapter 8, so we won't discuss them again here. However, in your cover letter to an academic institution, it is particularly important to address every point in the job announcement and to list your experience and commitment to diversity, distance learning, and research. We cannot stress enough that you should spend as much time working on your cover letter as you spend on any other part of the application packet.

Curriculum Vitae

Academic employers generally require a CV rather than a résumé. The CV provides a chronological listing of your academic life, from your undergraduate education through your graduate career. It chronicles your employment history, highlights particular aspects of your abilities and your educational accomplishments, and lists your publications. The titles and order of the categories change according to university and discipline, but in general the categories are similar to those of your résumé: educational background, grants and honors, and professional memberships. The CV also includes a chronology of your employment, a list of positions held, and a listing of your presentations and publications. As with the résumé, *never* include a picture, social security number, or other personal information.

There is no single "correct" style of CV (jobsearch.com offers at least 30 different examples). The best way to know the "right" style for your chosen field or subfield of anthropology is to ask a favorite professor for advice or go online and look at CVs of anthropology professors. If you are in the process of applying for particular positions and want to make sure that you are using the correct format, go to the websites of the departments and use the departmental CV style. If there is an inconsistency between styles, find a person within your field and use the style that person has used.

Once you have identified the general style of CV you want to use, make certain you don't create one that is all flash and no substance. CVs are simple. Be consistent with your font styles and use only one font type. You can highlight section headers by increasing the font size slightly or by using bold or italics. The font on your CV should match that on your résumé and cover letter. Try to find a good ratio of white space to text, and use line spacing to separate sections on the CV, for jobs, publications, presentations, and so forth. Analyze CVs that are pleasing to your own eye and try to emulate them. As with your résumé, when it comes to printing your CV, you should print it single-sided on a finer-quality, no-frills paper. If you are submitting your application via email, save it as a PDF before sending so that the format stays secure.

Writing Your CV

Work from the Stockpile Database (Chapter 7) you created for résumé construction, and identify the jobs that relate specifically to the type of position you are hoping to gain. Usually each section of the CV is presented chronologically, from most recent to oldest. You will generally want to list only those jobs that demonstrate experience directly related to the job you are applying for. However, you may list jobs that you've had that are outside of the field you are interested in, provided that the experience gained there is directly relevant to the job. For example, while a two-year stint in the Peace Corps is not "anthropology," the experience and the skills gained in working with different cultures directly relates to anthropology.

A minor difference between the résumé and the CV is that the résumé allows for a fairly detailed listing of the duties and responsibilities gained in each position, whereas the CV listing is much more limited. A job listing on a CV generally has the job title and the name of the company or organization that employed you. You can include a one- to two-sentence description of your job duties or other relevant information, but be judicious. You don't want the reader to lose interest by having to wade through too much information.

Once you have developed your original CV, keeping it updated is paramount for success. While you might not be looking for a new job right this moment, what would you do if your dream job became available at literally a moment's notice? If someone asks you to send them a CV, you have to be certain that it accurately reflects your current level of experience and accomplishments.

Joe usually tries to update his CV quarterly, saving one copy as a text file and then creating a PDF file from it. He has found that updating his CV this often is easier than trying to do so at the end of the year. (The older we get, the harder it becomes to remember: "What year did we travel to Australia to teach the ethnobotany field school in the Northern Territory?") Because of memory limitations and sheer quantity of information, between updating sessions Joe puts important items—publications, public and professional presentations, and other professional accomplishments—into a "Vita update file." Once the CV has been updated and the current version saved, he erases the information in the "Vita update file" and starts again. Even if there is nothing new to add to the CV, he changes the date on the CV and saves it as a new file. That way, he knows the CV is current as of that date and doesn't have to wonder whether he needs to update it or not.

It is also probable that you will need more than a single format of CV in your files at any one time. Different universities require different formats for internal reporting purposes. The University of New Mexico requires a different format than the University of Oklahoma, but each allows the individual professor leeway in the way the information is presented to outsiders.

Regardless of whether you are creating a CV or a résumé, be certain that you always list your job experiences as accurately as possible. If you find you have "holes" in your employment history, now is the time to clear them up (explain them). Also, while it usually is not necessary to list your supervisor on your CV, it pays to maintain those names within your master list; if you had a great term of employment, your supervisor will make a great reference! And, even though there will be some you will want to forget, having the name will make it easier *not* to take another job under that same person.

℘ *EXERCISE:* Create Your Curriculum Vita

You found the job announcement for the ideal position. It's the one you'd been hoping for, and there it is. You're ready to grab your cover letter and tweak your résumé when you read the bottom line, "To apply, please submit your curriculum vita to: Search Committee Chair, Department of Anthropology, P. B. & J. University."

Begin your CV creation process by looking online at the CVs of the anthropology professors in your department and those of other people in your network. If you did the exercises in Chapter 13, pull that information out now.

- Note the format, organization of information, and the headers used on the CVs that you are using as a reference.

- Open a new document and save it in a way that will let you know that it is your CV and the date it was created. For example: Ellick_CV_11-27-10.

- Put your name, address, phone number, and email address at the top.

■ Create sections for Education, Employment History, Grants and Awards, Publications, Papers and Presentations, and Organization Membership.

■ Use the information from your Stockpile Database to create your employment history, but remember: your CV should contain only the jobs relevant to anthropology. Unlike your résumé, your CV should list only the dates of employment, your position, company, agency, or organization that employed you, the job location, and your role. (Unlike the résumé, it does not contain a lengthy description of your duties and responsibilities.)

■ Provide a listing of your publications. If you have articles in press, list them first as "In press," along with the publisher and probable year of publication.

■ List the papers that you presented at meetings and conferences.

■ Complete your CV with a list of your organizational affiliations. Some CV styles list these organizational memberships before employment history, so again, check the models you are using for the appropriate order. ❧

Many of the CVs you will look at will be pages and pages long. Don't be discouraged if your CV is only a couple of pages! Remember: the CV is the entire anthropological employment life of an individual. After 30+ years in this field, Carol's CV is 11 pages and Joe's CV is 28 pages. Keep with it and yours will get there, too!

Before printing your CV, email it to a professor, adviser, or mentor, and ask that person to proofread it for you. As with everything else you produce for public viewing, you should always use an outside proofreader. One of our reviewers commented on this by saying: "Right! Very important! One time, I sent off a CV that listed 'Pubications' because I didn't have a proofreader!"

Writing Samples

Most academic job applications request that you provide examples of your writing along with your cover letter and other application materials. If you are submitting your application electronically, prior to sending your articles, save them as PDFs. If you have only hard-copy reprints, scan one, name it in keeping with the other components (Ellick_SAA

Record_2003), and save it as a PDF. If you are not yet published but have submitted some items for publication, include these, clearly designated on the top or on the cover page as "Submitted for publication to *journal x*." This way, reviewers will understand that you have already begun presenting your research to a wider audience. If you do not have any articles submitted for publication, include one of the "meatier" chapters of your dissertation. Your goal here is to demonstrate your ability to produce understandable, cogent arguments of sufficient quality that the department can see they need you in their midst as a colleague.

Knowing ahead of time that you will need writing samples should motivate you to start writing. Ruth Burgett Jolie, in her career story, mentioned that her husband (Ed Jolie) had numerous publications. "[O]ne reviewer noted that Ed had more publications as a third-year grad student than most tenured faculty do." Write. It's an important skill that needs cultivating early, one that may provide the extra point during the review process that gets you that job.

Letters of Reference

Your letters of reference can be one of the major reasons you make it beyond the initial screening of applicants and into the first round for consideration. Of course, your referees should know you and your abilities long before you apply for the position. Since you will likely be in the beginning stages of your career, think of the people who know you best: your graduate school instructors, the crew chiefs you worked for, the professionals you volunteered or interned for, and so on. As you have worked through your graduate career, you have undoubtedly made a good impression on a range of people who will want to help your career.

Help your referees make your job search easier. As we noted before, you should maintain contact with them often; keep them apprised of what you are doing and where you can be reached; ask them to review your written work (if both of you are comfortable with their reviewing your work) before you submit articles for publication. And above all, let them know how much you appreciate what they are doing for you. Everyone appreciates acknowledgment of their efforts. For more information on letters of reference or requesting them, refer to Chapter 8.

Important Note

After you have applied for the job, make certain to notify the job referees if any of your contact information changes. Joe recalls the voice mail message chiding him about not notifying the University of New Mexico that he *obviously* was no longer interested in interviewing for the position since the emails that had been sent to him asking for a convenient time to schedule a campus visit had gone unanswered. The person on the phone *knew* the emails had to have been delivered because they had not "bounced" and there was no error message. Joe was extremely interested in the UNM position, but during the time he had applied for the job, his Bureau of Indian Affairs email account had been blocked along with those of all other BIA employees as the result of a court case. Consequently, he never knew that UNM had emailed. It never occurred to him to email UNM from his personal email account and provide them with alternative contact information. A hurried and apologetic phone call settled the issue, but it was a near miss that might have had dire consequences!

MAKING THE FIRST CUT

If you have established that you are qualified for the position, and your cover letter and CV, combined with your writing sample and letters of references, have earned you a place in the top pool of applicants, you might be invited to give a presentation at the department to which you are applying. Don't panic! Now is the time to take a deep breath, outline your research interests, and create a PowerPoint presentation that will demonstrate your knowledge, skills, and abilities as well as your mastery of your research. Academic jobs generally require two very important components: the job interview and the job talk.

Some institutions include a third component, a phone interview for the top eight to ten candidates, before narrowing their list down to the top three to bring to campus.

The Phone Interview

Kelley Hays-Gilpin explains how the Anthropology Department at Northern Arizona University conducts phone interviews:

> The phone interview is really hard on everyone because it's usually five against one: the committee and the candidate. By law, we (the hiring committee) have to tape the interviews after asking the candidate's permission. The best advice I have for the phone interview is (1) schedule it for a time when you can be alone in your office or at home (no kids or dogs) and turn off all other phones and distractions. A land-line call will sound clearer than a cell phone call. (2) Know the university that's interviewing you—how many students, what kind of

diversity in the student body, who is on faculty, what courses are offered. (3) Have some questions ready to ask the interviewers: What kinds of classes would they like to offer that they don't yet? What is the ethnic or socio-economic or age profile of the student body (if you haven't found out from their website)? What's the cost of living in the area? What kinds of research opportunities do students there want? Is there support for international travel and research? Or is research expected to focus in the local area? What service learning opportunities do students have?, etc. (4) Practice answering questions with a peer. You want to answer in several concise, clear sentences and not drone on. Remember there will be eight to twelve questions asked of all candidates, and time for follow-up is limited. A phone interview should not last more than half an hour or attention wanders.

The Job Interview

Actually, the academic interview process begins with a series of one-on-one job interviews. Candidates (usually the top three, but occasionally four or more) are brought to campus to meet the professors, administrators, and students in the department. These interviews are usually semiformal, and are intended to give everyone the opportunity to meet the candidate, to discuss research interests, and to help everyone (including the candidate) get to know each other better. The interviews are often short, and the candidate can feel rushed from place to place and from person to person. When you meet the department chair or the chair of the hiring committee, it is okay to ask how many people are being considered for the position and how many have already visited or are yet to visit. It is also okay to ask when they expect to make a decision.

Take the time to review the information in Chapter 9, Applying for the Job. This chapter contains detailed information on dressing for an interview, interview questions, and how best to prepare for the day.

Preparation is the key to making a good impression on those professors. Remember, they might be your colleagues for life, and it is good for them to feel comfortable with you. Before the day of the interview, take the time to review the information you previously noted about the department, faculty, staff, programs, and so on. Take the time to research faculty interests. Get online and look at their publications, and see if you share similar research interests or whether your research is somewhat at odds with theirs. Try not to show off, but do engage the professors you meet with at least a minimal knowledge of who they are and what they do. Also, think in advance about how your research will fit within the program's research:

will it complement someone else's research or will it conflict with that of another? Either way, be prepared to offer suggestions about how your research will fit within the regional or theoretical research others are doing.

If you get a chance to talk with students, let them know what sort of research you do and how it might affect their course of study. Students count. While they may not have individual votes on hiring decisions, they do have a voice. It is important to remember that they are the ones who will be taking your courses, serving as research or teaching assistants, and helping you create your research program.

The Job Talk

In addition to these one-on-one interviews, you will likely be asked to present a "job talk" so that everyone can see how well you present yourself as a professional, what your research is about, and whether they like you enough to work with you for the next 30 (or 40) years. Remember, "tenure" can mean a lifetime commitment!!

The job talk is a mini-performance that can make or break a job application. If you do it well, people will talk about you and remember you when it comes time to vote on a hiring decision. If you do it poorly, people will talk about you and remember you as well. Sometimes, it's how you handle a difficult situation that earns you points. One of our reviewers commented, "I remember one candidate who had trouble with her laptop during her presentation. The power outlet wasn't working; she didn't know that, and the battery ran out halfway through her PowerPoint slides. She handled it with poise, taking just a minute or two to diagnose and fix the problem, and get back on track with a smile. The selection committee put it down as a point in her favor that she showed grace under pressure. She got the job."

Here is where you put to use all the suggestions we gave you in Chapter 12. Create a PowerPoint presentation that is not too showy but gets your points across. Stick to your time limits and show about one slide per minute. Keep the technology to a minimum so that, if things go wrong, you still have the opportunity to demonstrate your knowledge. Expect questions, so review the data and other research on your topic. Be personable but professional. Practice, practice, practice!

While your job talk is not the time to try out "brand new" data, it is also not the time to give a stale talk that someone is likely to have encountered either at a regional meeting or in someone else's class lecture. Try to give a presentation that shows how your research ideas fit within established research, but also how your research is different and exciting.

Follow-up

After the job interviews and job talk, and after you have flown back to your home base, take time to reconnect with those who have contributed to your experience. Notify your referees about how things went; follow up with any professors or students you talked with about research interests; if someone asked for a copy of a particular paper, send it along as soon as it is feasible to do so. A little bit of restraint is okay here, but don't forget to do the things you promised to do.

Then relax, do your current job (if you have one), or finish your dissertation if that needs doing. Most departments will make decisions within the week or two after the final job applicant has been wined, dined, and grilled. Don't make a nuisance of yourself, but don't fall off the radar either. Don't panic that you were the fourth person out of four interviewed. Kelley Hays-Gilpin says, "Now that I have served on many selection committees, I know that the job rarely goes to the first candidate on the list, and that if you make the top six or eight on the list, you have a good chance."

YOU'VE GOTTEN THE JOB OFFER!

Congratulations! You've done it! You've gotten the first academic job of your career. If this is your dream job, it may not only be the first job you applied for, it may also be the last. Some people actually do take a job and move through the ranks of assistant professor to associate professor, make tenure, and move through the process to full professor, all within the same department of the same institution. But, before you sign on the dotted line, there are some things about negotiating the contract that we think will be helpful.

Negotiating a Contract

Once the job offer has been extended, negotiations begin. Even though you might be excited about being offered the job, take advantage of this additional opportunity to get your new career off to the right start. There are some things to think about—office space, a research lab and equipment, spousal hires—in addition to basic salary and benefits. Now is not the time to price yourself out of the market, but it is the time to get what you will need to comfortably take on your new career. This first salary is the base from which all future salaries will grow. If all you receive in the future are cost-of-living adjustments, will this base salary not only cover your basic existence, but provide for potential changes in your lifestyle (including new additions to your family)?

Talk to people around you about where you should begin your negotiations. Depending on where in the country your new job is located, the cost of living might be a consideration. If so, a higher salary might be needed to make your transition easier. You should check current cost-of-living estimates online, prior to negotiations. Compare them with where you currently live and estimate the increase that will be needed. You might also consider a lower beginning salary if your spouse can be hired at the same university as well. Moving costs should be a part of your negotiations, as should a budget to purchase office and research equipment. There are no hard and fast rules about negotiating, but give and take on both parts is generally expected.

If You Don't Get the First Job

Few people actually get the first academic job they apply for, especially immediately out of graduate school. There are those lucky few who have prepared for their future and are able to make it work, but mostly those first jobs are stepping-stones to bigger and better ones. Networks often make as much of a difference as training and education, but, as they say, "Luck is where preparation meets opportunity!"

It never hurts to be polite. Follow up with the people who invited you to interview. Thank them. When the next job opens, you want them to keep you in mind.

SUMMARY

The information and exercises in this chapter are designed to assist you with the development of the components of your application packet, interview, job talk, and post-interview follow-up, but ultimately, it is up to you to make yourself shine. Deciphering a job announcement and creating an application that matches the employer's needs is a skill. Practice! Talk about the process to those who have succeeded. Use your network! And, be patient.

In summary, Kelley Hays-Gilpin offers the following advice for success.

> The successful candidate will be the one who shows some flexibility; do not signal neediness of the magnitude that you are willing to try anything just to make the committee happy. You have begun research in another state or country, but you have ideas about how to

involve students in similar research locally or in an existing study abroad program in an area that already interests you. You can teach a wide range of classes, but not take on the whole catalog. Your current focus is not the sum total of your career plan—you don't expect to spend the rest of your life gathering more data on the nasal bones of a particular species of lemur. You have a healthy balance of interests and experience, a coherent geographical, temporal, and theoretical focus, and a range of intersecting interests. If you say "here's how I can fill every gap in your program," you might be remembered as the candidate who criticized the program and claimed to have every band-aid in the box. Better to be remembered as the one who said, "I have skills and knowledge that complement your strong program, and I'd relish the opportunity to work with you—how can I contribute?"

The competition for academic positions is stiff, but there *are* jobs out there. If working in an academic setting is your dream, go for it with your full heart and soul.

FOR THE PORTFOLIO

Two products were produced through the exercises in this chapter. The first exercise, "Researching an Employer," produced information on at least two anthropology departments that you might consider working for. The second and probably more critical product of this chapter is your base curriculum vita. This CV will serve as the base into which you will enter all future professional anthropological involvements. Place each of these products within the appropriate section of your portfolio. In addition, if you have not yet completed the exercises in Chapter 8, do so now and place your letters in the appropriate sections as well.

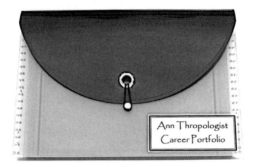

CHAPTER 15

KEEPING THE PORTFOLIO

"I let my résumé languish after landing a cushy government job, fig-uring I wouldn't need to worry about it for a while. Then one day I see the perfect job advertised and realized that the last entry in my résumé was over three years ago! I quickly learned that updating a résumé after years of neglect is an incredibly difficult and time-con-suming job that is better done in small pieces. Update your résumé as you gain new experiences or you'll end up trying to remember what you were doing three years ago—a difficult task on the best of days."
—Erin Hudson, District Archaeologist, USDA Forest Service

INTRODUCTION

This is it. This is where it all comes together. You've read the book and completed all of the exercises contained within. Now it's time to think ahead, not abstractly as you did when you created your five-year plan, but concretely, as in physically maintaining your employment documents.

Creating the portfolio was not simply an exercise; it was a process designed to assist you in creating the components necessary to the job procurement process. But the creation of the portfolio does not end here.

Maintaining the Portfolio

Unlike a filing cabinet, your portfolio is designed to be more than a deadzone for documents and files. It should be updated regularly and added to. The only documents and objects inside its covers should be those relating specifically to the job search and obtaining and maintaining your career. It is portable so that you can take it with you to interviews. At the point that it gets too beat-up to be presentable, buy a new one, but keep it going.

Your portfolio contains a minimum of ten sections, including spaces for your journal, personal contract, curriculum vita, résumé, biography, cover letters and letters of introduction, letters of reference, five-year plan and ethics statement, job application forms, and other. The following sections provide some suggestions relating to updating and maintaining each section within your portfolio.

Journal and Personal Contract

The journal you started in Chapter 1 should be kept up-to-date, documenting your ideas and notes as you follow your path toward a career in anthropology. As you do this, consider at what point during your employment you might actually assert, "I have a career in anthropology." It happens at different times for different people. You might declare that you've got a career when you've been hired in your dream job; you might consider it a career after ten years of continual employment; or it might be after you transition from temporary, part-time positions into one with benefits and vacation time. Whatever the path, make it yours and keep track of it. You never know when you will need to find a name, a number, an idea that you came up with when you were first starting out.

In Chapter 2, we suggested that you write a personal contract delineating what you hoped to achieve. This contract serves as the basis for assessing the products created and knowledge gained as you progressed through the book. Later in this chapter, there is an exercise to evaluate how you've done in relation to this contract.

"Before this I think I had a five-year-old résumé that I had lost, no CV, no five-year plan and was pretty rusty on writing cover letters and requests to professionals. Now, I have easy access to these things in my portfolio and strong templates to follow and build on for the future."
—Joseph (Woody) Aguilar, journal comment
Avenues to Professionalism class

Stockpile Database, Curriculum Vita, Résumé, and Biographical Statement

Your CV and résumé are the two most important components that need to be kept up-to-date. It is not always convenient to update these whenever you present, publish, join an organization, or win an award. We recommend that you add new information to your Stockpile Database or to a simple document in your computer. Since you never know where life will lead or when you might find a job announcement for that perfect position, it's good to stay on top of your updates. Take Erin Hudson's comment at the beginning of this chapter to heart. We concur and can simply say that falling behind is a pain!

The bio was noted for inclusion in your portfolio because even though it is not submitted as part of a traditional job application, it might be requested on a grant application or for inclusion in a proposal. Because the length and focus of your bio depends on how and where it will be used, you should have a number of versions available to be used as-is or to be modified on short notice. Develop a 50-word, a 100-word, and a full-page bio for these purposes.

Keeping hard copies is an important backup to the digital versions. Take it from people who've experienced the loss of the digital versions: it's hard to recreate years of employment and experience.

Letters

The letters you composed during the exercises in this book are the base for all future correspondence. Save these and any actual letters that you send to potential employers. The letters are helpful if you need to quickly see what you sent or when you sent it.

If you received letters of introduction or letters of reference from previous employers, professors, or colleagues, keep them. Keep all of them. If they get famous, you can say (and prove) you knew them when. ☺ If you get famous, well, you can look at the letters and remember who contributed.

Ethics Statement and Five-Year Plan

Your personal ethics statement should be your basic guide to your professional life. As you encounter more experiences, you will find that some things get easier and others get more difficult. Update your plan as you encounter new ethical situations. Keep thinking about what it means to be "ethical" and about the various communities of which you are a part or that your work impacts. Never let your personal ethics become stale and commonplace; your ethics say as much about who you are as your career and your education do (and remember, grandma is looking over your shoulder…).

Your five-year plan should never be considered a finished product. As each year passes, consult your plan. Over time, your goals and objectives will change as new information comes in and as you garner more experience. Use your plan as you would your personal contract. As each year passes, read through what you hoped to achieve and what you actually accomplished. Note the accomplishments. They are important, and we often forget to celebrate the positive achievements in our lives. Do this for yourself. Otherwise, there is a good chance that you will get bogged down with the never-ending life based on being behind and always having the deadline for the next project hanging over your head. Being successful does not mean that your job *is* your life. It's a job, so keep it in perspective with everything else that is important to who you are.

Other (Including Maybe This Book…)

This is your catch-all folder, the place where you can place things related to your job search and your career that do not fit in any of the other categories. Of course, if your portfolio has additional pockets, you can create additional categories and place the files in individually.

> *"I do feel the practical information given to us in class will benefit me by helping with attempting to get any job. It is sad that a class like this is not required in undergrad (upper class) programs because sometimes academics need these skills the most!"*
> —Monica Mondragon, journal entry, Avenues to Professionalism class

IN CONCLUSION

The information presented in this book is based on our personal employment success and the successes of those around us. It was based on the class we taught that was aimed at trying to bridge the gap for anthropology students between being a student and having a career. We were encouraged by the comments of our students to actually follow through with putting the content of the class into a book so that others could benefit. Part of the reason for teaching the class and writing the book was summed up in Monica's comment above and Matt Dawson's comment, "I give an 'A' for the creativity in designing this class and for its usefulness. It is quite true that there is no other class (that I am aware of) that actually gives you the tools and strategies for entering the job market or that gives you a map for getting where you would like to get."

In this book, we set out to provide you with information on the fields of anthropology and the options for employment. Through the information, recommendations, and the exercises, we hoped to provide you with the tools you would need to create documents relating to the job application process. Through the personal stories, we hoped to impart some of our experiences, good or bad, so that you could learn from our successes and mistakes and go forward into your career without some of the difficulties we experienced.

❧ CONCLUDING EXERCISE: EVALUATING YOUR PROGRESS

Remember that personal contract you constructed during Chapter 2? Well, it's time to reflect back on it and evaluate what you have accomplished as you progressed through this book. Look at what you wrote on the personal contract and at each of the components of your portfolio. Read through your journal entries. Did you accomplish what you set out to do when you entered into this process?

Write a personal narrative evaluation of your progress using the contract as your base. Describe each point you had hoped to accomplish and how you reached that goal. If you didn't achieve it, state what you will work on to make it happen. Conclude your assessment with a statement of how you plan to use what you have learned. ❧

REFLECTION

Did you need this book? Well, only you and time can be the judge of that. If we helped you discover one useful tool relating to obtaining a job, career, or dream job, then we'd like to think that the book probably paid for itself.

Our hope is that this book is useful to individuals as well as instructors of classes similar to Avenues to Professionalism. Book sale statistics will help us understand that, but won't be of much help in learning if we've left out the logic between what we were thinking and what was put down on paper. We don't know if it worked for you. If you got the job, then maybe the interviewer was as impressed by your pressed oxford shirt and tie as Richard Chapman was by the Avenues to Professionalism student (opening quote, Chapter 9).

Nine students completed the fall 2006 Avenues to Professionalism class. Of these students, we hear from and stay in touch with six. For those six, we continue to serve as committee members, advisers, mentors, and friends. We've watched as each of these students has been accepted into the graduate programs of their choice and get the jobs they desire. We'd like to think that the reason we haven't heard from the other three is that they've gotten their dream job and are too busy pursuing their careers to wonder where we are.

Even as teachers, we are learners. There is always something new. As such, we'd like to continue learning about what worked for you in transitioning from student to professional anthropologist. What did the employer say that he or she liked? What was useful that you learned within these pages? We'd love to hear from you so that we can update the book for a second edition. Let us know what worked and what didn't. Tell us of any extensions you created based on the exercises we provided. Provide constructive criticism so that we can make positive changes.

Send comments to us, care of Left Coast Press:
Carol Ellick & Joe Watkins
c/o Left Coast Press
1630 N. Main St., #400
Walnut Creek, CA 94596

And when it comes to your career, remember, there *is* such a thing as a pipe dream!

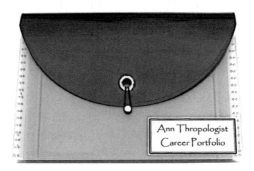

Ann Thropologist
Career Portfolio

APPENDIX 1

A PARTIAL LIST OF CURRENT ANTHROPOLOGY EMPLOYERS

In our quest to obtain data regarding the places that employ anthropologists, we contacted the American Anthropological Association. They were unable to provide us with the percentage of their members who are applied versus academic anthropologists, but they did give us a spreadsheet listing the affiliations of a previous annual meeting's attendees (minus those with university affiliation). This is the information people used on their name tags. The list is in alphabetical order, and the places that were represented by initials only and could not be readily identified on the Internet were removed from the list. We think this is an amazing piece of information, and so have reproduced it here for you, with the permission of the AAA.

A

Academy for Educational Development; Action Research; Aesthetic Realism Foundation; Affinis/San Diego Archaeological Center; African-American Research Library and Cultural Center; African Heritage Research Institute; African Population and Health Research Center; Aha Solutions; Aichi Cancer

Center; AIGA; Air Force Research laboratory; Alaska Native Epidemiology Center; Alaska Native Heritage Center; Alpine Archaeological Consultants, Inc.; AMATEA, LLC; American Environics; American Ethnography; American Foreign Academic Research; American Indian Center; American Indian Studies; American Institute for Yemeni Studies; American Institutes for Research; AMiCAS; Amnesty International; AMUCSS, MX; Andrew Mellon Foundation; The Antares Advisory; Anthro TECH, LLC; Anthropos Institute; Antioch Foundation; API Legal Outreach; Applied Sociocultural Research; ARC Associates; Archaeological Research, Inc.; Archaeologix, Inc.; ArchaeoPaleo Resource Management; Arid Lands Institute; Ariste Research; Asia Catalyst; Asia Research Institute, NUS; Aspen Institute; Austrian Academy of Sciences

B

Barcelona Centre for International Health Research; Barona Cultural Center and Museum; Barrow Neurological Institute; Basin Research; Battelle; Bavo Europoort; Beta Research Associates, Inc.; Bill Reid Foundations; Bioethics by & for the People; Bronx Guild

C

California Institute of Integral Studies; California Native American Heritage Cm; California Sea Grant; Calista Elders Council; Caminante Cultural Work; Campaign for Tobacco-Free Kids; Carnegie Foundation; Carolina Population Center, UNC; Cascade AIDS Project; CATIE; Clark Qualitative Research; Census Bureau; Center for Carbon-Free Power; Center for Community Research; Center for Digital Storytelling; Center for Disease Control and Prevention; Center for Health Research; Center for International Forestry Research; Center for Metropolitan Studies; Center for Partnership Studies; Center for Political Ecology; Center for Relationships & Sexuality; Center for Social Ecology & Public Policy; Center for Social Well Being; Center for the Study of Islam and Society; Center for U.S.-Mexican Studies; Center on Ecotourism & Sustainable Development; Centre for Modern Oriental Studies; Centre for Territorial Research; Centre for Tourism & Cultural Change; Century Foundation; CERAM Research; CERI-Sciences Po; Circa Cultural Consulting; Citizens Network; Chr. Michelsen Institute; Coastal Enterprises, Inc.; Coeur d'Alene Tribe; Cognitive Enterprises; Conservation International; Consumer Research Consultant; Context-Based Research Group; CRIA-Centre for Research in Anthropology (Portugal); Cross-Cultural Consulting Services; Crow Canyon Archeological Center; CSIC, Spain (Anthropology Research Group); Cultural Analysis Group; Cultural Diversities Consulting; Cultural Identification Laboratory, Hawaii; Cultural Integrity, LLC; Cultural Logic, LLC; Cultural Practice, LLC

D–E

Danforth Plant Science Center; Danish Institute for International Studies; Danish Institute for Advanced Studies; DBL-Institute Health Research and

Development; Desert Archaeology; Development Alternatives, Inc.; Department of Health and Human Services; Division of Research, Kaiser; Earthwatch Institute; EcoPlan Associates, Inc.; Electronic Ink; EnCompass, LLC; Energetics, Inc.; Environmental & Human Systems Management; Eufo-Institute (Regensburg, Germany); EVIA Digital Archive Project

F-H

Fafo Research Institute; Family & Community Research Center; Federal Acknowledgement, DOI; Feinstein International Center; Feminism and Legal Theory Project; Finnish Environment Institute; FLACSO Quito; Foundation for Environmental Security and Sustainability; Frobenius-Institute; Fusion Hill; Galisteo Consulting Group, Inc.; General Motors Corporation; Gentlestorm Productions; The Global Facilitation Network for Security Sector Reform; Group Health Center for Health Studies; GW Andrews Forestry Scientific Laboratory; Harborlight Management Services; HCQCUS, BCM & MEDVAMC; HealthPartners; Health Partners and Hennepin Healthcare; Henderson's Global Voices, LLC; Hershey Foods; Hewlett Foundation; HG Guggenheim Foundation; HIV/TB/STI Direct, W. Cape South Africa; Human Ecology Enterprises; Human Relations Area Files; Human Rights Watch

I

IBM; IIMAS-UNAM Research Institute for Applied Mathematics and Systems; ILAI Instituto Latin Americano de Investigacion; ILCAA Tokyo Research Institute for Languages and Cultures of Asia and Africa; Impact Assessment, Inc.; INAH National Institute of Anthropology and History, Mexico; Indigenous Water Initiative; INPA (National Institute for Amazonian Research); Inquiry & Learning for Change; Institut de Relations Internationales et Stratégiques; Institute for Community Research; Institute for Gender and Women's Studies; In-sync; Intel Corporation; Intelligent Research Solutions; Interactive Heterogenistics; International Center for Research on Women; International Institute for Population Sciences; International Institute of Art Culture and Democracy; International Organization for Migration; International Relief and Development; International Rice Research Institute; International Union for the Scientific Study of Population; IntraHealth International; IPI/Independence Park; Ipsos—UU North America; Israeli Coalition Against Housing Demolitions; IVIC Venezuelan Institute for Scientific Research

J-M

Japan Policy Research Institute; JB Intercultural Consulting; J.S. & J.L. Knight Foundation; JSI Research and Training Institute Inc.; Jumpstart/Project on Emergent Spiritual & Social Entrepreneurship; KAI-Research.com; Kaiser Permanente Center for Health Research; Kegging Shaulis and Associates; L.A. Landry & Associates, Inc.; La Cesta Consultants, LLC; Loeb & Loeb LLP; LSE Gender Institute; LTG Associates, Inc.; MacArthur Foundation;

Macro International Inc.; Max Planck Institute for Social Anthropology; Maya-K'ichee'; Mayo Clinic; Medical Care Development; Mediterranean Institute of Ethnology, European and Comparative; Microsoft Research; Middle American Research Institute; Molina Healthcare, Inc.; Motorola Labs; Myran Mack Foundation; Museum of Indian Arts and Culture

N

NADP Research Foundation; NASA Ames Research Center; Nathan Kline Institute; National Cancer Institute; National Center for Science Education; National Council for Research on Women; National Council of Scientific and Technical Research; National Endowment for the Humanities; National Institute of Education; National Institute of Mental Health; National Institutes of Health; National Jury Project; National Library of Medicine; National Research Council of the National Academies; National Science Foundation; Natural Resource Ecology Laboratory; National Centre in HIV Social Research; National Development and Research Institutes, Inc.; National Human Genome Research Institute; National Institute of Environmental Health Sciences; National Institute of Health and Human Development; National Institute of Immunology; National Institute for Occupational Health; National Museum of the American Indian; NE Fisheries Science Center; NOLA Investigations; NOPWorld; Nordic Africa Institute; Northern Land Use Research

O–R

Olhar Etnográfico; Overseas Development Institute; PA Consulting Group; Pacific Research Institute; Palo Alto Research Center; Pant Institute of Himalayan Environment & Development; Partners in Health; Pathfinder Research, Inc.; Patzisotz History Company; People Path, LLC; Perutz Enterprises; Philips Research; Planning Alternatives; Population Services International; RAND Corporation; RAW Ethnographics, Inc.; REAP Change Consultants; Recuerdos Research; The Reed Foundation; Rehabilitation and Research Center for Torture Victims; Research for Action; Research International; RIKEN BioResource Center; Rio Grande Foundation

S–W

Sandia National Laboratories; School for Advanced Research; Sentrum Moderner Orient (a German Research Institute); SETI Institute; Smithsonian Tropical Research Institute; Social Science Research Council; Social Solutions, Inc.; South Atlantic Fishery Management Council; Spencer Foundation; SRI Foundation; SW Foundation for Biomedical Research; Swiss Tropical Institute; Two Hawk Institute; UNESCO; The Urban Institute; U.S. Department of Health and Human Services; Waitt Family Foundation; Wendel Ethnographic Research; Wenner Gren Foundation

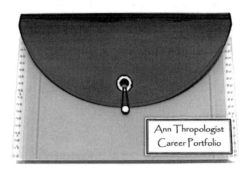

APPENDIX 2
ANTHROPOLOGIST CAREER STORIES

In keeping with the structure of this book, the career stories are listed in three categories: Applied, Academic with Applied, and Academic. The career stories within each category are in alphabetical order by last name.

Elizabeth K. Briody, Ph.D.
Founder and Principal, Cultural Keys, LLC

My Transition from Graduate Student to an Applied Career
I was in my last year of my anthropology Ph.D. program at The University of Texas at Austin. A friend of mine came back from the ASA (American Sociological Association) Meetings and said she had met a guy there from General Motors (GM) who was looking to hire an anthropologist. She told me that she thought I should apply for the job.

My first question was, why didn't he go to the Anthropology Meetings? She replied that he had and that he hadn't found anyone who was interested in applying! Then I made some comment about how I wasn't really interested because I was going to be a professor. My friend had a quick comeback—that I should not be ridiculous and that I should go ahead and contact the man.

It was the end of the summer of 1984. Anthropologists graduating with Ph.D. degrees sought tenure-track appointments but only some were successful. As I recall, there were about 300 applicants for each academic job during the mid-1980s. The culture of graduate anthropology programs had not kept pace with the changing times. The ideology of "academia or bust" prevailed, despite the decreasing number of positions in anthropology departments, and the growing number of non-academic opportunities for those trained to apply the "anthropological toolkit."

Paying little attention to these difficult job market characteristics, I took my friend's advice and followed up with the man from GM. It turned out that Dr. Carroll DeWeese was a sociologist looking for a researcher experienced in qualitative research. He persisted in contacting me on several occasions that fall to get a copy of my CV, writing samples, and letters of recommendation. I was stunned when he tracked me down at my parents' home over the Christmas holidays. He wondered if I would be willing to come and interview at the GM Research Laboratories and do a seminar for my industrial research audience consisting of four parts: (1) my background and training, (2) my dissertation research, (3) my research interests, (4) a discussion of why GM should hire an anthropologist. Oh, and I should limit my remarks to 20 minutes since the Q&A would likely last at least 40 minutes. I agreed, thinking that the visit would provide me with good experience for my anticipated academic interviews.

To prepare for my seminar, I began thinking about how my research interests related to work and occupations might overlap with GM's own interests. Very quickly I decided that part 4 of the seminar should focus on work issues in a corporate setting. An MBA student I knew reviewed the content of my talk, cut out the jargon, and helped me to frame my remarks so that they were relevant for GM. I ended up arguing that my own graduate research projects (e.g., involving janitors, migrant farm workers, Catholic sisters and priests) had exposed me to an array of work conditions and strategies. The work patterns I would identify among GM designers, engineers, or assembly line workers would serve as a baseline for understanding the organizational environment; from there, it would be possible to offer specific recommendations to help those groups become more effective.

The interview day was a whirlwind. After a meeting with the physicist department head, I gave my seminar. It was very well received. Then, throughout the day, I met with a variety of researchers (e.g., economists, mathematicians, psychologists, a demographer) in half-hour intervals. Their research interests were fascinating, eclectic, and problem-oriented. The energy level in the department was high. The research projects I learned about seemed innovative and useful. By the end of the day, I had done a complete 180-degree turn and was sold: I wanted to become a part of this exciting research organization. About six weeks later I was offered the position of Senior Research Scientist. I completed my Ph.D. work in Austin by the summer of 1985 and began my research career at the end of August—about one year to the day when I first learned about the GM job opportunity. This great career lasted 24 years!

What I Found Most Useful from Graduate School

Three aspects of my graduate training have been particularly valuable to my career. First, I had numerous opportunities to work on several different research projects involving field data, census data, or a combination of the two. Prior to leaving graduate school, I was able to present a number of papers at conferences and publish a couple of articles.

Second, I participated in interdisciplinary research teams of anthropologists, demographers, and sociologists. Most of these opportunities stemmed from campus research assistantships, though one involved a contract research project. I found both that my anthropological training was viewed positively by those from other disciplines, and that they were eager to help me understand their perspectives and approaches.

Third, I was lucky to receive one-on-one mentoring. Most students get some attention from faculty through their coursework, independent studies, dissertation research, and research or teaching assistantships. I benefited in all these ways, but I also had the opportunity to assist my undergraduate adviser with her fieldwork one summer when I was in graduate school. I learned an enormous amount simply by observing how she built social relations within the two communities she was studying, and how she gathered data about the changing environmental context. All of these experiences played a role in shaping my training and in preparing me to make the transition from graduate school to professional researcher.

Advice to Graduate Students

It is always tricky to give advice, since the conditions faced by one person are likely to be very different from those faced by another. However, I have four suggestions that are fairly general, so they should be useful to anthropologists with an interest in applied work.

First, it is important to target your anthropological skills to problems that are relevant to your audience—the group, organization, or community with whom you are working. That audience has certain interests, faces particular challenges, and has the potential to benefit from your analysis, insights, and proposed solutions. Corporate managers, for example, are likely to value research that improves business opportunities or enhances organizational effectiveness, while residents and staff members of an assisted living facility are likely to appreciate research that leads to an improvement in the quality of their lives. Focusing on what matters to your audience helps you to be viewed as someone who listens, understands, and appreciates their concerns. It also positions you to be effective in working with them to develop solutions—in part because you have already built key relationships and secured their confidence and support.

Second, prepare to move from fieldwork and analysis into the arena of recommendations. Anthropologists are quite comfortable describing and explaining phenomena, and situating findings within a theoretical context. However, a problem-solving orientation is necessary to figure out the best ways of addressing a particular problem. Therefore, additional knowledge and effort are necessary. The cultural patterns that you document must be linked with actionable recommendations. Try putting yourself in the shoes of the group or organization you are trying to help (to the extent that is possible). Think about what resources they control, what decisions they are responsible for, and what level of influence they have over others. Use that information to guide your suggestions.

Third, develop simple, clear, and concise ways of expressing yourself—both orally and in writing. Test your ideas with others to gather some feedback on their usefulness, persuasiveness, and importance. Ask others to critique your verbal remarks, presentations, or writing samples for their understandability as well as content. Eliminate all jargon and define any unusual terms or phrases so that ordinary people can grasp your message.

Fourth, network as much as possible. Building and maintaining social and professional networks inside your group or organization is an excellent way to help others learn from you, and to help you learn from them. Knowing the key roles, those with influence and control, and the extent of alignment and division among individuals and groups enhance any applied effort. Networking with anthropologists—whether locally or through a professional association—helps you, your anthropology colleagues, and anthropology as a discipline. In addition to sharing knowledge and applications, such networks can be valuable sources of internship placements, consulting arrangements, research collaborations, and hiring opportunities.

Michelle M. Carnes, Ph.D.
Cultural Anthropologist/Federal Project Officer

I am a rather new graduate, so my career has only begun, but the transition from student to career is fresh in my mind. I started my degree wanting to be an anthropology/women's studies professor. I loved school and I loved my teachers. I suppose most people who would choose to spend so much time in school (to get a doctorate) come into that decision with a high level of affection and respect for the academy. In fact, I entered in awe of the academy and faculty members. I understand now that I had a romantic image of being a professor: seemingly limitless time to think, write, and spend time with students sounded like a great way to spend my working life.

Once I became a doctoral student, I woke up. I found that many of my colleagues and I shared similar characteristics: hard on ourselves, hard on each other, absorbing criticism straight to our hearts, pursuing approval at all costs from those we worshipped (faculty) in the process of becoming like them (PhD'ed). It felt hard to "have fun" when the papers and readings needed to be done, and many of my friends turned down invitations to go out and frolic (have a beer, see a movie) simply because we all had such difficulty putting the assignments out of our heads for long enough to enjoy the time. It was a common dance to ask friends to join me in frivolity, listen to their laundry list of assignments weighing on them, remind them of how much they've accomplished, how "good" they've been this week (or month), and hope they would be convinced to take a break. After all, if I was the only one taking a break to "goof off," I'd feel guilty too.

This is one important lesson I learned early on in my work life: to set and maintain boundaries. When I gave myself permission to work on something for a set period of time, it prevented me from allowing it to take over my life. I started working full-time while I was finishing my dissertation. While my adviser was horrified that I would work 40 hours while writing (and at a non-academic job—how could you, Michelle!?), it actually helped me finish faster. It took the pressure of rent/food money off my brain, allowed me spending money to treat myself when I finished a chapter, and, most importantly, it demanded that I set boundaries on my time to finish the dissertation. Unlike the years leading up to writing (when I was fully "being" a grad student in classes), the dissertation could not "take over my life" because eight hours of my day were already spoken for. Thus, I had to use my time wisely and be prepared to write when the time came, knowing that the same eight-hour block was already spoken for tomorrow.

While writing my dissertation, I also learned to cope with delayed success—as in, delayed for years. And years. It felt stifling to report that I "wasn't quite done yet" at holidays and casual conversations with non-academic friends (fellow grad students rarely asked, sharing the anxieties wrapped up in such questions). I had to come up with my own reward system to acknowledge and celebrate my successes, on my terms. I had to stop seeking approval from my committee; they did not have time to clap their hands about my latest breakthrough. Their job was to seek out and point out the weaknesses, omissions and gaps—so that I may fill them. Thus, I had to throw my own "little parties" when I finished a chapter, started a new one, when I wrote 25 pages in a single day, when I finished the bibliography. I learned to reward and congratulate myself (and to no longer wait for my committee to acknowledge or value it). Not only was this important for finishing my degree, it was an important lesson personally—and one that translated into a healthy workplace presence as well.

I've worked many jobs to survive school. As an undergrad, I served my colleagues meals in the dorm cafeteria, worked the counter at a video rental store, at a record store, at an ice cream shop—various temp jobs and under-the-table "off the record" gigs. As a grad student, I taught courses on anthropology, feminism, and linguistics while working as a contractor for the government—which later became a full-time federal position as I finished my dissertation.

I finished my degree in 2009 and work for the federal government on American Indian health and wellness issues. While I have sometimes had to educate many employers about what my anthropology training is about ("No, I don't raid pyramids or solve crimes"), I was fortunate to find a boss who not only knows what social-cultural anthropology is, but clearly saw the match to the position I hold. Instead of starting over at the bottom of the academic totem pole as a professor, the federal government offered me a way to make a contribution to people's lives on a large scale.

I am glad to be out of the academic environment for many reasons. To me, the federal system seems to reward advanced degrees with exciting projects, job security, recognition for excellent work, financial stability—including the ability for working-class Ph.D.s to pay the student loan debts we acquire during the process. In my experience, an academic post would not have done any of these for me. Now that some time has passed, I would love to come back to campus to teach as an adjunct. I would enjoy it because I don't need the (low) paycheck and I can share my growing experience in the field with students (which I would have appreciated when I was in their shoes). I do plan to come back to teach, and I know it will be a great experience for me: *it will be on my terms.*

In my work for the federal government, I've found that my anthropology training in qualitative interviewing methods and analytical skills is invaluable when working with tribal communities who may have a strained relationship with data gathering and evaluation efforts (at best), whose gender norms vary from tribe to tribe, whose cultural roots hold the key to future collective health. Again, fortunately, my work colleagues understand qualitative data to be as valuable as quantitative. This is another translation that we sometimes need to do for those who employ us. Numbers can feel like The Truth, but they're not the whole story. You need to know the context, the story, the origins of those numbers. Without anthropology, numbers are just numbers.

However, there are a wide range of other things I picked up besides the "doing" of anthropology, thanks to school. Because we spend so much time in grad school, around other grad students, we can begin to take for granted what we do and what we've learned.

In my view, what many of us don't realize is that when we leave grad school, we've amassed a giant toolbox of abilities that we bring with us to a job (and which employers crave): sharp writing skills, public speaking practice, course curriculum development, teaching experience (translating complex concepts for laypersons), self-directed learning/research capabilities, independent work styles requiring little supervision/guidance, strategies to manage multiple projects/priorities, interpersonal/group facilitation skills, ability to maintain records for long-term projects (if a dissertation isn't a "long-term project," I don't know what is!), knowledge of IRB requirements and responsible handling/protection of sensitive research information. We've dealt with customer service issues (irate students, complaining parents), created and enforced policies (classrooms need 'em). We've managed bosses (ahem, advisers) and taken sole responsibility for our work, stood by it, answered questions about it, and been prepared to be criticized for it.

When you start working in the applied field, I think you'll notice that these are skills that others will come to count on you for—and they are skills which make you a huge asset. These are skills which grad students must possess in order to successfully complete a graduate program, so ultimately, think of your experience as a job. In many ways, it is. This will help you translate your training for an employer if they ask you what you can do for them. Translating anthropology is important, but having been a doctoral grad student is a badge of honor all its own too! Don't sell yourself short—it's not just about your content knowledge. We have skills, we are valuable . . . and the world (desperately) needs us.

Liana S. Hesler
Graduate Student, Native American Studies

I began my undergraduate career with hopes of fulfilling an interest in archaeology that I have had since childhood. What began as a liking of "digging in the dirt" quickly turned into so much more. As I progressed in my undergraduate career, and as my own ideas of archaeology began to take shape, I wondered, "Where are all the Indians?" It dawned on me at that time that is exactly why my grandmother encouraged me to be a "Native American archaeologist". . . because there were not many at all.

Being an American Indian, I always felt odd in the Anthropology Department as well as strange when telling other American Indians that I "studied" archaeology. The concentration on science in archaeology contradicted what I had been taught as a child—the past is the past, let it go. So who am I to serve? The archaeological community or the American Indian community? I wanted to find a balance between the two, and I felt that balance would come from the Native American Studies Department M.A. Program at the University of Oklahoma. I would be able to stay connected and be sensitive to

American Indian ideas and concepts, while still being able to continue my study of archaeology, albeit different than the original perspectives of archaeology. I hope to work in the future as an archaeologist who would be inclusive of other indigenous perspectives.

Carolyn J. McClellan, Assistant Director
Community and Constituent Services
National Museum of the American Indian

I began my college career as a nontraditional student. Growing up on my grandparents' allotment in the northeast portion of the Cherokee Nation in Oklahoma, getting a college degree was not a priority, but getting married and having a family was. We later moved to California, and it was not until my oldest daughter began attending UC Berkeley and I still had two children at home—a daughter in high school, and a son in middle school—that I seriously considered going back to college. As a single parent and with the encouragement of all three children, I transitioned from a full-time real-estate career to three part-time jobs to allow me to begin my college career. I chose anthropology for a number of reasons, but it wasn't my first choice. I originally intended to be a civil engineer, based on economic factors and the fact that an advanced degree was not required to earn a livable wage. However, after taking some anthropology and American Indian Studies classes, I discovered my passion in cultural anthropology.

After completing two years at Palomar Community College in San Marcos, California, I transferred to the University of Arizona and finished my B.A. in cultural anthropology there. One of the biggest life-changing events of my college career was when I applied for and was accepted as an intern in the American Indian Program at the Smithsonian National Museum of Natural History, the summer prior to my senior year. I worked for Dr. JoAllyn Archambault on the Mohave Tribal Catalog Project, researching the Mojave collections, not only at their museum but across the country. Dr. Archambault then asked me to stay on for the fall semester of my senior year, and the university allowed me to earn credit for my research project, which allowed me to graduate in the spring of 1996. This experience taught me the value of research, of the vast amount of data available at other repositories, and working with tribal communities other than my own.

Realizing that to earn a living in my career field I needed an advanced degree, I applied to a number of Ph.D. programs in anthropology but received the best incentive package from the University of Oklahoma (OU) Anthropology Department. During my time at OU, the emphasis of the Ph.D. program was to get students into an academic career. After doing some research, I discovered that an academic career was not in my personal best interest, as I was already in my early 40s. Over the course of my college career, I had acquired student loan debt to pay for living expenses, and the starting salary of a tenure-track professor was not conducive to paying off that debt and having a lifestyle that I desired. I saw much more potential using applied anthropology as a career choice, which I also thought would afford me a better lifestyle. With that in mind, I ended my education with my M.A. in cultural anthropology, with an emphasis in American Indian studies. I continued to work for Dr. Archambault in Washington, DC, at the National Museum of Natural History, and she offered me a contract after my graduation from OU in 1998.

Seeking a permanent federal career, later that year I applied for and was accepted as a historian for the Bureau of Indian Affairs (BIA) in the Branch of Federal Acknowledgment. This branch researches groups of individuals that seek to be federally recognized tribes by the U.S. government. My research experience provided me with the skills to be successful as a historian. Later, a promotion opportunity arose when the BIA hired me to be its first Native American Graves Protection and Repatriation Act (NAGPRA) Coordinator, a position I held for four years. This experience was tremendous and allowed me to work with a number of repositories that housed BIA archaeological collections removed from tribal lands during the American Antiquities Act of 1906 and prior to the passage of the Archaeological Resources Protection Act (ARPA) in 1979. During the course of tribal consultation, I was able to build many lasting relationships with museum and tribal representatives that still serve me well today.

In 2004, I left the Bureau of Indian Affairs for another promotional opportunity to become the Division Chief for Cultural, Paleontological Resources and Tribal Consultation with the Bureau of Land Management. In this position, I had oversight not only for NAGPRA, but National Historic Preservation Act Section 106 and Section 110 and paleontological resource protection compliance activities.

In 2008, I accepted my current position as Assistant Director, Community and Constituent Services for the Smithsonian National Museum of the American Indian. This position is the highest GS level in federal service in terms of salary compensation. Each of my prior positions has served as a springboard for my job responsibilities. I oversee community and tribal outreach; seek out partnerships with other organizations that will mutually benefit both parties; and supervise internships and the resource centers at both of our museums with an emphasis on family activities. The museum's mission is to provide outreach for the entire Western Hemisphere; therefore, we seek to build relationships in Canada and all of Latin and South America. I just coordinated a multi-day Living Earth Festival that concluded on August 8, 2010. The festival combined several existing museum programs and brought together cotton weavers from Hopi and Veracruz, Mexico (Totonaca); Lumbee and Karuk basket weavers; and a farmer's market featuring locally grown organic vegetables and meats. It also held an Iron Chef–like cooking competition and demonstrated family activities including making biodegradable seeded paper and spinning string from raw cotton.

I'm glad I chose an applied anthropology career, as it has allowed me to achieve personal and career goals beyond my wildest dreams through meeting the myriads of wonderful people I've had the opportunity to work with and the financial rewards to afford me a lifestyle that will carry me through retirement when I choose to retire.

Jim McDonald, USDA Forest Service
Eastern Region Regional Environmental Coordinator

It really began with the need to earn money to pay for graduate school. When I arrived at University of Arizona (UA) in 1973, I already had some contacts in the department as a result of being a student at the field school in 1972. The contacts included Valetta Canouts and Jim Rock. Val helped me get a job with the Arizona State Museum, working on the Tucson Gas & Electric El Sol to Vail Transmission Line, and I may have done one or two other small projects with the museum. Somewhat later, Jim Rock helped me get a job at the Western Archeological Center ("Conservation" was not part of the name at the time), working on an archaeological overview of Canyon de Chelly National Monument, and later on the Canyon del Muerto Survey. Both National Park Service projects supported the Management Plan for the Monument. So I was hanging out in places where there was a lot of discussion of the Moss-Bennett Bill, and what it might mean for federal support for archaeology.

I happened to be in the graduate program office at the department one day, and heard the secretary on the phone with the department secretary, helping her spell a doctoral student's name on his degree. It was troubling that the department secretary seemed not to know the Ph.D. candidates very well; it was a sign that the department was just too damn big. Which got me to thinking about the demographics of anthropology at the time: in any given year, a few large departments were turning out far more Ph.D.s than there were decent openings. On the other hand, it appeared that there would be quite a few federal job openings, so I firmed up my intention to take a terminal M.A. in archaeological resource management and find a job with the feds. Once I got the degree, I went full-time with the National Park Service, but on a term appointment.

In those days, permanent federal hiring was done mostly from the Professional and Administrative Career Examination (PACE), which I had taken. I received occasional "inquiries as to availability," which were sent to candidates for open positions. The inquiries helped Office of Personnel Management (OPM) avoid creating rosters full of people who were not interested in a particular position or who were no longer seeking employment. There was no guarantee that the positions would relate to one's interests or training. Two inquiries stand out in my memory. One was for a Logistics Management Specialist at Vandenberg Air Force Base. I had visions of overseeing a warehouse of toilet paper and janitorial supplies, since once they found out about my high school chemistry experience, I was pretty sure they wouldn't allow me around rocket fuel. So I said "no thanks" to that. I also remember an inquiry for a Bureau of Land Management (BLM) archaeologist position in Battle Mountain, Nevada. After talking to a fellow UA grad who had gone to work for the BLM, I turned that down as well. The polite way of characterizing his description was that Battle Mountain was small, isolated, and something of a hardship post.

A third inquiry was more intriguing. It was for a Forest Service Realty Management Specialist position on the Klamath National Forest. At the time I received it, I was in a spike camp working on the del Muerto Survey, with no ready access to a phone (which I really needed, since in the interim, Jim Rock had gotten the job of Klamath National Forest Archaeologist, and I knew he was recruiting an assistant). I really wanted to call and find out what was going on. But instead, I responded by mail, saying I was available for the Realty Specialist position.

Apparently, a couple of weeks later, Jim's boss walked over to Jim's desk and said, "You won't believe this. We have an archaeologist at the top of our Realty Specialist roster." Rock said, "Oh, who is it?" When he found out it was me, he and his boss called OPM and asked if they could use the Realty Specialist roster to fill the Archaeologist position, and send up a new roster for the Realty Specialist position. OPM wouldn't allow that, but they would allow the Forest Service to request me by name on the roster for the Archaeologist position. I placed well enough that the Forest was able to hire me. And that is how I ended up as a Forest Service Archaeologist.

Maria Michalczk, M.A., R.N.
Oregon Health Science University

I am a registered nurse and worked for nearly ten years before I got a master's in anthropology. I received my master's at Portland State University (PSU) in 1989 in physical anthropology, all the while working as a registered nurse. I was lucky, as there was a position to develop the Healthcare Interpreter Program at Oregon Health Science University. I developed the program, and it became a national icon for many years. During this time, I worked with Oregon legislation to create a law to certify interpreters in our state. I meanwhile went on to work on national policies on healthcare interpreting and remain doing this work, working on national certification. I believe that my education in anthropology gave me great tools to work on policy issues related to health and culture and could speak to cultural concerns and disparate health policies in our country. In 1986 I was awarded the Governor John Kitzhaber Public Health Award. Although my nursing background gave me tools to actually take care of patients, it was the anthropology discipline that provided me the background to critically think about and apply anthropological principles to the work I now do. I could indeed write a book on my journeys after my graduation from PSU, and I firmly believe that this education was the turning point in my career.

Jeanine Pfeiffer, Ph.D
Ethnoecologist

Knowing that I would face stiff competition for academic and research-oriented jobs when I graduated with a Ph.D. in integrated ecology from UC Davis, I worked hard to augment my CV with teaching, scholarship, and grants. I taught undergraduate and graduate courses in a range of cross-disciplinary subjects: environmental science, environmental biology, research methods, women in science, herbal medicine, ethnobotany, and ethnoecology. Some of those classes I designed and taught with other graduate students, some I co-taught with junior and senior faculty, and two courses I designed and taught entirely on my own. To expand my professional networks, I obtained funding and put on a number of seminars and conferences on topics such as environmental ethics and biological invasions and biocultural diversity. The biological invasions conference ultimately turned into a review article published in *Environmental Conservation*.

I also set a goal for myself to have at least five publications either published or submitted by my final academic year, and I formatted the chapters of my Ph.D. thesis as publishable units. For example, one chapter was published as a book chapter in an anthropological anthology on communities in Southeast Asia, another as a gender review article for an ethnobiology journal, and a third chapter as a scientific article in a special issue of *Environment, Development, and Sustainability*. My previous international work, after I obtained my M.Sc. (in international agricultural development, also from UC Davis), as a social scientist for the United Nations and other international development organizations helped me learn how to conduct fieldwork and expedite report-writing, skills that served me well in my doctoral fieldwork in Indonesia, where I ultimately dedicated ten years of my life to collaborative research and conservation programs with indigenous communities.

In the year following my graduation, I participated in co-writing three interdisciplinary grant proposals with large groups of researchers for the National Science Foundation and the National Institutes of Health. Two of those proposals were successful: one employs me part-time, with ongoing fieldwork in Indonesia; the other involves substantial volunteer work that keeps me current with online teaching methods in ethnobiology.

In the second and third years following my graduation, while lecturing at UC Davis and San Jose State University (SJSU), I applied for and obtained interviews for three positions: two as tenure-track academic faculty at non-USA universities, and one at an international nonprofit conservation organization. Ultimately I accepted the position as a social science research director at the nonprofit (because I thought they had the most to offer me), but I resigned eighteen months later when I perceived that my core values were being compromised by the organization's policies and practices.

After returning to California (now five years after my graduation), I was fortunate to have continued my research position at UC Davis and my lectureship at SJSU while employed at the nonprofit, so I could work professionally while seeking additional employment and trying to figure out what my next professional steps would be. I began attending community-based meetings for a state marine conservation initiative, and was recruited by local government officials to the position I now hold as a county contractor for public outreach efforts. I have also been approached by local tribal communities to write position papers on traditional ecological knowledge and indigenous science, something that really excites me because it allows me to directly apply my expertise as an ethnoecologist and to do something that is highly relevant, useful, and timely.

Looking back on my postgraduate career path, I wish I had received more professional assistance from my thesis committee members and academic advisers. I applied for only a few jobs because I really didn't know how many possibilities were out there. It wasn't until I was several years out of the university, when colleagues linked me into critical list-serves like the environmental anthropology (E-ANTH) list-serve of the American Anthropological Association and the social science working group (SSWG) list-serve of the Society for Conservation Biology, that I really began to comprehend the wide diversity of professional positions I could apply for as an ethnoecologist (or "environmental anthropologist" or "cultural ecologist"). I also wish that I had developed a list of core values *before* I began applying for positions, as that would have helped me ask more penetrating and insightful questions during the interview process, and to make better choices.

Patricia Sachs, Ph.D.
President, Social Solutions, Inc.

There was not an abrupt transition from being a student to having a career for me. It took me many years to complete my doctorate (from B.A. to Ph.D. took eleven years), because I needed to work the entire time, and I also had two children during that time. One factor that did play a part in my thinking was that in my first year in grad school, a couple of professors talked about how there would be fewer academic jobs for us due to the demographics of departments. There simply were lots of people in academic departments who had fairly long careers ahead of them, and not much churn was expected. That made me realize I would need to think more broadly about a career. This didn't affect any specific actions on my part; I would say it was part of my consciousness. In addition, since I was working, and studying the anthropology of work, I witnessed many workplace situations that I thought could be handled differently, yet I was not in a position at the time where I had much legitimacy for making suggestions. I could see, at work, that possessing a third-party validation (such as a Ph.D.) provided legitimacy for insights and ideas that could produce change of some sort. Again, I have to say these were somewhat silent observations, yet ones that allowed me to see the possibilities for an unfolding career. I would add that one reason my observations were silent was that I really had no one to talk to about them! My grad school peers were intent on going after academic jobs; "applied" work was seen as being for people with fewer brain cells, and I was further constrained geographically: I had kids to raise, and academic opportunities were generally not tenure tracked, not local, and often very short-term. The process of becoming a practitioner was, in fact, practical. I needed to support my kids! I needed to stay in one place geographically.

From that perspective, I was rather opportunistic, if aided by awareness. A chance for a postdoc in developmental and cognitive psychology came my way, which I took on for a couple of reasons (money was certainly not one at the time—I took a reduction in pay). I took the position because (1) they were actually looking for an anthropologist who specialized in work—and at the time, the mid-eighties, there were a handful of us. (2) I wanted to better understand issues from a psychological perspective, because I could see the power it had in workplaces (as distinct from an anthropological or social view, which held no sway whatsoever). It was fortuitous that the postdoctoral work, which became a job, was in an area that was really ripe for consulting and for a synthesized view of psychological and anthropological knowledge, and workplace change. That area was in expert systems—I sort of consider myself a sociogeek! In the postdoc period, our research revealed that technology was seen as a cure-all for workplace woes, decisions were made on that basis, and yet actual success in working out problems was socio-technical. The human part was categorized in workplaces as a "source of errors," and expert systems were envisioned as "perfect" thinking systems not fraught with human error. As this five-year period of research came to an end, I had the opportunity to join an expert systems lab as a "visiting professor" (!), and within two months, I saw the chance to help them rethink expert systems, not as technologies that do the thinking, but as sophisticated systems to support expertise in human systems. Anthropological understanding (and cognitive and developmental understanding) was very important here in helping engineers learn to look at workplaces as more than body parts (or highly segregated tasks). So, I carved out work, and founded a lab to do so, that focused on understanding the nature of work in real settings, the role of technologies, and helping engineers and managers and workers learn to see that people work in systems, not just in tasks, and that technologies are part of those systems. It always seemed fundamentally anthropological to me, as much as understanding stone tools in social systems. The tools and systems were just more complex.

I will say that as time has gone on, I have treasured the direct interaction I have with clients. I work now mainly with small businesses and their founder/owners, on strategic issues. I have an inherently systems view, and it is harder for me to identify what is "anthropological" and what is "consulting" or "strategic thinking" about what I do; they are very integrated for me.

APPLIED AND ACADEMIC

Kelley Hays-Gilpin
Associate Professor, Northern Arizona University

I didn't plan to become an academic archaeologist. I wanted to do museum work, enjoyed most of the CRM projects I'd worked on, and didn't think I had the stamina for a full teaching load. I knew there weren't many tenure-track positions available, and getting one would be very competitive. It's hard to offer advice about how to land a professorship because, for me, I'm sure that following my interests and taking advantage of unique opportunities worked out better than single-mindedly pursuing a tenure-track job from the get-go would have.

When I entered the Ph.D. program at the University of Arizona, I spent only one semester as a teaching assistant before switching to the research assistant track in the Arizona State Museum. I wanted a museum career, but I was more interested in method, theory, and area studies in anthropology than in museum methods classes. I assumed I could complete a four-field academic program, start writing my dissertation, and then take museum methods. But the Museum Studies program was disbanded before I got around to those classes. I was immersed in research and getting hands-on experience with collections. After completing the Ph.D., I had several job offers in private-sector cultural resource management, state parks, and national parks, and did not apply for any academic positions. I accepted an offer from the Navajo Nation Archaeology Department (NNAD) and worked happily for seven years as a tribal archaeologist. I served as the ceramic specialist for compliance projects on the Navajo reservation, analyzing pottery from road projects, and water and housing improvements. I got to do a little fieldwork, lots of lab work, write research designs, and write and edit reports. Most rewarding, I helped train Navajo and other Native American students to become archaeologists so they could perform CRM clearances for their own communities. I taught ceramic analysis at Northern Arizona University as an adjunct professor because I enjoyed teaching small seminar-style classes, and developed a class for the Women's Studies Program called Women in Prehistory. That way, I got some valuable teaching experience, got to know the NAU Anthropology Department close-up, and learned to value applied anthropology and service learning.

Partly due to the NNAD-NAU student training program's success in training Navajo successors, and partly due to economic shortfalls in BIA funding for roads projects, I started to look for other opportunities, but did not want to leave my home in Flagstaff. A tenure-track position in Southwest archaeology opened up at Northern Arizona University after a long-time faculty member retired, and I applied. The first offer went to another candidate who already had a tenure-track position at another university, but was seeking a position for her spouse. Her university counteroffered with such a position, so she and her spouse stayed where they were, and I got the next offer. Now that I have served on many selection committees, I know that the job rarely goes to the first candidate on the list, and that if you make the top six or eight on the list, you have a good chance. At that level, all the candidates on that short list are qualified, and selection is mostly about "fit"—which candidates will make good colleagues, can they teach classes that need to be taught, do they understand the needs of the students already in the program and those the program hopes to recruit? Acceptance by the top candidates can depend on salary, spousal hire (exceedingly rare on a first offer, better chances later in the career track, per the above example), laboratory start-up space and equipment, and cost of living. (Can a junior faculty member afford to buy a house in Flagstaff on a starting salary from a third-tier state university? No. In Iowa? Yes—so the out-of-town candidate accepts the offer in Iowa.) In my case, assets included a solid record of part-time teaching, service, and publications—several edited volumes published, a few peer-reviewed articles, lots of compliance reports, demonstrated commitment to applied anthropology and to diversity issues. As a two-income family with student loans paid off, we already had a house in the community. NAU and I were a "fit."

The first few years of teaching full-time and trying to develop a coherent program of research and publications were very difficult and the work time-consuming. Junior faculty are expected to carry a high teaching load, with new preparations and lots of large introductory courses that do not necessarily play to one's expertise. Human evolution is not my strong subject, but it needed to be taught; it needed to be taught to reluctant freshmen. The youngest students typically turn in negative reviews that comment on an assistant professor's age, appearance, clothing, accent, and all sorts of irrelevant details, so one has to work hard to sift through student reviews to find areas that really do need improvement. It's difficult—probably impossible—to find a balance between catering to the seekers of the "easy A" (not a good way to get tenure) and making the course interesting and challenging for those who really are there to learn.

In my experience, after the first few years, the work does not get easier, but one has more flexibility, more choice in course selection and development, and more opportunities to contribute to curriculum development, collaborative lesson plans, and interdisciplinary ventures. You find out where the external and internal funding sources are. You start to serve on grant and fellowship selection committees and learn how to write better proposals and what other universities are doing that might be useful in your own program. You develop a network of colleagues and former students that you can rely on for ideas and information. You stop worrying about whether your students "like" you and focus on whether they are gaining the skills and knowledge they need to succeed. Their successes make you proud to have been a part of their lives and careers.

I still don't think I have the stamina to teach three classes a semester every semester, the standard teaching load at NAU. I negotiated a new job description, in which the Museum of Northern Arizona (a private nonprofit regional museum) uses the income on a small endowment to buy out two courses a year so I can serve as Anthropology Curator there. The university gets enough money from the museum to hire part-time instructors for a couple of classes, or can aggregate my buyout with sabbatical-release savings to hire a full-time instructor on a one- or two-year contract. Everyone gains. For me, the time and energy commitment is like having two full-time jobs, but then, a full teaching schedule and research program is no less than that. But now I have my museum job and students, as well as tenure, sabbatical release every seven years, and two institutional support networks for grants and contracts. I can bring the museum and the students together by facilitating collections research, service-learning opportunities, contract and grant work, and internships.

Lori L. Jervis, Ph.D.
Sociocultural Anthropology
Associate Professor, University of Oklahoma

I began working in nursing homes when I was fifteen years old for extra spending money, progressing from "water girl" to "nursing assistant" to "therapeutic recreation assistant" over the course of the next decade. Although there were aspects of this work I found fulfilling, as a whole I couldn't wait to escape it, finding it to be a back-breaking, dead-end career path. As an undergraduate in college, anthropology seemed a route to a more exotic, intellectually stimulating place. Yet, from time to time, it occurred to me that the kinds of insights and methods ethnographers applied to the "exotic" locales in which they prototypically worked could and should be applied to the nursing homes in our backyards that were, in their own way, equally interesting but often overlooked.

Nonetheless, years later as an anthropology graduate student, I initially intended to work in a faraway locale, investigating topics as far away from aging, illness, and nursing homes as I could get. In my classes, I was bombarded with postmodern theory . . . and eventually came to wonder what the point of the discipline was. I took a year off from graduate school, went to work at a geriatric unit in a psychiatric hospital, and loved it. I returned to the idea of doing research in my own backyard, and wrote a dissertation on the chronic mentally ill residents of a nursing home and the staff who cared for them.

Since that time, I have continued to work in the area of psychiatric anthropology and gerontology, and the themes from earlier phases of my life have continually resurfaced. I worked for eleven years in a Department of Psychiatry at the University of Colorado in an American Indian and Alaska Native research program. There, I led projects on tribal nursing homes, cognitive impairment, and elder mistreatment. After eleven years, I took a position at the University of Oklahoma, where I now have appointments in Anthropology and the Center for Applied Social Research.

In the end, I am not sure whether I chose an "applied" career or whether it chose me. I guess I must have chosen it, albeit unconsciously, by selecting topics of study with a practical dimension. Working with American Indians provides a further impetus for research with potential to shed light on real-world problems, as in most cases the acquisition of knowledge for knowledge's sake is simply no longer enough of a compelling motivation for engaging in further research—communities want action!

Frances Norwood, Ph.D.
Assistant Research Professor, George Washington University

In these difficult times, it is all about networking. One of the best pieces of advice that I got during my job hunt was if you find a place you want to work, create reasons for being there. Drop in if you can, attend brown bag lunches, call and have coffee with people who work there. My mentor said she just started showing up to meetings at this one organization, and eventually they got so used to seeing her there, they offered her a position. Be willing to piece together your existence until you get where you want to go.

I currently work full-time as Director of Research in a nonprofit doing interesting work that does not pay very much. I teach one course per semester as an adjunct at George Washington University, and I was able to get a research appointment there that allows me to write grants to create my own dream job. I have submitted two grants so far (one for NIH funding) and have two more in the hopper. I hope to one day teach and do research full-time through George Washington University. To get there, I hang out and network with professors in the Department of Anthropology and the Institute for European, Russian, and Eurasian Studies as often as possible.

Teresa Tellechea, Ph.D.
Department of Anthropology, University of Northern Colorado, Greeley, CO

I am an applied anthropologist from Madrid, Spain. I studied and learned about the field of applied anthropology in Boulder, Colorado. When I finished the defense of my dissertation, I knew a whole world of opportunities had opened for me because I realized that anthropology had given me the main tools to connect with the world, which are to be engaged, open to many and different perspectives, connecting dots across disparate fields, to learn from others, and do something together to solve human problems.

So I started by looking into what were the needs around me and how I could be part of community initiatives. As a result, I have worked in public health as a community health specialist and health educator on education campaigns, coalition building, and policy change. I have also used my ethnography skills to do criminal defense investigation for the Public Defender's Office. Building rapport with witnesses during interviews was crucial in the biggest case I worked, where I contributed with a team of lawyers and other investigators to avoid a death penalty sentence. I also worked in education using my anthropological knowledge and applied skills as a Latino/a achievement adviser for a school district.

I now teach at a university where I bring multiple field experiences and applied perspectives to the classroom. Since academia sometimes makes me feel a bit isolated from the type of work I am used to, I stay involved in the applied world, consulting and working on multiple projects in my community.

Agencies, institutions, and organizations are in need of applied anthropologists, but they do not know it. That is why I always make a point of saying that I am an anthropologist doing such-and-such work.

ACADEMIC

Darna Dufour, Professor
University of Colorado at Boulder

By the end of my undergraduate degree, I was quite tired of being in school, excited to learn more about the world, and inspired by President John F. Kennedy's call for service. It was the late 1960s. I joined the Peace Corps and was assigned to Venezuela. It was there I learned about anthropology from a book, Edward T. Hall's *The Silent Language*. It was one of the books in the Peace Corps "book locker" I had been given, and one I picked randomly as I read my way through the locker. The book is about nonverbal language and helped me enormously in understanding my experience in Venezuela. It was also the start of my lifelong interest in anthropology. A trip to the Gran Sabana region of Venezuela and the opportunity to spend a week with local indigenous people added to my interest in understanding cultural differences, and was probably the tipping point in my decision to apply to Binghamton University to do an M.A. in cultural anthropology. In working on the M.A., I realized that my interests were in biocultural approaches, and so changed to biological anthropology for my Ph.D. I did my dissertation fieldwork with native peoples in the northwest Amazon, and completed my dissertation while on a Fulbright Fellowship in Colombia teaching biological anthropology. I took a postdoctoral fellowship in the UK (London School of Hygiene and Tropical Medicine, and Glasgow University) to gain depth in research methods, and then a position as an assistant professor at the University of Colorado. I am still at Colorado, and a now a full professor in anthropology and Associate Dean for Faculty Affairs.

Erica Gibson, Ph.D.,
Assistant Professor, University of South Carolina

I was the first graduate from the medical anthropology track in the new Ph.D. program at the University of Alabama, and felt some pressure from my department about getting a good job upon graduation. While doing my dissertation research, I obtained adjunct positions at both Rollins College and the University of Central Florida, where I was able to rediscover my passion for teaching (I had previously taught high school).

Upon graduation, I was not sure what type of career I wanted to pursue. As a medical anthropologist, I could work in the traditional field of academia or I could work in the public or private sector for numerous organizations focused on health. Due to the fact that I defended my dissertation in the summer and would not be receiving my diploma until December, I was unable to apply for academic jobs that wanted a degree in hand by September. I began looking for other options and was told about a postdoctoral fellowship in an NIH program focused on pain research at the University of Florida.

My dissertation focused on birth practitioner choice and stress during pregnancy; however, one of the main themes that emerged was that of pain during labor. Although it was not my main research focus, I was able to use this experience to gain a two-year fellowship as a postdoctoral researcher. I hoped to be able to design and conduct my own research study while at the University of Florida, but was unable to do so. The fellowship was guided by the Pain Research Center under the auspices of the College of Dentistry, so I was straying quite far from anthropology. This experience helped me focus on what I truly wanted—getting back into an anthropological teaching setting in a university rather than being a token anthropologist on a multidisciplinary project. During my first year as a postdoc, I applied for many academic positions in anthropology departments, and I was ultimately hired in a tenure-track position by the University of South Carolina.

I am currently working 50/50 in the Department of Anthropology and the Women's and Gender Studies Program. Being in two departments has pluses and minuses: I have to balance service and teaching commitments in both departments and attend two faculty meetings each month, but I also have double the number of supportive colleagues to help me through the tenure process!

My recommendation to anyone pursuing a career in anthropology is to find a mentor in the type of job you think you would like to have as early as possible in your education. This way you can go to them for help or answers to questions about their duties, likes and dislikes, and general help in choosing how to proceed through your career.

Ruth Burgett Jolie
Assistant Professor of Anthropology, Mercyhurst College

We [my husband Ed Jolie and I] were lucky—yes, we worked really hard, but let's not ignore luck. Mercyhurst happened to be expanding their program, we happen to fit their requirements (including willing to work in Erie. Honestly).

Networking: Those who work in textiles know each other. Ed's work, in particular, is amazing, and it's hard not to know of his work. He really is good at what he does, and he has numerous publications to prove it (I believe one reviewer noted that Ed had more publications as a third-year grad student than most tenured faculty do). We have always kept a "hand in the pot," so to speak. Every year we made certain that we were presenting at a meeting(s) and working on publications. Being on boards at meetings and other places, I think this is what really got Adovasio's attention when he was looking for new faculty, and he had a long list to choose from, but he wanted people who were doing good research. So you asked how we stayed in touch. Well, it was easy because, as I mentioned, it's a small world. We saw Adovasio (the dean and the individual who ended up hiring us) at the regional and national conferences. He saw our presentations and read our publications. He is in the same field, so that was lucky in a way.

We also diversified our research areas. Yes, textiles are jolly good, but we also knew that one skill area wouldn't cut it. So I focused on gender and urban anthropology as well, and Ed expanded to anthropological ethics. This was not a hardship, as we really enjoy what we do, and I like switching from, let's say, textiles as markers of social hierarchy to parental identity, in the course of a year. It's a lot more work, but it is rewarding, too.

We also tried to get as much teaching experience as possible without falling into the trap of only teaching and not "dissertating." We really worked on that aspect of the academic career, since we knew that we wanted to work at a small college or university where teaching is emphasized. Carol, you are an amazing teacher, but as you know, for some of us it is a steeper learning curve!

Not partying. I know this sounds obvious, but we sacrificed a lot of fun times because we knew we had to work Saturday morning (or whatever). We had a great time in grad school and made a lot of friends, but we also worked really hard. Probably harder than we had to! But then, I know that I am far from brilliant, so I need to work! And we still do. Tenure isn't guaranteed and as I am learning (much to my chagrin) that, I still find myself in the office late at night and on weekends. It doesn't stop in grad school—which is why an academic position isn't for everyone. It is a really greedy job. Rewarding, yes, and I wouldn't change it for anything, but everything that I did in graduate school was just a practice for this career. And we wanted to get through as quickly as possible, too. I mean, I had a plan—a Ph.D. in less than a decade—because I knew that I needed to start saving for retirement! Haha!

Advice? Work on those publications now. Go to conferences and get to know other academics' research and see where your skills and research interests fit in. It is never too early to get your foot in the door and then keep it in there! Even if it squishes your toes, keep that foot in the door! I don't know that I have any "anthropological skills" that set me above the rest. I know a lot of truly brilliant, hard-working, amazing anthropologists out there, and just because they don't have academic jobs does not make those jobs any less worthy. But I'm sure you have that in your book already.

Also, when we were negotiating these positions, I did a bit of research to see what other members of the social sciences at Mercyhurst were involved in, and then when we interviewed in person, I was able to make an argument that my research meshes with some of that being conducted in the Social Work Department, the Gender Studies Department, as well as the Anthropology Department—which I guess falls under the "diversify your research interests" heading. So I was able to quickly (and hopefully eloquently) suggest cross-listed classes, new classes that I could teach that would fit the core, and so forth. Ed did the same.

Dress conservatively. Twinsets are good, as are knee-length skirts. No one wants to hire a woman with questionable attire. Ed actually irons his shirts. Shocking, I know. I'm not sure this should make it into the book, but I feel that cleavage ought to be kept out of the classroom!

Be friendly. Don't be snooty. Somebody always does something better than you! Play and work well with others. Okay, I'm stretching here. Sorry.

Amanda Minks
Assistant Professor, University of Oklahoma

I started applying for academic positions in the fall of 2005 while preparing for my dissertation defense at Columbia University. I applied for every job and postdoc that I could possibly connect to my interests and training. This required reframing my application materials for every position, which is time-consuming but necessary. I was fortunate to get an offer relatively quickly for a tenure-track position in the Honors College at the University of Oklahoma, and I decided to withdraw from the other searches and accept it.

The job I accepted was advertised as a position in cultural anthropology, but the Honors College is an interdisciplinary unit with an emphasis on American Studies. My research is in Latin America, and my Ph.D. is in ethnomusicology, although my work is oriented more toward cultural and linguistic anthropology. I wrote my "job talk" with a broad audience in mind, emphasizing the interconnections between the U.S. and the Caribbean coast of Nicaragua, where I carried out my dissertation research. I prepared for the campus interviews by reading about the research and teaching of other Honors College faculty and thinking about how I could connect with them and also add something new. At the time I was going on the job market, I was adjunct teaching an undergraduate linguistic anthropology class at the New School (my first stand-alone teaching experience), which helped me to articulate a teaching philosophy.

Moving to a new institution always requires some adjustment, but I have been very happy with my job in the OU Honors College. The flexible curriculum is a good fit for me because I have been able to design courses around my interdisciplinary interests and move into new research areas. I like teaching motivated undergraduates in small classes at a public institution, which draws many first-generation college students. I am also grateful to have time for research and writing as well as teaching.

For Ph.D. candidates seeking an academic job, I would recommend starting to apply while you are in the middle of writing your dissertation. It is a good experience even if you don't get called for interviews, and you never know when you will get a "bite." It is also important to think about long-term stability (if you are someone who likes stability!). Now that the job market has tightened up so much, I am glad I dove into a tenure-track position right away rather than undertaking a multi-year postdoc. I would also recommend keeping an open mind about locations and positions. Apply for everything, everywhere. Some out-of-the-way places have hidden benefits, such as a low cost of living. If it is a good job, you should have the resources to travel when you are not teaching.

If you are thinking about entering a Ph.D. program with the goal of becoming a tenure-track professor at a research institution, you might want to think again. The structure of universities is changing, and when tenured professors retire, they are often replaced with adjunct instructors. The number of Ph.D.s on the market far exceeds the number of tenure-track positions available in most fields. You should undertake a Ph.D. only if you can avoid getting into a lot of debt, and only if you are totally committed to the learning experience (including coursework, research, reading, and writing) for its own sake, knowing that it may not increase your job options or earning power. But if you have the determination and imagination to complete a Ph.D., these skills will also help you find a way to make a living, hopefully doing something you like. You never know what you may enjoy doing (and where) until you give it a try.

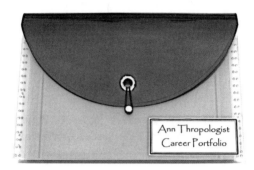

APPENDIX 3

RESOURCES

The following resources have been found by us, or identified by our colleagues, as being potentially useful. This list, organized by categories similar to those used in this book, is in no way comprehensive, nor are these resources set apart as "better" than any others. These are offered merely as examples of the types of resources available to students who wish to develop their career materials and searches.

CAREERS IN ANTHROPOLOGY

Archaeology magazine website. *"Protector of the Past." http://www.archaeology. org/online/interviews/eubanks.html* (accessed December 2, 2010).

This article in a popular magazine details the career of archaeologist Thomas Eubanks. It gives some insights into the training, experiences, and background that help archaeologists do their jobs.

Boites, Salvadore Z., Pamela Geller, and Thomas C. Patterson. "The Growth and Changing Composition of Anthropology 1966–2002." http://dev.aaanet.org/resources/departments/upload/Changing_Composition.pdf (accessed December 2, 2010).

This article describes some of the changes in the field of anthropology as evidenced by the changes in anthropology programs between 1966 and 2002. The data is derived from the AAA's *Guide to Departments of Anthropology* during that time period.

Briller, Sherylyn H., and Amy Goldmacher. *Designing an Anthropology Career: Professional Development Exercises*. Lanham, MD: AltaMira Press, 2009.

This book provides exercises for students as a means of helping them think through and create materials they will use in their professional careers.

Cal State Fullerton website. "Job Opportunities for Anthropology Majors." http://anthro.fullerton.edu/JobOpportunities.html (accessed December 2, 2010).

This website from the Department of Anthropology at California State University, Fullerton, offers information for students interested in careers in anthropology.

eHow.com website. "How to Become a Museum Curator." http://www.ehow.com/how_12539_become-museum-curator.html (accessed December 2, 2010).

This website article offers suggestion for students interested in becoming a museum curator—suggestions such as getting involved in professional organizations, interning, and having superb writing skills.

Ferraro, Gary. "An Essay on Careers." http://www.wadsworth.com/anthropology_d/special_features/anthro_careers.html (accessed December 2, 2010).

This website article offers information on the various careers within anthropology, coupled with some video clips about a forensic anthropologist, an applied anthropologist, and a corporate anthropologist.

Forensic Magazine, http://www.forensicmag.com/ (accessed December 2, 2010).

This is a general website about the various fields within the forensics boom, ranging from forensic chemistry to forensic anthropology, and other aspects of forensic sciences.

Gwynne, Margaret A. *Anthropology Career Resources Handbook*. Boston: Pearson Education, 2003.

This book offers information primarily for the undergraduate student interested in a career focused on some aspect of applied anthropology. It includes a very good list of resources that existed at the time of publication. While we did not investigate the websites to see if they are still active, they provide suggestions of places students can search for contemporary information.

Robbins, Elaine. "Archaeological Crime Fighters." *American Archaeology, Summer 2006.*

This article describes the work of forensic archaeologists who apply their skills to help law enforcement agencies at crime scenes and major disasters.

Schuldenrein, Joseph. "Changing Career Paths and the Training of Professional Archaeologists: Observations from the Barnard College Forum, Part I." *SAA Bulletin* 16 (3). *http://www.saa.org/Portals/0/SAA/publications/ SAAbulletin/16-1/SAA20.html* (accessed December 2, 2010).

This article is a summation of the Bernard Forum, a program that brought together many archaeologists in the New York City area to discuss the ways that archaeology has changed from that of primarily an academic endeavor to one where cultural resources management plays a major role in employment opportunities.

Schwartz, Shelly K. "Anthropology Majors Can Capitalize on the Growing Global Marketplace." CNNMoney.com website, Working Your Degree. *http://money.cnn.com/2000/11/17/career/q_degreeanthropology/,* November 17, 2000 (accessed December 2, 2010).

This online article discusses job opportunities for anthropology graduates in a global marketplace. Of particular use is an inset that offers "Top 10 occupations that employ persons with only a bachelor's degree in anthropology and archeology."

Society for Historical Archaeology website. "Careers in Historical Archaeology." *http://www.sha.org/students_jobs/career_types.cfm* (accessed December 2, 2010).

This web page of the Society for Historical Archaeology defines historic archaeology and the types of jobs historic archaeologists do across the United States today. It is a good glimpse into the myriad of opportunities available to those who choose this subdiscipline of archaeology.

Stephens, W. Richard. *Careers in Anthropology: What an Anthropology Degree Can Do for You.* Boston: Pearson Education, 2002.

This volume contains the character profiles of fifteen anthropologists who are currently working in the field. The book is organized to help students understand the wide range of areas where anthropologists work today and to help students better understand the uses to which a degree in anthropology can be put.

Strang, Veronica. *What Anthropologists Do.* New York: Berg, 2009.

This book presents a discussion of the ways that anthropology contributes to a very wide range of fields, from environmental issues, to museums, communications technology, crime scene investigation, and business, among others

Wagner, Robin, "Careers for Ph.D.s in Museums." *The Chronicle of Higher Education* website, *http://chronicle.com/article/Careers-for-PhDs-in-Museums/46302/* (accessed December 2, 2010).

This article provides information for students interested in breaking into the field of museum work. It suggests volunteering and internships as one important step. It also provides information on the various job opportunities one can find within the museum field.

Walsh, Sharon. "Corporate Anthropology: Dirt-free Research." CNN.Com/Career website, *http://archives.cnn.com/2001/CAREER/dayonthejob/05/23/corp.anthropologist.idg/* (accessed December 2, 2010).

This article dispels the myth that all anthropologists are of the "Indiana Jones" archaeologist type. It discusses the jobs of some anthropologist in the corporate world, from "studying consumers in their natural habitats (the home, usually) to advising industrial design teams."

Warner, Faith, Joanna Salicki, and Judith Steinhilper. "How Do I Become a Professional Anthropologist? Advice to Undergraduates on Graduate School and Career Development." *Anthropology News* 49 (9): 37.

This article in *Anthropology News* offers suggestions from anthropologists on how undergraduate students can better gain experience and skills to help them become professionals. The advice and suggestions of meeting and survey participants are provided in this article.

Wasson, Christina (editor). *Making History at the Frontier: Women Creating Careers as Practicing Anthropologists.* NAPA Bulletin 26. American Anthropological Association.

This collection of articles describes ways that various women anthropologists have developed their careers as practicing anthropologists. The articles offer suggestions that can help students understand ways that they can develop their career paths.

Wienker, Curtis W. "Physical Anthropology in Multidisciplinary Biomedical Research." *Medical Anthropology Quarterly,* New Series, 3 (4): 368–376.

This article provides the reader with information concerning ways that physical anthropology and its practitioners are used within biomedical research.

JOB SEARCHES AND
JOB OPPORTUNITIES INFORMATION

American Anthropological Association (AAA) website, *http://careercenter. aaanet.org* (accessed December 2, 2010).

This web page of the AAA is devoted to offering students information on the ways that an anthropology degree can further career opportunities.

American Anthropological Association. E-Guide to Departments (AAA members only): *http://www.aaanet.org/membership/eguide_search.cfm* (accessed December 2, 2010).

The E-Guide is an electronic copy of the *AAA's Guide to Departments of Anthropology*. Available only to AAA members, it is a convenient way of searching for professional sources, contacts, and information on numerous departments of anthropology in the United States as well as within certain countries elsewhere.

American Association for State and Local History (AASLH) website, *http:// www.aaslh.org* (accessed December 2, 2010).

This website is a portal to information about the association as well as its programs, areas of interest, and more. Interested students are encouraged to use this site as a means of garnering understanding of the ways that history can merge with historical archaeology and archaeology of contemporary populations.

American Association of Museums website, *http://www.aam-us.org/aviso/ index.cfm* (accessed December 2, 2010).

This website is primarily for AAM members, but it offers contacts and job announcements that will help identify some job opportunities for those interested in pursuing museum jobs. It also offers opportunities for organizations to recruit interested individuals.

American Association of Physical Anthropologists website, *http://physanth. org/career* (accessed December 2, 2010).

This website is a portal for the American Association of Physical Anthropologists and directs students to information on graduate programs in physical anthropology, jobs in biological and physical anthropology, careers in museums and government agencies, frequently asked questions about physical anthropology, and more.

American Board of Forensic Anthropology website, *http://www.theabfa.org/* (accessed December 2, 2010).

The American Board of Forensic Anthropology is the licensing agency that offers certification in forensic anthropology. In purpose and organization, the ABFA functions in much the same way as do certifying boards in various medical specialties and other scientific fields. This website is a portal to information on various career opportunities and information for practicing forensic anthropologists.

Government Jobs website, *http://www.governmentjobs.com/* (accessed December 1, 2010).

This website is a commercial site that offers information on a myriad of job possibilities within the government sector across the United States. It offers information for job seekers, employers, and others.

Jobsearch.Com website, *http://www.jobsearch.com/. 2010* (accessed December 2, 2010).

This website is a country-wide commercial website that offers searches by state and specialty. Its opportunities are limited, but its information is applicable in terms of cost-of-living information as well as broader markets.

National Association of Tribal Preservation Officers website, *http://www.nathpo.org/mainpage.html* (accessed December 2, 2010).

This website offers information on the 100+ Native American tribes that have taken over the responsibilities of the State Historic Preservation Officer as part of the federal historic preservation compliance requirements.

Society for Applied Anthropology website, *http://www.sfaa.net/sfaajobs.html* (accessed December 2, 2010).

This website offers job openings in government, academia, and the private sector for anthropologists and social scientists, as well as opportunities for employers looking to hire an applied anthropologist.

USDA Forest Service website. Working for the Great Outdoors, Student Programs, *http://www.fs.fed.us/fsjobs/forestservice/scep.html* (accessed December 1, 2010).

This website explains the student programs within the USDA Forest Service. As the primary source for external recruitment for entry-level hires in the Forest Service, SCEP provides work experience that is directly related to the student's academic program or career goals.

US Department of Transportation Federal Highways Administration website, *http://www.fhwa.dot.gov/webstate.html* (accessed December 1, 2010).

This website is the portal for every state Department of Transportation office in the United States. From here, interested people can search for information on local and regional transportation systems nationwide. Each state website varies by content and information.

Virginia Association of Museums website, *http://www.vamuseums.org/ Resources/ForMuseumStudiesStudents/TypesofMuseums/tabid/160/Default. aspx* (accessed December 2, 2010).

This website offers information about the various types of museums within the broader field of museum studies, types of museum jobs, information about museum jobs, and the steps students should take in order to gain the qualifications for such positions.

FIVE-YEAR PLAN

Malone, Erin. "Planning Your Future." Boxes and Arrows website, *http://www. boxesandarrows.com/view/planning_your_future* (accessed December 2, 2010).

This online article offers a template to help students understand that it is important to devise a realistic plan within the framework of one's interests and career path as a means of shaping a vision toward reaching a future goal.

McKay, Dawn Rosenberg. "Writing a Career Action Plan." About.com website, *http://careerplanning.about.com/od/careeractionplan/a/action_plan_ln. html* (accessed December 2, 2010).

This article talks about how an action plan can be considered a road map to get you from Point A—choosing an occupation—to Point B—becoming employed in that occupation. It even helps you get past Point B, to Points C through Z, as you grow in that career.

McKinley, Elizabeth. "Write a Career Plan in Five Steps." Aol jobs website, *http://jobs.aol.com/articles/2009/09/07/write-a-career-plan-in-five-steps/* (accessed December 2, 2010).

This online resource offers five essential steps to help you craft a career plan to fit your professional needs in order to help you focus on your goals and get you where you want to be as a professional anthropologist.

Quintessential Careers website. "Developing a Strategic Vision for Your Career Plan." *http://www.quintcareers.com/career_plan.html* (accessed December 2, 2010).

This online article provides some basic guidelines for both short-term and long-term career planning, as well as exercises to help students develop strategies for creating realistic goals and objectives that one can accomplish in the near future.

CURRICULUM VITA AND RÉSUMÉS

Résumés

Examples Resumes website, *http://www.exampleresumes.org/* (accessed December 2, 2010).

This website offers a multitude of résumé examples from numerous different types of careers and professions.

University of Utah example:

http://careers.utah.edu/downloads/SocScisocservsampleresume.pdf (accessed December 2, 2010).

This downloadable PDF is an example of a social scientist's résumé. It is meant to be an acceptable example of structure, style, and format for student use.

Indiana University-Fort Wayne example:

http://www.ipfw.edu/career/assets/_files/resumes/Anthropology%20Resume%201.pdf (accessed December 2, 2010).

This is another one-page sample of an acceptable social scientist's résumé, It is meant to be a good example of structure, style, and format for student use.

The Evergreen State College website, Career Development, Resume Writing page, *http://www.evergreen.edu/career/resume/home.html* (accessed December 2, 2010).

This website offers information for the student on many of the various aspects of creating a social scientist's résumé. Other pages within the site give examples, types of résumés, as well as many possible headings to be used in the résumé.

The Evergreen State College website, Career Development, Power Verbs page, *http://www.evergreen.edu/career/resume/verbs.htm* (accessed December 2, 2010).

This list of "Power Verbs" contains suggestions for helping students develop more powerful résumés.

Curriculum Vitae

Job Searching, About.com website. "Curriculum Vitae." *http://jobsearch.about.com/od/curriculumvitae/Curriculum_Vitae.html* (accessed December 2, 2010).

This website is a portal to information on writing the CV, when to use a CV instead of a résumé, tips for writing a CV, as well as tips for producing cover letters to accompany the CV.

Karen Olsen Bruhns (San Francisco State University) example:

> *http://userwww.sfsu.edu/~kbruhns/howtocv.htm* (accessed December 2, 2010).

This interactive website offers a template for a CV as well as information on particular topics (denoted by a blue star on the website).

University of Washington example:

> *http://careers.washington.edu/ifiles/all/files/docs/gradstudents/pdfs/ AcademicCareers-Curriculum_Vitae_07-08.pdf* (accessed December 2, 2010).

This downloadable PDF contains information on offering basic skills that help students develop a CV that highlights experience and training. It also offers a series of sample CVs in varying styles from which students can choose.

INTERVIEWING SKILLS AND SUGGESTIONS

Collegegrad.com website. "Fifty Standard Interview Questions." *http://www. collegegrad.com/jobsearch/Mastering-the-Interview/Fifty-Standard-Interview-Questions/* (accessed December 2, 2010).

This website offers 50 standard interview questions for the job hunter.

Doyle, Alison. "Top 10 Interview Blunders: How Not to Interview." About.com website, *http://jobsearch.about.com/od/interviewsnetworking/a/interviewblund. html* (accessed December 2, 2010).

This online article offers what it perceives to be the top ten mistakes regarding interviewing for a job.

The Evergreen State College website, Career Development Center, *http://www. evergreen.edu/career/interview/home.html* (accessed December 1, 2010).

This is a portal website that has separate pages on preparing for the interview, tips for better interviews, reminders about preparing for interviews, telephone techniques in job hunting, informational interviews, as well as questions most frequently asked by employers.

The Evergreen State College website, Career Development Center. "Questions Often Asked by Employers," *http://www.evergreen.edu/career/interview /interviewemployerquestions.html* (accessed December 2, 2010).

This is a list of 50 questions most commonly asked by employers during the job interview process.

Helpguide.org. "Interviewing Techniques and Tips: Putting Your Best Self Forward and Getting the Job." *http://www.helpguide.org/life/interviewing_techniques_tips_getting_job.htm* (accessed December 2, 2010).

This article offers information aimed at helping people put their best foot forward during job interviews as a means of "selling" themselves to potential employers.

Martin, Carole. Special Report, "Dress for Interview Success." Monster com website, *http://career-advice.monster.com/job-interview/interview-appearance/10-interview-fashion-blunders/article.aspx* (accessed December 2, 2010).

This report details the ten most common interview "fashion blunders" and how to dress for success.

Scribd.com website. "55 most frequently asked interview questions." *http://www.scribd.com/doc/239734/55-Most-Frequently-Asked-Interview-Questions* (accessed December 2, 2010).

This page contains 55 of the most commonly asked questions by employers during the job interview process.

INTERNSHIPS AND VOLUNTEERING

American Anthropological Association website, *http://www.aaanet.org/ar/internopps.html* (accessed December 2, 2010).

This is a portal to many internship opportunities offered in anthropology, from museums to private industry and fellowships.

GoAbroad.com website, *http://www.internabroad.com/search/anthropology* (accessed December 2, 2010).

This website is a portal for many different programs and internship opportunities in various locations outside of the United States.

Phoebe A. Hearst Museum of Anthropology website, *http://hearstmuseum.berkeley.edu/employment_opportunities/volunteers.php* (accessed December 2, 2010).

This website details opportunities for students who wish to work, volunteer, or intern at the Phoebe A. Hearst Museum of Anthropology in Berkeley, California.

Smithsonian Institution website, *http://anthropology.si.edu/outreach/internsh.html* (accessed December 2, 2010).

This website is for students interested in internship opportunities within the Smithsonian Institution in Washington, DC.

Presenting and Writing

Achert, Walter S., and Joseph Garibaldi. *The MLA Manual of Style.* Modern Language Association, 2008.

This is a classic guide for writers who create manuscripts that use the MLA (Modern Language Association) writing style. It offers suggestions for writing, as well as guidelines for formatting manuscripts within this style.

Becker, Howard S. *Writing for Social Scientists: How to Start and Finish Your Thesis, Book, or Article.* 2nd edition. Chicago: University of Chicago Press, 2007.

This book offers suggestions for people writing within social science. Its tips and suggestions can help authors get past common sticking points that hinder writing and manuscript production.

Butcher, Judith, Caroline Drake, and Maureen Leach. *Butcher's Copy-editing: The Cambridge Handbook for Editors, Copy-editors, and Proofreaders.* 4th edition. New York: Cambridge University Press, 2008.

This guide is intended to help copy-editors as they work on other authors' manuscripts to get them ready for publication. It is a classical guide for professionals who work in the fields of publishing and editing.

Chicago Manual of Style. Online edition, *http://www.chicagomanualofstyle.org/16/contents.html* (accessed December 2, 2010).

This is one of the major style guides for professionals creating academic texts. It offers suggestions on writing style, as well as citation styles used by many different publication houses and disciplines.

Ellick, Carol J. "Against the Clock: Introducing Archaeology in Time-Limited Situations." In *The Archaeology Education Handbook: Sharing the Past with Kids,* edited by Karolyn Smardz and Shelley J. Smith. Walnut Creek, CA: AltaMira, 2000.

This article discusses ways that presenters of information and educational opportunities can and should customize their presentations depending on the amount of time available to the students and the presenter.

Ellick, Carol J. "Audience, Situation, Style: Strategies for Formal and Informal Archaeological Outreach Programs." In *Past Meets Present: Archaeologists Partnering with Museum Curators, Teachers, and Community Groups,* edited by John H. Jameson and Sherene Baugher-Perlin. New York: Springer Press, 2007.

This article outlines strategies of practicing professionals to help them present their findings to various audiences as well as information on formal and informal styles.

Fagan, Brian. *Writing Archaeology: Telling Stories about the Past.* 2nd edition. Walnut Creek, CA: Left Coast, 2010.

This book offers suggestions and tips to archaeologists who are interested in creating written material for the general public.

Hoffman, Paul. "Accommodating Color Blindness." *Usability Interface* 6 (2), October 1999. *http://www.stcsig.org/usability/newsletter/9910-color-blindness. html* (accessed December 2, 2010).

This article discusses the types of color-blindness, as well as ways of ensuring that many of the common confusions that can arise because of color vision deficiencies do not occur or can be minimized.

Strunk, W., and E. B. White. *The Elements of Style.* 4th edition. Needham Heights, MA: Allyn and Bacon, 2000.

This is a classic style guide for writers—not only for professional authors but also for students.

Turabian, Kate L. *A Manual for Writers of Research Papers, Theses, and Dissertations: Chicago Style for Students and Researchers.* 7th edition. Chicago: University of Chicago Press, 2007.

This is also a classic style guide for writers. It offers suggestions, tips, and common hindrances to clarity.

Zimmerman, Larry J. *Presenting the Past.* Archaeologist's Toolkit, Vol. 7. Walnut Creek, CA: AltaMira, 2003.

This book offers suggestions for general writers, tips for presenters at national and local conferences, as well as suggestions and tips for engaging the general public in archaeological stories.

COMMUNICATION STYLES AND CROSS-CULTURAL COMMUNICATION

Elliott, Candia. "Communication Patterns and Assumptions of Differing Cultural Groups in the United States." Lunar and Planetary Institute website, *http://www.lpi.usra.edu/education/lpsc_wksp_2007/resources/elliott.pdf* (accessed December 2, 2010).

This downloadable PDF is a succinct presentation of ways that ethnic groups in the United States interpret and react to various presentation styles, public involvement, interpersonal interaction, and other culturally influenced communication and interpretation factors.

Elliott, Candia, R. Jerry Adams, and Suganya Sockalingam. *Multicultural Toolkit. Toolkit for Cross-Cultural Collaboration.* Awesome Library website, *http://www.awesomelibrary.org/multiculturaltoolkit.html* (accessed December 2, 2010).

This study offers a plethora of information about the effects of culture on communication style and comprehension as well as how to better increase understanding between cultures.

Florida Association of Community Health Centers. "Normative Communication Styles & Values for Cross-Cultural Collaboration." *http://www.fachc. org/pdf/mig_Normative%20Communication%20Styles.pdf* (accessed December 2, 2010).

This downloadable PDF offers a handy chart on broad and general communication styles for cross-cultural communication by ethnic groups in the United States.

U.S. Peace Corps. *Culture Matters. The Peace Corps Cross-Cultural Workbook. http://multimedia.peacecorps.gov/multimedia/pdf/library/T0087_culture-matters.pdf* (accessed December 2, 2010).

This volume is used by the Peace Corps as a training manual to provide information on the various communication styles and context features of various cultures across the world. It offers suggestions, information, exercises, and ways of gathering information concerning the ways that culture influences not only our understanding of others, but also the ways we interpret different cultures.

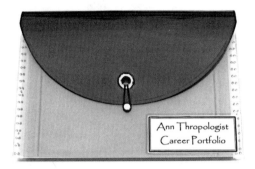

APPENDIX 4

SAMPLES AND EXAMPLES

This appendix provides samples and examples of a résumé, biographies, five-year plans, a cover letter, letter requesting a reference, a letter of reference for a student and an employee, and job applicant evaluation rubric.

RÉSUMÉ

The following résumé is fictitious. Ann Thropologist and her life have been created specifically for this book. Ms. Thropologist hopes to work as a cultural anthropologist with indigenous peoples. Her résumé contains her job history, including both her anthropological positions and those relating to anthropology that she feels would help her in achieving her goals.

Ann Thropologist
1234 Culture Cross Rd., Indiana, OK 76543
(123) 456–7890
ann.thropologist@gmail.com

GOAL STATEMENT:

My career goal is to use my anthropological training to work with indigenous communities and to assist them with achieving benefits as defined by the community itself.

RELEVANT EXPERIENCE:

June 2010–Present: Anthropological Assistant, Southwest Native Council, NSW, Australia

Assisted the Council's Senior Anthropologist with research relating to native title. Did ethnographic, archival, and genealogical research.

June–September 2009:   Assistant Researcher, Native for Native, Phoenix, AZ

Conducted community interviews. Assisted the staff anthropologists with data input and produced a descriptive report on the field procedures.

January–May 2009:   Research Assistant, Maxwell Museum of Anthropology, Albuquerque, NM

Helped inventory and catalog ethnographic collections. Used the inventory database to help create an online searchable catalog for public use.

June 2006–May 2008   Sales Person, East Coast Camping Outfitters, Alexandria, VA

Sold backpacking and camping equipment, advised customers on camping equipment based on need, helped lead backpacking adventures, maintained the rental equipment, took inventory and restocked shelves, and helped train new employees.

VOLUNTEER EXPERIENCE:

June–September 2008: Volunteer, For the People Foundation, Wilmington, DE

Helped create PR for the Foundation's website. Assisted with redesigning the Foundation's website to highlight their mission and reach more people. Did data entry on the mailing list. Worked on a team to help design an "infomercial" for public television.

Ann Thropologist / Résumé- 2

EDUCATION:

M.A., University of New Mexico, Anthropology, with a Socio-Cultural Specialization, 2010

B.A., American University, *Magna Cum Laude* in Anthropology, 2008

PROFESSIONAL ORGANIZATIONS:

2008–Present American Anthropological Association.

2008–Present Plains Anthropological Society, Student Board Representative.

SKILLS:

Proficient with Dreamweaver web design tools and Microsoft Office programs, for both Mac and PC. I am logical, efficient, and organized, and I work well as a member of a team or independently. Hold current American Red Cross Basic First Aid and American Heart Association CPR certification.

HOBBIES AND INTERESTS:

Reading, international travel, backpacking, wilderness camping, personal fitness, and drawing.

REFERENCES:

Upon Request

BIOGRAPHY (BIO)

The following two examples were composed as class assignments by students in the Avenues to Professionalism class.

Monica Mondragon

Monica Mondragon holds a B.S. in anthropology from the University of New Mexico (2004) and recently completed her Master's of Science in anthropology, with a specialization in osteology and bioarchaeology, from the University of New Mexico where she was a Spuhler Fellow. Her current work includes providing information concerning body donation, managing laboratory databases, and cleaning and labeling skeletons for the Laboratory of Osteology at the Maxwell Museum of Anthropology. Other duties include developing osteobiographies for modern, historical, and prehistoric human skeletons brought into the osteology laboratory.

Her current study interests include the archaeology and bioarchaeology of the Scandinavian and Germanic tribes in the Iron Age and Medieval periods in Europe, as well as bone and muscle biology, bone histology, bone biomechanics, and the functional morphology of the skeleton. Previous research has centered on ontogeny and musculoskeletal markings in prehistoric New Mexican populations.

Ms. Mondragon's publications include abstracts found in annual professional meeting editions of the *American Journal of Physical Anthropology* in conjunction with Dr. Osbjorn Pearson. She is also a member of Phi Beta Kappa, Phi Kappa Phi, and Golden Key Honor societies.

Ian Thompson

Ian Thompson is an anthropology graduate student at the University of New Mexico who is of Choctaw, Muskogee "Creek," and European heritage. Ian was fortunate to find his passion early in life: the traditional arts (flint-knapping, bow-making, traditional hide-tanning, pottery, etc.). By age sixteen, his work was being used by several museums, and he was serving as a research consultant for an anthropology master's thesis on traditional hide-working.

For the last eight years, Ian has run Little Blue River Traditional Arts, selling his artwork part-time. This has been complemented with hundreds of hours of teaching traditional arts informally and through displays, public demonstrations, and formal classes at a number of venues, including the 2006 Choctaw Nation of Oklahoma culture camp. Additionally, Ian has worked as an archaeological field technician and private contractor in excavations at Fort Osage, Missouri, and a number of sites across New Mexico.

Ian has been an active student leader, serving as treasurer for UNM's Kiva Club, one of the nation's oldest Native student organizations, and previously as vice-president of From the Four Directions, the equivalent organization at the University of Missouri. He has been heavily involved in planning, fund-raising, and hosting dozens of activities to help benefit Native students and the local community, including concerts, lectures by indigenous scholars, Native pageantry, benefit art auctions, protest marches, and Traditional Craft Night. The latter was conceived by Ian as a forum for Kiva Club members to share and learn about one another's traditional cultures and arts.

Ian's publications include: "Cutting Edge Technology," an experimental study of stone arrowpoint performance (*Missouri Archaeologist*, 2003) and "A Reexamination of Indian Bows and Arrows," an experimental study of Native American archery equipment (*Missouri Archaeologist*, 2002). Titles in press include "My Own Personal Kennewick Man" (in the *Kennewick Man Reader*, edited by Joe Watkins and Dorothy Lippert) and "Indigenous Archaeology: An Encounter with the Other" (*Southeastern Archaeology*).

Currently, Ian is working on his doctoral dissertation, entitled "Chahta Intikba Im Aiikhvna (Learning from the Choctaw Ancestors): Integrating Indigenous and Experimental Approaches in the Study of Mississippian Technologies." Under the guidance of a committee chaired by Joe Watkins, he will be using experimental replication to study the traditional arts of Choctaw peoples during the time immediately preceding European contact, attempting to provide a number of specific benefits for both Native Americans and archaeological communities. Ultimately, Ian hopes to build on his experiences and studies to create a full-time business dedicated to making and teaching the traditional arts.

FIVE-YEAR PLANS

The following are sections of two five-year plans submitted by Avenues to Professionalism students. At the time, Debi was an undergraduate student and Matt was a graduate student.

Debi

Today: September 13, 2006

Dream

To be a director of a museum with collections from the Classical world.

Right Now

Physical Location: Albuquerque, New Mexico

Job Description: Full-time undergraduate student at the University of New Mexico. Working on a bachelor's degree in anthropology and history. Also working part-time at Defined Fitness as a customer service representative.

KSAs: I have extensive experience in customer service and also with computer programs such as Microsoft Suite and Mac operating systems. I also have experience with filing, data entry, multi-line phones, scheduling, and sewing. I have past experience with managing staffs of between 5 and 20 people. I can work under pressure and with difficult personalities. I have the ability to keep 25 children entertained in a safe setting and am certified to perform CPR.

One Year

Physical Location: Storrs, Connecticut (1st choice graduate school, location optional)

Job Description: Full-time graduate student working on a Ph.D. in museum studies. I also hope to be working as a graduate assistant. At this time I will know what I want my dissertation to be on, and will have already started the research.

Needed KSAs: Obviously, all the skills I have now, plus at least a couple of months of volunteering experience at a museum. Hopefully, I will gain the basic knowledge of how to run a museum, how to properly set up exhibits, and how to preserve artifacts when not on display. I would like to specifically work with artifacts from the Classical time period and Near East geographic location. At this time, I will be starting to learn the Latin and Italian languages.

Three Year

Physical Location: Storrs, Connecticut (or other)

Job Description: Full-time graduate student working on a Ph.D. in museum studies. I also hope to still be working as a graduate assistant or to have gained a part-time job in a museum.

Needed KSAs: Everything I've gained to date, plus a more enhanced understanding of how to conduct research. In addition to the basic skills I picked up while volunteering in my undergraduate career, I will have a strong understanding of everything involved in the successful running of a museum. I hope to be able to write grant proposals as well as to have a strong foundation for my dissertation. In addition to these crucial skills, I also hope to have a reading knowledge of the Latin language, as well as being fluent in Italian. Around this time, I will also have a beginning knowledge of another language, possibly a form of modern or ancient Greek.

Matt

Today's Date: September 8, 2006

The following is an outline of the goals and a plan for achieving those goals over the next five years. It begins with the present and immediate future, and projects to approximately six months, then to one year, three years, and ultimately five years from the above date. It includes personal and professional goals, and is a "living document." In other words, this plan is adaptable and fluid. Goals will be maintained, yet they will be augmented as various opportunities or difficulties arise.

Dream

I want an academic teaching position in an anthropology department at a major university.

Three Months

Within the next three months I must: completely and "legally" organize my committee. I must also investigate what I will need to complete for my "skill" requirement (archaeometallurgy) and how to go about it. Finally, I need to meet with the professor to complete my language requirement.

I need to take Proposal Writing in the spring of this year. Goal #1 is to locate the readings for all of the different sections I need to include in my proposal. Goal #2 is to organize and practice these topics and techniques with my Chair until I feel comfortable and fluent enough that I can work with the professor in the Proposal Writing class to put together a solid foundation for my Dissertation Proposal, organize it, and defend it. Goal #3 is to successfully defend the proposal and be able to begin research.

At work, I am the Lab Director. I would like to have the lab organized, cleaned, and ready to be functional within three weeks. This will take some planning and dedicating of several hours of overhead time. Goal #1 is to get that time approved. Goal #2 is to get some equipment replaced and get the obsolete equipment out. Goal #3, obviously, is to complete the project.

Five Year

By year five, I plan to be close to completing my Ph.D. or to have obtained it. It may or may not be a lofty goal to achieve by this point, but it is my goal nevertheless. However, one of the "KSAs" I have that will aid me in obtaining these goals is a drive and the ambition to complete it. I have been many things in my lifetime, but this is the first time I've really known what I want to be. Whether or not I am complete or within reach, I will begin seeking university/college tenure-track positions at institutions I can foresee myself spending a good amount of time in or be taken into permanently. There are websites and literature to be found now on almost any campus, large or small. These will form the basic toolset in my arsenal in searching out potential victims to send my CV and résumé to. Connected intimately to this idea is to research the areas in which the schools are located. I will investigate crime rates, costs of living, and how the "Romans" view living in town as opposed to outside of it or in another area completely. Another hurdle will be conversing, planning, and hopefully agreeing with my mate on which of these institutions and towns will support her needs, dreams, and goals.

I plan to maintain ties and research opportunities with my friends and colleagues in Spain and Ireland by interacting with them in the manner I already do, and by spending professional and personal time with them. A KSA I possess that will help me in this endeavor is my ability to speak Spanish, and I am learning Irish.

With plans to complete my Ph.D., or with having the degree in hand and planning to relocate and establish myself at a university, I will begin a plan to sell our house and look for a new one in that target area.

Cover Letter

October 4, 2006

Dr. H. Jones, Jr.
President, Albuquerque Archaeology, Inc.
1234 Albuquerque Rd.
Albuquerque, NM 12345

Dear Dr. Jones:

I learned of this position through the professors at the Department of Anthropology at the University of New Mexico (UNM). I immediately became interested in this opportunity. I believe that my drive and my enthusiasm for this job and the field of archaeology will uniquely qualify me for this position.

I am completing my B.A. in archaeology at UNM and will be graduating in May of 2008. This educational experience in archaeology has been valuable in preparing me for this job. I have taken courses that have trained me in surveying, grid layout, and excavation. These same courses have trained me in proper procedure for lab analysis, too. In addition, I have taken courses that deal with the theory and concepts of archaeology. I am also double majoring in art studio drawing. This has given me exceptional experience in sketching and illustration, should your company need these skills.

My current job as the Assistant Director of Community Experience has given me experience in leadership, organization, responsibility, and delegating work. For this job, I organize and operate events and programs that involve UNM students doing community service. This is with a staff of seven paid positions and twenty-five volunteers. My other job experiences as a cook and janitor have prepared me for hard work and long hours. I am now looking for a job that involves practical job experience that allows me to apply my classroom experience in archaeology.

Thank you for taking the time to review my application. I am excited to work with your company and look forward to meeting with you on October 4, 2006, at UNM to further discuss my qualifications.

Sincerely,

Doug Rocks-Macqueen
Enclosed: Résumé, List of References

Letter Requesting a Reference

Dr. Joe Watkins
Department of Anthropology
University of Universities
Anytown, OK 12345

Dear Dr. Watkins:

I am writing to ask if you would write a letter of reference for me. I will be graduating in the spring and would like to request a letter for future use. I understand that a "generic" letter might not be as strong as one written for a specific purpose, but I would like to be able to use the letter as a general letter for "emergency" situations. If you agree, I would also like to be able to list you as a reference for future situations.

I have taken four classes with you over the course of the last two years and have really learned a lot in them. The Contemporary Issues class helped me better understand the issues that Indigenous groups face today. I will continue to use the information and skills I learned in the Method and Theory class as I go forward in my educational and professional career. I put the information presented in the Museum Studies class to immediate use during my Research Assistant position at the Maxwell Museum. Finally, I believe your Research Methods class has had the most impact on my educational career, especially since it led to my involvement with the Southwest Native Council in New South Wales, Australia.

My immediate goal is to use my scholastic training to help Indigenous communities with achieving the benefits defined by the community itself. My degree and educational background should be a tool I can use to help the groups who will ask me.

I am enclosing copies of the papers I wrote for the Contemporary Issues and the Research Methods classes. I really appreciated your comments and the opportunities to revise and resubmit them—it really made me aware that a writer's job is never done!

Thank you in advance for the letter. If there is any additional information you need from me, please feel free to contact me at *ann.thropologist@ gmail.com* or by telephone at 555–5555.

Sincerely,

Ann Thropologist

GENERIC LETTER OF REFERENCE

December 13, 2006

To Whom It May Concern:

It is with great pleasure that we provide to you this recommendation for Erin Hudson. Ms. Hudson was a graduate student in the "Avenues to Professionalism: Obtaining a Career in Anthropology" class during the fall semester 2006.

The goal of the "Avenues to Professionalism" class is to provide students with the knowledge and skills necessary to transition from their lives as students to a career in anthropology. During the semester, students were required to actively participate in individual and cooperative projects. They performed research relating to their individual career paths; wrote one-, three-, and five-year plans that clearly delineated their goals and objectives; identified local, state, and national or international professional anthropological societies; composed their résumé, curriculum vita, and personal biography; and developed and presented a 15-minute PowerPoint presentation on a research topic of their choice. Students participated in a mock job application and interview process, playing the role of the applicant and the employer. Students utilized constructive criticism techniques and evaluation rubrics when evaluating products and presentations. They learned about teaching-styles and learning-styles, business organizational structure and management, and about writing a proposal based on a request-for-proposal.

In addition, graduate students researched the presentation requirements for a professional conference and composed a submission containing a title and abstract for the next annual meeting. They also organized and hosted the first annual University of New Mexico Department of Anthropology Career Fair which was attended by more than 25% of the anthropology majors and graduate students. The undergraduates in the class assisted at the Career Fair.

Ms. Hudson actively participated in all individual and cooperative requirements. She completed all aspects of the course requirements and utilized her network to provide assistance on projects. She exhibited excellent organizational skills and produced only the highest-quality work. Ms. Hudson was able to step into leadership roles, but was equally able to participate in a team capacity. Erin has been a delight to work with.

With this letter and the job portfolio that she created, Erin enters the profession of archaeology with the essential skills necessary to build a successful career. She brings these skills and more with her to any job or activity she pursues, and she would be a positive asset to any employer.

If you have any questions or would like additional information, please do not hesitate to contact us.

Sincerely,

Joe E. Watkins, Ph.D., RPA   Carol J. Ellick, M.A., RPA
Associate Professor   Adjunct Lecturer
Department of Anthropology   Department of Anthropology

Job Applicant Evaluation Rubric

BIOARCHAEOLOGIST POSITION

NAME: _____

Submitted prior to or brought to interview: Cover letter: ___ Résumé: ___ References: ____

Professional Experience

KNOWLEDGE AND SKILLS	Extensive	Strong	Some	Minimal	None
General survey experience					
General excavation experience					
Excavation: Human skeletal remains					
Past work within the region					
Project director supervisory experience					
Crew chief experience					
Program administration					
Laboratory management					
Laboratory assistant-general					
Laboratory: Human skeletal analysis					
Cooperative work					
Independent work					

Education

DEGREE	Ph.D.	M.A.	B.A.	Associate	None
Anthropology: Subfield _____					
Social science					
Other					

Computer Program Experience

DATABASES	Extensive	Strong	Some	Minimal	None
Access					
Excel					
SOFTWARE					
MS Word					
Outlook Express					
Photoshop, Illustrator, Paint Shop, etc.					
GENERAL COMPUTER					
Problem resolution					

Writing Experience

TYPE OF WRITING	Extensive	Strong	Some	Minimal	None
Research designs					
Plan of work or field plans					
Descriptive reports					
Synthetic reports					

Comments & Questions:

INTERVIEW NOTES

Applicant Name: _____

Interviewed by: _____ Interview Date: _____

1. The individual showed up to interview on time.   Yes___ No___

Comments:

2. The individual was neat in appearance.   Yes __ No__ Somewhat __

Comments:

3. The individual was at ease with the questions asked. Yes __ No__ Somewhat __

Comments:

4. The individual took time to think about the question prior to answering.

Comments: Yes ___ No___ Somewhat___

5. The individual asked questions regarding the position.   Yes___No___

Comments:

6. I would recommend this person for consideration.   Yes___No___

Comments:

Questions:

1. What are your long-range career goals?

2. Why did you choose the career for which you are preparing?

3. What do you consider to be your greatest strengths and weaknesses?

4. Why should I hire you?

5. Create one other question based on résumé and cover letter:

Answer:

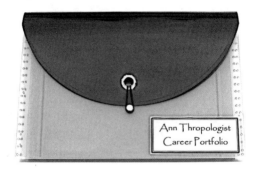

REFERENCES

American Anthropological Association
  2009 "AAA Code of Ethics," February 2009. *http://www.aaanet.org/
  issues/policy-advocacy/upload/AAA-Ethics-Code-2009.pdf*
  (accessed December 2, 2010).
American Anthropological Association
  2009–2010 *American Anthropological Association 2009–2010 Guide to
  Departments of Anthropology.* Arlington, VA.
American Anthropological Association
  2010a "Anthropology for Businesses," PowerPoint, August 2010. *http://
  www.aaanet.org/profdev/careers/* (accessed December 2, 2010)
American Anthropological Association
  2010b Blog post by Jona Pounds, "So, How Long does it take to find a
  job?" on August 10, 2010, online at *http://blog.aaanet.org/
  2010/08/10/so-how-long-does-it-take-to-find-a-job/* (accessed
  December 2, 2010).

Berman, John
  2009   "Got Work? College Graduates Face Toughest Job Market in Years."
          ABC News online May 20, 2009, *http://abcnews.go.com/Business/
          story?id=7636561&page=1* (accessed December 2, 2010).
Fagan, Brian
  2010   *Writing Archaeology: Telling Stories about The Past.* 2nd edition.
          Walnut Creek, CA: Left Coast Press.
Fiske, Shirley J.
  2008   "Working for the Federal Government: Anthropology Careers." In
          Careers in Applied Anthropology in the 21st Century: Perspectives
          from Academics and Practitioners. *NAPA Bulletin* 29: 110–130.
Fiske, Shirley J., Linda A. Bennett, Patricia Ensworth, Terry Redding, and
          Keri Brondo.
  2010   "The Changing Face of Anthropology: Anthropology Masters Re-
          flect on Education, Careers, ad Professional Organizations."
          AAA/CoPAPIA 2009 Anthropology MA Career Survey. Arlington,
          VA: American Anthropological Association.
Guerrón-Montero, Carl.
  2008   "Introduction: Preparing Anthropologists for the 21st Century." In
          Careers in Applied Anthropology in the 21st Century: Perspectives
          from Academics and Practitioners. *NAPA Bulletin* 29: 1–13.
Hahn, Robert A.
  2009   "Going Where No Anthropologist Has Gone Before." *Anthropology
          News* 50(3): 31.
Jenkins, Rob.
  2009   "Tenure and the Two-Year College." Chronicle of Higher Educa-
          tion, online at *http://chronicle.com/article/Tenurethe-Two-Year/
          44474/* June 11, 2009 (accessed Dec 2, 2010).
June, Audrey Williams
  2010   "Anthropology Groups Restyles Its Offerings to Lure Nonacade-
          mics". Chronicle of Higher Education, online at *http://chronicle.
          com/article/Nonacademic-Members-Push/125440/?key=
          G2N1cFE4NCcSbS00ZG1FZz4APXBgZUh3ZyNDaHx1bltdGQ%
          3D%3D*. November 18 2010 (accessed December 2, 2010).
Jones, Peter N., and Darby Stapp
  2008   "Half a Century of Collaboration: Articles Concerning Native
          Americans in Human Organization, 1941–2008 and Practicing An-
          thropology, 1978–2008." Boulder, CO: Bäuu Institute and Press.
          Paper available at *http://ssrn.com/abstract=992456.*
Jordan, Brigette and YutakaYamauchi
  2008   "Beyond the University: Teaching Ethnographic Methods in the
          Corporation." *Anthropology News* 49(6):35.

Kedia, Satish
2008   "Recent Changes and Trends in the Practice of Applied Anthropology." In Careers in Applied Anthropology in the 21st Century: Perspectives from Academics and Practitioners. *NAPA Bulletin* 29: 14–28.

Littlefield, Carla N., and Emilia González-Clements
2008   "Creating Your Own Consulting Business." In Careers in Applied Anthropology in the 21st Century: Perspectives from Academics and Practitioners. *NAPA Bulletin* 29: 152–165.

Montell, Gabriella
2000   "A Look at the Job Market for Anthropologists." Chronicle of Higher Education in 2000, November 17, 2000. Online at *http://chronicle.com/article/A-Look-at-the-Job-Market-for/46333* (accessed December 2, 2010).

National Council for State Historic Preservation Officers Website: *http://www.ncshpo.org/* (accessed December 1, 2010).

National Park Service. Secretary of the Interior's Standards and Guidelines for Historic Preservation.
2010   *http://www.nps.gov/history/local-law/Prof_Qual_83.htm* (accessed August 15, 2010).

Nolan, Riall W.
2003   *Anthropology in Practice: Building a Career Outside the Academy.* Boulder, CO: Lynne Rienner Publishers.

Peace Corps
1999   *Culture Matters.* Peace Corps Information Collection and Exchange.

President Barack Obama, Office of the White House
2010   Presidential Memorandum, Improving the Federal Recruitment and Hiring Process, May 11, 2010.

Register of Professional Archaeologists
2010   Code of Ethics. *http://www.rpanet.org/displaycommon.cfm?an=2* (accessed December 2, 2010).

Robbins, Elaine
2006   Archaeological Crime Fighters, *American Archaeology*, Summer 2006.

Schlatter, Elizabeth N.
2008   *Museum Careers: A Practical Guide for Students and Novices.* Walnut Creek, CA: Left Coast Press.

Shelton, Donald
2008   "The 'CSI Effect': Does it Really Exist?" *NIJ Journal,* No. 259. Washington, DC, March 2008, *http://www.ojp.usdoj.gov/nij/journals/259/csi-effect.htm* (accessed December 2, 2010).

Society for American Archaeology
  2010   Principles of Archaeological Ethics. *http://www.saa.org/ AbouttheSociety/PrinciplesofArchaeologicalEthics/tabid/203/ Default.aspx* (accessed December 2, 2010).
Sontag, Larry C.
  2006   "The CSI Effect? The Albuquerque Police Crime Lab Responds." *Forensic Magazine,* June/July 2006. Online at *http://www. forensicmag.com/node/94 (accessed* December 2, 2010).
Young, Philip D.
  2008   "Practicing Anthropology from within the Academy: Combining Careers." In Careers in Applied Anthropology in the 21st Century: Perspectives from Academics and Practitioners. *NAPA Bulletin* 29: 56–69.
Zimmerman, Larry J.
  2003   *Presenting the Past.* Archaeologist's Toolkit, Vol. 7. Walnut Creek, CA: AltaMira Press.

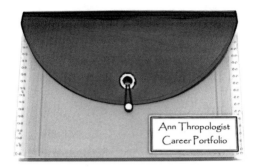

INDEX

customer service, 65, 215, 251
data collection/analysis, 35, 45, 73,
85, 100, 133, 141, 211, 214, 248,
251
ethnography (ethnographic), 33, 34,
37, 46, 100, 130, 227, 248
inference, 63, 141, 143
interview, 33, 35, 62, 121, 125, 214, 214
journal (-ing), 22, 25, 130, 134, 144
market research, 46, 73, 131
observation, 33, 63, 123, 140, 141
records search, 34
report writing, 35, 220
research, 25, 34, 39, 43, 51, 55, 64, 220
teaching, 42, 63, 64 85, 179
videography, 34
writing, 64, 146, 151, 215, 220, 234
application form(s) (*see also:* job application), 27, 200
application packet, 110, 116–119, 126,
186, 187, 196
confirmation, 117, 118–119
digital submission, 117–118
written submissions, 116–117
web, 118
applied anthropology (*see also:* practicing), 40, 41, 42, 83, 170, 217, 218,
224, 227, 234, 238
archaeology, 16, 31, 75, 216, 218, 250, 256
applied, 41
associations and societies, 53, 54,
135, 136, 167, 235, 237
career in, 37, 42, 43, 170, 215, 235,
224
field of, 36
associations and societies (*see also:* organizations and conferences):
American Anthropological Association (AAA), 13, 33, 40, 46, 47, 52,
55, 74, 101, 137, 155, 160, 170,
185, 205, 221, 237, 242, 249
American Association for State and
Local History, 72, 237
American Association of Physical
Anthropologists, 53, 71, 237
National Association for the Practice
of Anthropology (NAPA), 13, 54,
67, 166

National Association of Tribal His-
toric Preservation Officer(s)
(NATHPO), 73, 238
Register of Professional Archaeolo-
gists (RPA), 52, 56
Society for American Archaeology
(SAA), 53, 102, 135, 167, 168
Society for Applied Anthropology
(SfAA), 9, 46, 54, 66, 73, 137
Society for Cultural Anthropology, 53
Society for Historical Archaeology,
235
Society for Linguistic Anthropology, 53
Avenues to Professionalism, 9, 17, 62, 66,
67, 68, 88, 148, 204, 249, 251, 256
avocational society, 52, 135, 136

bachelor's (B.A.; B.S.), 13, 171, 254, 257
in career stories, 43, 102, 216, 221
what you can do with, 32, 37–38, 39,
41, 43 235
bioarchaeology, bioarchaeologist, 249,
250, 257
bio, biography, biographical, 26, 47, 180,
249, 256
examples, 102, 103, 249–250, 263
creating, 79, 93–94, 101–104
updating, 200–201
biological anthropology (*see also:* physical anthropology), 38, 39, 174, 229
Briody, Elizabeth K., 156, 209
Burnett, Deborah (Debi), 251
business cards, 164, 167

career story (stories), 17, 42, 65, 170,
209–232
academic, 227–232
applied, 209–223
applied and academic. 223–227
Carnes, Michelle M., 36, 64, 68, 87, 212
communication, 51, 62, 63, 74, 85, 108,
127, 139–151, 158, 244, 245
email (*see also:* email), 148–150
high and low context, 142–143
direct and indirect, 142, 143–144
non-verbal, 144–145, 229
written (*see also:* writing), 145–146
crew chief, 16, 38, 43, 44, 90, 257

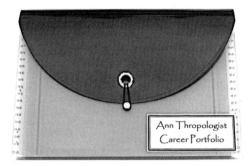

Ann Thropologist
Career Portfolio

ABOUT THE AUTHORS

Carol J. Ellick is founder of Archaeological and Cultural Education Consultants (ACECs) and serves as adjunct faculty in the Native American Studies Program at the University of Oklahoma. Ms. Ellick has a B.A. in anthropology from The Evergreen State College and an M.A. in education from Chapman University. She has worked in cultural resource management (CRM) for over 30 years, starting the first full-time public outreach program in 1995. She is one of the leading experts in archaeological education in the United States. Ms. Ellick's publications include articles in professional journals such as the National Park Service's publication, *Common Ground*, and the Society for American Archaeology magazine, *The SAA Archaeological Record*. She also has chapters in The *Archaeology Education Handbook: Sharing the Past with Kids* (2000) and *Past Meets Present: Archaeologists Partnering with Museum Curators, Teachers, and Community Groups* (2007).

Joe E. Watkins is the Director of the Native American Studies program and Associate Professor of Anthropology at the University of Oklahoma. Dr. Watkins received his B.A. in anthropology from the University of Oklahoma and his M.A. and Ph.D. from Southern Methodist University. He has been doing archaeology for more than 40 years and has published extensively on his research interests: the ethical practice of anthropology and anthropology's relationships with descendant communities and aboriginal populations. His book *Indigenous Archaeology: American Indian Values and Scientific Practice* (2000) is a seminal work in Indigenous Archaeology. His second book, *Reclaiming Physical Heritage: Repatriation and Sacred Sites* (2005), written for high school and early college students, draws attention to important Native American issues.